Global Convergence Cultures

G000155459

Today's convergent media industries readily produce stories that span multiple media, telling the tales of superheroes across comics, film and television, inviting audiences to participate in the popular universes across cinema, novels, the Web and more. This transmedia phenomenon may be a common strategy in Hollywood's blockbuster fiction factory, tied up with digital marketing and fictional world-building, but transmediality is so much more than global movie franchises. Different cultures around the world are now making new and often far less commercial uses of transmediality, applying this phenomenon to the needs and structures of a nation and rethinking it in the form of cultural, political and heritage projects. This book offers an exploration of these national and cultural systems of transmediality around the world, showing how national cultures – including politics, people, heritage, traditions, leisure and so on – are informing transmediality in different countries. The book spans four continents and twelve countries, looking across the UK, Spain, Portugal, France, Estonia, USA, Canada, Colombia, Brazil, Japan, India and Russia.

Matthew Freeman is Reader in Multiplatform Media at Bath Spa University, UK, where he is also Co-Director of the Media Convergence Research Centre. He is the author of *Historicising Transmedia Storytelling: Early Twentieth-Century Transmedia Story Worlds* (2016) and *Industrial Approaches to Media: A Methodological Gateway to Industry Studies* (2016).

William Proctor is Senior Lecturer in Media, Culture and Communication at Bournemouth University, UK. He has published on numerous topics of popular culture and is the author of *Reboot Culture: Comics, Film, Transmedia* (2018) and the co-editor of *Disney's Star Wars: Forces of Production, Promotion and Reception* (2019).

Routledge Advances in Internationalizing Media Studies
Edited by Daya Thussu, University of Westminster

For a full list of titles in this series, please visit www.routledge.com.

Global Convergence Cultures

Transmedia Earth

**Edited by Matthew Freeman and
William Proctor**

LONDON AND NEW YORK

First published 2018 by Routledge

2 Park Square, Milton Park, Abingdon, Oxfordshire OX14 4RN
52 Vanderbilt Avenue, New York, NY 10017

*Routledge is an imprint of the Taylor & Francis Group, an
informa business*

First issued in paperback 2020

Library of Congress Cataloging-in-Publication Data
CIP data has been applied for.

ISBN: 978-1-138-73238-4 (hbk)
ISBN: 978-0-367-59100-7 (pbk)

Typeset in Sabon
by codeMantra

Contents

List of Table

Foreword
Earth to Transmedia

Toby Miller

Transmedia storytelling is both ordinary and extraordinary, ancient and modern, mundane and fun, normal and transformative. Why?

Cultural work has always covered a multiplicity of terrains. Marxism first lived in the form of pamphlets, journalism, correspondence and meetings, as well as academic treatises. Dickens' novels emerged from chapters published in magazines. From its very first days, Hollywood drew on plays, paintings and novels; once sound became standard, playwrights and other writers were hired to produce dialogue for cinema.

Many studio stars also worked in radio, frequently reprising or anticipating their roles in cinema, and music transmogrified with radio's advent from printed scores to recorded formats. Newspaper reporters, especially gossip columnists, doubled as broadcasters, and distance education via the radio blended forms almost a century ago. Prior to the domination of sealed radio sets, choral-response genres produced by leftists proliferated – workers changed the texts they were listening to by speaking back to them (Johnson 1988), with Brecht (2000) an early champion and dramaturg.

Sometimes new cultural technologies seemed threatening rather than obviously additive and accretive. The televisualization and suburbanization of the United States after the Second World War initially appeared to imperil the movie industry because theatrical attendances quickly waned. But then it became apparent that twenty years of films – hitherto disregarded as back catalog, and seemingly doomed to oblivion or second-run and repertory houses – had potential new lives when screened on television. Something similar happened, of course, when deregulation and satellite technology thrived, starting in the 1980s. Established television networks and genres were thought to be in real trouble. But television shows themselves began new lives because thousands of hours of programing were needed in hundreds of countries, and the major powers stood ready to sell them. Television had become the 'warehouse of culture' (Newcomb 2005).

Today, YouTube is doing for the culture industries what television did from the 1950s – finding new ways for Hollywood and its kind to get free marketing (in the case of so-called piracy) and new audiences for old programs. It's a warehouse, too.

Meanwhile, the cross-pollination of media and genres continues: autobiographies signed by athletes, celebrities and politicians are excerpted in newspapers, continuing a long tradition. Genres such as talent quests have morphed between the stage, radio and television into their current Newspeak life as 'reality' shows. Newspapers, magazines, radio stations and television networks produce podcasts for the delectation and demographic targeting of their audiences. Reporters for NBC also generate copy in the form of spoken, filmed and written material for US affiliates, international CNBC stations and MSNBC. They frequently do so minus the old retinue of a producer, cinematographer and sound recordist to accompany them on location shooting. Museums vend toys, maps, books, paper, postcards, games and other merchandising, both as forms of income and surveillance and in order to engage their visitors.

In academic circles, twin theories of intertextuality help us to understand all of these signifying movements – and indeed the function of transmediality across them.

One theory is concerned with hermeneutic interpretation. As per Kristeva (1997), it argues for an inevitable mosaic of conscious and unconscious quotations and influences animating cultural production. This intertextuality is decipherable hermeneutically, by 'knowing the code'. The other theory is driven by political economy. It examines the incarnation of popular figures across and between various institutions, whether amateur or professional: intertextuality as per literature's James Bond, dating back to the 1950s (Bennett and Woollacott 1987), or television's *The Avengers*, from the 1960s (Miller 1997). Both of these franchises had of course lived across theater, radio, comics, fiction, music, games, fanzines, television, toys, sunglasses, figurines, paintings, lighters, clothing, fragrances, applications, cups and cinema. I must have left some things out... The point is that they all drew upon, and contributed to, the signification of 007, John Steed, Cathy Gale, Emma Peel et al. While many of these articulations were the property of corporations, such work both borrowed from and was supplemented by fan creations.

Today, looking globally and in less commercial spheres, we now find noncorporate and nongovernmental institutions proliferating ways of telling and sharing stories by drawing on the internet as well as on oral and other traditions. One of the best-established and longest-lasting is Sarai, which is dedicated to exploring urban life in South Asia by sharing new technologies with those who have been traditionally excluded from digital pleasures. Colombia's community-radio network, meanwhile, is promising to facilitate indigenous and African-descended survivors of colonialism, *mestizaje* and the conflict to work together and share stories.[1] On Brazil, too, Grupo Cultural AfroReggae[2] and Olodum[3] have strived to give racialized Brazilians dance, song, film and education as both outlets and resources by embracing practices of transmediality. To understand these particular sites, be they in South Asia or South America, one needs to appreciate both the hierarchies that structure their structuring media environments and their lived experience as cultural alternatives.

The methods of analyzing the forms and manifestations of transmediality explored in this volume fit the bill. Matthew Freeman, William Proctor and their contributors give readers the relevant political-economic contexts to their work as well as very particular, granular research. This allows us to learn about institutional settings along with cultural practices and meanings, allowing us to read about the popular classes as well as the dominant ones. The first approach emphasizes structural power and the second alternative forms of life. Their interplay is evidenced internationally across the volume. Such generous globalism allows us to go some way in transcending the effortless extrapolations from the global North that dog the study of globalization, where one language rules and one set of stories dominates.

Notes

1 See https://colombia2020.elespectador.com/pais/radio-comunitaria-dos-decadas-llevando-mensajes-de-paz.
2 See http://www.afroreggae.org/.
3 See http://olodum.com.br/.

Bibliography

Bennett, Tony and Janet Woollacott. *Bond and Beyond: The Political Career of a Popular Hero*. Basingstoke: Palgrave Macmillan, 1987.

Brecht, Bertolt. *Brecht on Film and Radio* (translated and edited by Marc Silberman). New York: Bloomsbury, 2000.

Johnson, Lesley. *The Unseen Voice: A Cultural Study of Early Australian Radio*. London and New York: Routledge, 1988.

Kristeva, Julia and Kelly Oliver. (ed.). *The Portable Kristeva*. New York: Columbia University Press, 1997.

Miller, Toby. *The Avengers*. London: British Film Institute, 1997.

Newcomb, Horace. "Studying Television: Same Questions, Different Contexts." *Cinema Journal* 45:1 (2005): 107–111.

Acknowledgements

Freeman:

It may be a cliché, but it is often said that travelling broadens the mind – that immersing yourself in different cultures around the globe can open your eyes to the true potentials and possibilities of the world. Cliché or not, it is absolutely true. Toward the end of 2015, I was invited to teach on the Masters in Transmedia Communication program at EAFIT University in Colombia, which serves as the first postgraduate degree devoted to transmediality in Latin America.

We discuss this institution in more detail in the introduction, but allow me to set the scene for the idea of this book by saying that, having worked on the content of the Masters program in the autumn of 2015, I then flew out to teach in Colombia, delivering workshops about the different models, strategies and techniques of transmedia storytelling – focusing primarily on US and UK contexts. The primary aim here was to lay out the core characteristics and tendencies of transmedia stories so that the students could then apply particular conceptual ideas and strategies when developing their own transmedia projects. However, what struck me about the whole experience was that when working in a Colombian environment, many – though not all – of my ingrained ideas about what transmediality actually is were largely irrelevant. When understanding transmediality, in other words, travelling really does broaden the mind. As such, I thank this trip for opening my eyes to some of the true potentials of transmediality.

And, of course, I wholeheartedly thank my co-editor for his efforts, as well as each of our contributors for providing such rich and fascinating chapters that fulfilled our vision of globalizing transmedia studies.

Proctor:

I have been enormously fortunate to work with Matthew Freeman on various occasions, and I would like to thank him for our many conversations about transmedia, which, of course, ended up leading to this book and the genesis of our Transmedia Earth Network (stay tuned!).

Matthew's rapid rise to Reader is testament to his passion and energy for academic work, and I consider myself a better scholar because of our collaborative activities.

I am also grateful for the many conversations I have had with scholars over the past seven years or so on all things transmedia, and I would like to take a moment to express my gratitude. In no particular order, thanks to Jessica Austin, Martin Barker, Justin Battin, Lucy Bennett, Paul Benton, Will Brooker, Steve Canon, Dan Hassler-Forest, Jonathan Gray, John Paul Green, Colin B. Harvey, Matt Hills, Henry Jenkins, Rob Jewitt, Julia Knight, Ann Luce, Richard McCulloch, Mark McKenna, Neil Perryman, Tom Phillips, Jim Pope, Martin Shingler, Andrew T. Smith, Clarissa Smith, John Storey, Bronwen Thomas and Mark J.P Wolf.

And, of course, many thanks to all our contributors that have made editing this book such a joy.

Introduction

Conceptualizing National and Cultural Transmediality

Matthew Freeman and William Proctor

Across the globe, people now engage with media content across multiple platforms, following stories, characters, worlds, brands and other information across a spectrum of media channels. And yet perhaps the biggest challenge and the biggest opportunity for understanding this transmedia phenomenon right now is the sheer breadth of its interpretation. In the contemporary era of media convergence where the sharing of media across multiple platforms is increasingly accessible, transmediality has emerged as a global strategy for targeting fragmentary audiences and spreading content across a spectrum of media channels. But while scholarship continues to dwell on the commercial industry contexts of transmediality, smaller national communities and often far less commercial cultures around the world are now beginning to make very different and altogether nationally specific uses of transmediality, applying alternative modes of the transmedia phenomenon to the needs and structures of a nation or rethinking this phenomenon entirely by reapplying it to nonfictional-, cultural-, political-, social- or heritage-based projects.

Consider Colombia, a country that will be interrogated later in this book. Here, transmediality is not – or rather should not be – any kind of commercial practice of storytelling, promotion, world-building, franchising and the like. Instead, it is a political system that is nothing short of pivotal to developing social change in local communities; for some Colombians, transmediality is about reconstructing memories (Freeman 2016c). In opposition to the giant media conglomerates underpinning many examples of commercial transmedia franchises in the USA – characterized by the likes of Star Wars, Marvel and Batman – in Colombia, it is independent producers and universities who serve as the key drivers of that country's current transmedia trend. One project, for example – developed at EAFIT University in Medellín in 2015 – aimed to create nonofficial narratives of the Colombian armed conflict from the victims' point of view. By using different platforms such as games, maps, web series, books and museums, the Medellín victims were able to communicate their thoughts and memories about the Colombian armed conflict to both local and national public spheres. In short, in the context of contemporary Colombia, transmediality goes beyond social change – it is a blessing born out of a long history of cultural tradition and community-building that can help Colombians reconstruct the country after more than fifty years of armed conflict. As one of the postgraduate students at EAFIT University asserts,

> I strongly believe that transmedia in Colombia can contribute to creating processes of memory, recognition and solidarity for the victims of the Colombian armed conflict. I think that using transmedia with local communities can be the clue to starting real processes of reconciliation in the country.

The emphasis, then, is on using transmediality – most broadly describing 'the increasingly popular industrial practice of using multiple media technologies to present information … through a range of textual forms' (Evans 2011, 1) – for something *real*, going beyond fictional and commercial contexts of storytelling, branding, marketing and franchising. If nothing else, the Colombian project above signals the importance of beginning to fully interrogate transmedia cultures – in the plural – and to establish a cultural specificity approach to transmediality.

Not only do these more localized, cultural perspectives on transmediality remain considerably under-documented in academic circles, but so far there has been very little attempt to analyze, theorize and to fully understand a national or cultural idea of transmediality. Convergence culture is really only an umbrella term for making sense of the proliferation of interconnected screens and media texts that dominate our contemporary media culture. And as has been rightly pointed out by James Hay and Nick Couldry, 'international differences are obscured by the generality of the term "convergence culture", and it can be helpful to consider convergence "cultures"' in the plural' (2011, 476). *Global Convergence Cultures: Transmedia Earth* aims precisely to pluralize understandings of both convergence culture and transmediality, and in turn to redress the gap by contributing new frameworks and taxonomies from international contexts.

Specifically, and in establishing a cultural specificity approach to transmediality, the book looks across four continents – Europe, North and South America and Asia – and a total of twelve countries, spanning the UK, Spain, Portugal, France, Estonia, the USA, Canada, Colombia, Brazil, Japan, India and Russia. In doing so, it explores how the national media structures, agendas, policies and cultures of these countries (including their institutional systems, politics, heritages, social traditions, leisures, ideologies, etc.) are informing nationally specific models and meanings of transmediality. As such, this book aims to greatly enrich current understandings of transmediality, moving far beyond commonly studied scenarios of Hollywood convergences and globalized digital communication giants by instead beginning to map and to theorize how the rising prominence of transmediality across cultural borders has been used in very different ways to engage and to reshape local cultural communities and their national stories around the world.

Rethinking Transmediality

The transmedia phenomenon has led to the burgeoning of transmedia studies in media, cultural and communication studies departments across the academy, not to mention across a spectrum of creative and cultural industries. And yet the definition of transmediality remains decidedly in flux, indeed meaning different things to different people at different times. Since Marsha Kinder (1991) first used 'transmedia' to describe the multiplatform and multimodal expansion of media content, the term has seen increased academic and industry attention. Henry Jenkins (2006) reintroduced the term within the context of digital change, and 'transmedia storytelling' has subsequently seen widespread adoption and interrogation. Jenkins' updated definition of transmedia storytelling as 'a process where integral elements of a fiction get dispersed systematically across multiple channels for the purpose of creating a unified and coordinated entertainment experience' (2011) has become one of the dominant ways by which the flow of entertainment across media is understood, especially in a digital and commercial context. The correlation between transmedia storytelling and the commerce of entertainment has since been reinforced in industry and discursively. As *Heroes* creator Tim Kring asserts, transmedia storytelling is 'rather like building your Transformer and putting little rocket ships on the side' (Kushner 2008). By providing audiences with more and more content, transmediality is characteristically seen as a practice intended to appeal to migratory audiences; hence why scholars including David Alpert and Rick Jacobs (2004) and Jay Lemke (2004) theorized transmediality as that which produces a 'marketing assault' designed to 'maximize profits'.

Accordingly, Jenkins' model of transmedia storytelling (of a single narrative that is only complete when elements from multiple media forms are brought together into a coherent whole) is still most closely associated with what Birkinbine, Gómez and Wasko refer to as the global media giants – those being 'the huge media conglomerates such as Disney and Time-Warner, [which] take advantage of globalization to expand abroad and diversify' (2017, 15). Outside of the conglomerates, though, transmedia storytelling has evolved in more experimental spaces – into a brand-development practice, or as a way to support traditional media content through transmedia franchising (Johnson 2013), to name just a few of its commercial purposes. But transmediality has equally gained wider scholarly relevance as digital screen technologies have multiplied where the so-called old media of film and television are now experienced through transmedia distribution practices (Evans 2015), integrating with social media and other online platforms. Other terms such as 'multiplatform' (Jeffery-Poulter 2003), 'cross-media' (Bechmann Petersen 2006) and 'second screening' have joined it (Holt and Sanson 2014), but transmediality remains a dominant concept for both scholarly and industrial attempts to understand fundamental shifts that digital technologies have wrought on the media industries and their audiences.

However, the more that transmediality has broadened its definition and practical use – growing into both a distinct subfield of scholarly investigation and a cross-disciplinary theoretical concept that underpins work in film, television, digital media, game studies, communication studies, cultural studies and beyond – the more that it has arguably become something else entirely. While in the USA and the UK transmediality has evolved into an established marketing and brand-development practice (see, for example, Grainge and Johnson 2015; Gray 2010), emerging research across Europe paints a different picture of transmediality. In Europe, transmediality can occupy the role of a promotion tool for independent filmmakers, or that of a site of construction for social reality games, or even serve as a means of political activism (see Freeman 2016b; Scolari, Bertetti and Freeman 2014). In countries such as Spain, meanwhile, entire curricula are now being developed around the potential application of transmediality as a tool for educational and literacy enhancement for students seeking advanced global citizenship skills (Scolari 2013).

Hence one thing starts to become very clear: when conceived of or utilized as a cultural practice – rather than as a commercially minded industrial one – transmediality is suddenly no longer about storytelling, at least not in a traditional fictional sense. Instead, it is about something more, something more *real* – that is to say, something more political, more socially minded and more ideologically profound. So while Jenkins famously theorized transmediality within a digital and industrial context, what does it really mean to study transmediality from a *cultural* perspective?

From Global to Cultural

In one sense, examining transmediality from a national and cultural perspective first means acknowledging the innate multiplicity of its potential. And so in another sense, examining transmediality from a national and cultural perspective also means establishing a whole new *cultural specificity model* or approach to understandings of transmediality, taking into account the politics, peoples, ideologies, social values, cultural trends, histories, leisure and heritage of individual countries and their smaller communities. Taking a cultural approach to analyzing transmediality really means mapping the many faces of transmediality in different countries.

In some ways, the idea of mapping the many faces of transmediality around the world flies in the face of globalization, which most broadly describes the growth of media on a worldwide scale. The process of global integration concerning the international influence of economies and cultures has led to a change in the way that scholars now discuss present-day media as that which is 'produced, distributed, marketed, exhibited and consumed in many different countries, and which intends to reach international audiences and provide international conglomerates with profit' (Mirrlees 2013, 2). Media globalization has of course led to a rise in the number and size of multinational media corporations, but also in a proliferation of cross-border transactions of media products, such as the same film characters and stories being distributed globally or the same news being watched globally. As such, scholars such as David Machin and Theo van Leeuwen have emphasized the close association between globalization theory and the idea that 'cultural differences are disappearing as a result of globalization' (2007, 26). The disappearance of cultural differences, otherwise known as homogeneity, is linked to the interconnectivity between previously separate audiences and media forms that is itself part of the globalization process. If homogeneity is seen to be a potential cultural impact of globalization most broadly, then interconnectivity between industries, platforms and even products very much shapes media on a textual level. For instance, Doris Baltruschat (2010) understands global media ecologies as connections between television networks, as co-productions in the film industry (between the USA and China, for example), as international news coverage, or as format franchises (*The X Factor*, to name just one). Put simply, globalization may well equate to a standardizing of media culture.

In contrast, however, the chapters in this book – showcasing the diverse, localized practices, meanings, policies, expectations, limitations and cultures of transmediality around the world – aim to collectively free transmediality from its standardized, globalized and highly Western-centric understanding. The oft-cited model of transmediality – that is, the one seemingly based on convergences in the name of commerce – is not the only one. As Freeman has demonstrated elsewhere, 'past builders of fictional story worlds employed many different strategies that showcase just how many possibilities there really are for telling tales across multiple media' (2016a, 189–190). Similarly, we claim that only by looking to other countries and by localizing understandings of transmediality can one truly begin to comprehend all of the strategies that can be used – and indeed are being used – to communicate media messages across multiple platforms. For as Machin and van Leeuwen note, 'in globalization theory, the "national" and the "international" are closely interrelated ... Historically, as the world "universalized", people began to hank for "the particular", the reinvention of differences' (2007, 29). This book is about the cultural particularities of transmediality, showcasing a reinvention of its national differences.

Toward a Cultural Specificity Approach

So, again, how might one examine transmediality from a cultural perspective? Or to put it another way, how do the unique cultures, politics, heritages and social traditions specific to a given country and its media systems and audiences inform specific workings of transmediality? In identifying a conceptual framework for exploring the multiplicities of transmediality, it is crucial to turn to the discipline of cultural studies – in this case, particularly, its long-standing concept of 'Culturalism'. Introduced by sociologist Florian Znaniecki in the early 20th century, Culturalism is an ontological approach that ultimately aims to eliminate simple binaries between seemingly opposing phenomena, such as nature and culture. For our purposes, this approach is important for remembering that all sorts of cultural factors, including the likes of politics, peoples, ideologies, social values, heritage, etc., are not opposing factors but rather contributing factors in the building of a larger (trans)media system. Znaniecki proposed that a Culturalism approach allowed him to 'define social phenomena in cultural terms' (Halas 2010, 2), noting that our culture shapes our view of the world and our thinking (Dulczewski 1984, 187–188). Similarly, and as will be demonstrated in different ways throughout the pages of this book, the cultures of individual countries work to shape the meanings, models and functions of transmediality in distinct ways. Importantly, Znaniecki argues that while the world is composed of physical artefacts, such as films, television programs, corporate offices, policy documents and so on, we are not really capable of studying the physical world other than through the lenses of culture (Dulczewski 1984, 189) – just as the peoples of each of the countries examined in this book are prone to understanding their transmedia system through the lens of their culture.

Cultural studies, of course, has always sought to explore the forces within and through which people conduct and participate in the construction of their everyday lives. As a field of study, it is based on observing the narrower or more personal cultures that people create; it understands communities – or, in this case, cultures of transmediality – as unique communities, which while still part of larger systems, operate independently. A turn toward cultural studies and to interrogating the cultures of transmediality is in many ways only a logical continuation of what is already happening in other areas of media studies. In *Production Studies: Cultural Studies of Media Industries*, for example, Vicki Mayer, Miranda J. Banks and John Thornton Caldwell sought to 'dig deeper into this notion of production as a culture', looking at 'how media producers make culture' (2009, 2). Here, Mayer, Banks and Caldwell conceived that 'the off-screen production of media is itself a cultural production, mythologized and branded much like the onscreen textual culture that media industries produce' (2009, 2). Conceptualizing media production in this way has become crucial to our understanding of media industry studies, for it points to ideas that media industry workings can all be analyzed, textually, in much the same way that a film or a television program might be analyzed textually. Going a step further, then, it figures that by exploring different manifestations of transmediality through the lens of cultural studies, we can not only understand transmediality as a culture, or as a set of cultures, but also assess the relationships between the workings of a given culture and its transmedial formations, with the ethnographic turn toward studying social spaces such as shopping centers and museums equally useful here for analyzing the cultural mappings of transmedial zones.

When thinking discursively and through the lens of Culturalism, moreover, it is likely to be the case – as it so often is in the chapters of this book – that 'transmedia' is not actually the focus of study at all but is instead the theoretical framework through which a different though no less significant area of enquiry can then be investigated and analyzed. For example, Chapter 4 positions transmediality as key to understanding transformations in the cultural heritage sector in France, Chapter 5 sees transmediality as a mechanism for supporting cultural heterogeneity and for understanding cultural semiotics in Estonia, Chapter 8 unravels the role of transmediality in generating processes of social memory construction in Colombia, Chapter 10 argues that transmediality is central to the workings of national branding in Japan and so on. Or to put it another way, this book's cultural specificity approach is about rethinking transmediality as something else – transmediality as slow journalism, transmediality as social identity construction, transmediality as cultural heritage, transmediality as national branding, transmediality as documentary, etc. That is not to say that we ignore industry, however; Chapters 1 and 2 are rooted in explorations of the UK and Spanish media industries, respectively. But in both of these cases, the authors seek to showcase the different systems of transmediality that exist within these media industries – systems that are entirely specific to those two country's media infrastructures. And this positioning of transmediality, alongside or within the context of some other media, cultural and industrial phenomena altogether, speaks of the sheer diversity that now makes up the very fabric of transmediality around the world, and reiterates the extent to which transmediality is now beginning to thoroughly reshape our media and cultural landscape.

Nevertheless, even as our cultural specificity approach implies a rethinking of transmediality as some other cultural phenomenon, it is still necessary to pinpoint what we mean by 'culture' in this context. Earlier we indicated an interest in studying how the likes of politics, heritage, traditions, ideologies, leisure and war might lend themselves to the workings of transmediality. But all of these cultural phenomena are of course quite different entities; and so is it possible to map different cultural phenomena to different approaches of transmediality? The answer, as the ensuing chapters will demonstrate, is yes – but for now allow us to summarily map the approaches to transmediality taken throughout this book to Raymond Williams' three theories of culture.

Back in 1958, Raymond Williams published *Culture and Society*, a seminal work exploring how the notion of culture developed in the West, especially in the UK, from the 18th through the 20th centuries. Williams proposed that culture can be defined according to one of three categories: culture as 'the ideal' (meaning culture as a process of intellectual, spiritual and aesthetic development), culture as 'the social' (meaning culture as a specific way of life) and culture as 'the documentary' (meaning works and practices of intellectual and artistic activity).

Logically, the cultural phenomena interrogated in our book (people, politics, heritage, social values, ideologies and so on) fit most comfortably into Williams' second category, indicating that we are exploring the meanings, functions and workings of transmediality as *a way of life*. Chapters devoted to the transmedia brand narratives surrounding Portuguese port wines and to the role of transmediality in the radicalization of Canada, for example, exemplify understandings of transmediality as 'the social'. But that is not to suggest that our book is limited to social perspectives on culture. Other chapters devoted to the use of transmediality in reconstructing social memory in Colombia and to building national branding in Japan, for example, can be seen to embody Williams' notion of 'the ideal', with both of these chapters positioning transmediality as a form of intellectual, spiritual and aesthetic development. And each of the other chapters can be said to be exploring the cultures of transmediality through the lens of what Williams calls 'the documentary' – interrogating how the creative works and how practices of a country are being crafted as intellectual and artistic exercises in communicating messages across multiple media platforms.

The Structure of the Book

The book is divided into twelve chapters and split into three parts – 'European Transmediality', 'North and South American Tramsmediality', and 'Asian Transmediality'. Within these three parts, each of the chapters interrogates a different country. However, our goal is certainly not to cover all transmedia-producing countries around the world; that would be encyclopedic and an impossible task for one edited collection. We also do not intend each chapter to represent the practices that are most characteristic of a given nation. Instead, our chapters show that there are multiple versions of transmediality emerging around the world, even within the same country. In broadening understandings of transmediality from its oft-cited US-centric model, our book pays particular attention to forms of transmediality that are not tied to the globalized media industry, focusing on ways in which transmediality takes on cultural, social and political impacts locally.

In 'Part I: European Transmediality', then, Matt Hills' chapter asserts that transmedia studies can (and should) be extended beyond its customary focus on film, television and video games by instead tackling pop music and, more specifically, the cultural mythos surrounding the UK band the Justified Ancients of Mu Mu and their 2017 'comeback'. Showing how the band transmedially aligned themselves with a mythos of grandly elemental (but hidden) conflict played out through popular music, Hills delves into the transmedia aesthetics of popular music. The chapter argues that the band's 'Welcome to the Dark Ages' events occupy the status of a complex self-reflexive transmedia undertaking – spanning the forms of novels, merchandise, film, fan-created art and events – that embraces contradictory discourses between art and folk, subversive and on-brand.

Also centered on European transmediality, Chapter 2 sees Carlos A. Scolari, Mar Guerrero-Pico and María-José Establés examine present-day Spanish transmediality. This chapter presents what the authors call a 'state of the art' of transmedia production in Spain, focusing on fictional narratives. Despite the explosion of transmediality, Scolari, Guerrero-Pico and Establés-Heras argue that Spanish productions feature a number of limitations compared to projects from broader markets. They explore differing attitudes toward transmediality in the Spanish media industries, introducing and describing a first generation of transmedia productions – led by *Águila Roja* (2009) – before reflecting on the emergence of a more advanced second generation of transmedia fictions – as exemplified by *Isabel* (2012–2015) and *El Ministerio del Tiempo* (2015–2016), among others. The authors pinpoint the significance of public service broadcasting and crowdfunding on the narrative and promotional expansion of media across platforms in Spain.

Chapter 3, by Matthew Freeman and Ana Margarida Meira, considers how the transmedia narratives surrounding Portuguese port wines have forged affective connections with people via their cultural connections with the collective memories of a Portuguese culture heritage. The chapter explores how transmedia brand narratives convert the relationship between consumers and products in cultural spaces. Transmedia narratives are typically built by brands to tell the stories that define the essence and identity of their products, but Freeman and Meira analyze how consumers construct a bridge between the tangibility of products, producers and brands, and a more intangible dimension enclosed by emotions and collective memories. More specifically, the chapter analyzes how the work of cultural intermediaries ties consumers into a moment of sharing individual and collective memories that transform this dynamic into a fluid transmedial dimension formed by cultural spaces. Since few products are quite so closely tied to Portuguese tradition, culture, history and memory as port wine, the chapter focuses on the transmedia brand narratives of two port wines – Kopke and Vasques de Carvalho – to understand how these brand narratives are interwoven into the culture, heritage and memory of the Portuguese people.

Chapter 4, by Mélanie Bourdaa, moves on to document the role of transmedia storytelling as cultural heritage in France, exploring how new technologies and their uses have changed the way that culture is apprehended in the French context. Bourdaa aims to specify the relationship between museums and other institutions that preserve local, national or international cultural patrimony – in a broad sense, including exhibitions, historical monuments and facts, folklore, etc. – and the rise of a participatory culture. To do so, the chapter focuses on the 'Media-Num' (Digital Media for Patrimony and Culture) project, analyzing the role of transmedia storytelling in terms of the valorization of patrimony and cultural heritage in France. By examining how Jenkins' canonical definition of transmedia storytelling ['a process where integral elements of a fiction is dispersed systematically across multiple delivery channels for the purpose of creating a unified and coordinated entertainment experience' (2006), 95–96)] can be applied to educational projects, museum exhibitions and the valorization of cultural patrimony, Bourdaa shows how French projects use strategies of transmedia storytelling to better communicate the cultural heritage of the country and in turn to engage a younger, participatory audience in the process.

Chapter 5, by Indrek Ibrus and Maarja Ojamaa, considers the dual role of transmediality in Estonia, showing it function as both a mechanism for supporting cultural heterogeneity and for enforcing coherence and stability in culture via maintaining the relevance of historical media texts. The chapter delves into both of these two distinct contexts – exploring transmediality in the local film and television industries and also showing how the transmedia concept evolved within the Tartu-Moscow semiotic school's conception of cultural dynamics. Ibrus and Ojamaa argue that, more than any other rationale, transmediality in Estonia is expected to serve as a strategy for converging with the much more successful Information and Communication Technology industry, largely on account of the small scope and relative lack of funding for media in Estonia. But the chapter also outlines the key cases of transmedial development in this country, pointing to the importance of the public sector (for example, the Estonian Film Institute), whose neoliberal agenda has facilitated a commercial efficiency and global reach for parts of the local audiovisual sector. In doing so, the chapter offers a comparative analysis of these two different yet complementary frameworks for transmediality in Estonia, ultimately arguing that what connects both frameworks are the dynamics of change in the country's local cultures and markets within the globalized world.

In 'Part II: North and South American Transmediality', William Proctor's chapter challenges the current 'no adaptation rule' (Dena 2018) in transmedia storytelling by drawing upon the imaginary world of US author Stephen King as a case study, focusing on literature. As with Hills' comments in his chapter regarding music being largely occluded from work on transmedia, Proctor argues that studies of transmediality have often excluded literature from the media ecosystem, considering the way in which the contemporary fetishization of transmedia storytelling, especially the utopian model proposed by Henry Jenkins (2006), has prioritized platform migration over other elements, especially what Richard Saint-Gelais (2011) describes as 'transfictionality.' Redressing this, Proctor examines the way in which King developed and deployed his imaginary world not with coherent world-building in mind and design but in hindsight, through various narrative techniques including trans-fictional storytelling, 'retroactive linkages' (Wolf 2012), 'ontological rules' (Ryan 2017) and a distinct version of what he terms *reflexive transmedia storytelling* whereby authors and proxy authors evoke the ontological rules of the story world in 'orienting paratexts' (Mittell 2015) to enable and activate various transmedia elements toward imagined coherence and 'stratified hyperdiegesis'. In doing so, Proctor demonstrates the way that binaries between adaptation and transmedia, between licensing and transmedia, are complicated and confounded by the King multiverse, showing that such transmedia expressions are but one element in a lengthier chain of trans-associations.

Chapter 7, by Marie-Ève Carignan and Sara Marcil-Morin, analyzes the media coverage of the terrorist attacks of Canada in 2014 in order to understand the role of transmediality in the radicalization of Canada. Politically, these attacks were linked to the Islamic State of Iraq and the Levant activities in the media, and Carignan draws on this political context to examine the implications for transmediality in terms of how we understand radicalization and terrorism in Canada. Specifically, this chapter outlines the media coverage of the shooting that took place on Ottawa's Parliament Hill on 22 October 2014. Carignan and Marcil-Morin argue that the way that traditional media related what was said on social media, including by the perpetrator, which was integrated with the live broadcasting of a speech to the nation by Canadian Prime Minister Stephen Harper, raises questions about the coverage of the events as a transmedia experience. In short, the chapter takes this situation as a jumping-off point for assessing how transmediality is implicit in citizens' understanding of terrorism and religious radicalization in this country.

Chapter 8, by Camilo Andrés Tamayo Gómez and Omar Mauricio Velásquez, builds on Carignan's study of Canadian radicalization by exploring how the peace politics in Colombia have led to cultural projects that unite displaced citizens via the communicative power of transmedia messages. The chapter analyzes the communicative and expressive dimensions of civil society's collective action as a mechanism to restore a sense of citizenship through the development of transmedia projects. Gómez and Velásquez show how collective belonging and human rights are constructed through processes of memory, recognition and solidarity, where the development of transmedia projects is key in order to catalyze social cohesion in fragile Colombian communities. The city of Medellin serves as the chapter's case study, analyzing two projects: the transmedia social project 'Memory, Territory and Peace' and the Antioquia Museum's exhibition 'Exile and Reparation'. A key aim is to understand what kind of citizen processes these two transmedia projects can open up within contexts of armed conflict and how these practices have affected human rights in Medellin from a civil society perspective. Gomez and Velasquez argue that it is evident in the Colombian context that the development of transmedia projects for different civil society groups can generate processes of social memory construction and political solidarity.

Chapter 9, by Felipe Muanis and Rosane Svartman, examines the experimental boundaries between fan and corporate content in relation to Brazilian telenovelas. With television changing – artistically, socially and economically – this chapter considers the role and power of audiences in the new era of Brazilian transmedia television. If in the past only the 'cold' audience rating or information gathered through qualitative research (focus groups, for example) influenced the television stations and content producers, nowadays a campaign made by fans online can help a program build audiences and prestige. Muanis and Svartman explore this contemporary context in Brazil, and by reflecting on the relationship between the audience and telenovelas, this chapter discusses how the former can – in addition to influencing the development of the latter, which is the most traditional product in Brazilian television – interfere in the production and consumption of those narratives. Using empirical research drawn from audience engagement and crowd-sourcing projects for telenovelas in Brazilian television – namely TV Globo, Brazil's biggest media firm – this chapter reflects on the renewal possibilities of Brazilian television in its quest for relevance today, demonstrating how telenovelas have been changing in their forms of participation and spectatorship amidst national and international media transformations.

In 'Part III: Asian Transmediality', Manuel Hernández-Pérez's chapter explores transmediality as institutional communication and national branding in Japan. The chapter uses narrative theory as the main axis for a communicational and rhetorical study of Japanese media and its transmedia culture. To do so, Hernández-Pérez explores the main Japanese communication agents and the current state of the convergence process in this country, taking into account both technological and sociological aspects. In particular, he assesses how the reformulations of non-fictional national branding strategies aligned to the popular 'Cool Japan' fictional narratives in Japan work together to create the Tokyo 2020 Olympic Games discourse as a transmedia narrative. Pointing to the function of fictionality and the role of fictional characters in seemingly nonfictional cultural narratives, Hernández-Pérez argues that it is almost impossible to build effective cultural (or nonfictional) messages across multiple media platforms that avoid referencing elements from other communication structures, notably fictional entertainment.

Chapter 11, by Matthew Freeman, considers questions of location in relation to transmediality, explored against the backdrop of digital technologies and mobile devices in contemporary India. Freeman's chapter focuses on *Priya's Shakti*, a transmedia project that uses comic books, exhibitions, augmented reality and street art to call attention to the struggles faced by women in Indian society. It uses *Priya's Shakti* as a lens through which to explore the significance of interactive mobile devices and augmented reality technology on the role of transmediality, thinking about what it now means to conceptualize the transmediation of reality and arguing that *Priya's Shakti* exemplifies the way in which transmediality can be used to reshape how we see the world. In short, Freeman demonstrates how mobile devices, comic books, augmented reality and street art murals are all used strategically and creatively in this transmedia project to draw attention to the line standing between worlds of reality and fantasy simultaneously, using the separation and technologically aided overlap between these worlds to provoke emotions.

Chapter 12, lastly, by Renira Rampazzo Gambarato, examines the ways in which transmedia storytelling strategies have come to operate as new forms of political activism in Russia. To do so, Gambarato's chapter examines *Grozny: Nine Cities*, a transmedia experience created by a team of Russian documentary photographers, journalists, filmmakers and photojournalists. This collaborative project depicts the hidden layers of Grozny, the capital of Chechnya, a city coping with the aftermath of two wars. It is a nonfictional cultural project that aims to raise awareness of the postwar suffering that the population is facing and to begin the much-needed dialogue between Chechens and Russians, fighting against their mutual prejudices, and to unify both communities. The chapter discusses the forms of interactive documentary and slow journalism as the theoretical background through which the transmedia analysis of the *Grozny: Nine Cities* project is founded. The methodological approach to analyzing this project is the transmedia project design analytical model established previously by Gambarato (2013), which outlines the features of the design process behind transmedia experiences in order to, in this case, understand the diverse facets of the *Grozny: Nine Cities* story world in the midst of convergence cultures.

Looking forward a little, two overarching themes link the chapters of this book. The first theme concerns the importance of conceptualizing transmediality as a series of systems for building and capturing memory. Colin Harvey (2015) argues that memory is a key component of transmedia storytelling insofar as audiences are required to remember the specifics of a story world across media, and also in terms of the remembered set of expectations with which audiences encounter and engage with transmedia artefacts – a mechanism that certainly relates to Chapter 1's exploration of the Justified Ancients of Mu Mu's 'comeback' and Chapter 6's study of the Stephen King universe. But beyond this individualized definition of memory, this book's chapters collectively highlight a notion of transmediality as the capturing of a broader, more collective *cultural* memory. While Chapters 3, 4 and 5 all deal with questions of cultural heritage, Chapter 8 explicitly explores transmedia projects that were designed to preserve the memory of the Colombian population. Chapter 10, too, is rooted in memories of Japan's past. The second theme concerns the way in which a number of chapters depict transmediality as something that helps people. Chapter 8 certainly conveys this theme, as do Chapters 11 and 12, which both deal with transmedia projects designed to help citizens cope with oppression and grief. Regardless of its different systems, practices and meanings around the world, the idea that transmediality is a method for helping people and for holding onto fading cultural memories is a powerful thought.

Looking even further forward, the book's diverse approach to analyzing transmediality according to specific cultures does raise some important questions about the future of transmediality, particularly in terms of its definition in academic circles and what it actually *is*. This book paints an enormously varied picture of transmediality, but as Henry Jenkins asserts,

> this does not mean that transmedia means everything to all people and thus means nothing to anyone. Rather, it means that we need to be precise about what forms of transmedia we are discussing and what claims we are making about them.
>
> (2016)

It is our hope that the chapters of this book have successfully grounded their interpretation and manifestation of transmediality in the local cultural context of the country being studied. Nevertheless, given that our cultural studies approach is based on observing the narrower or more personal cultures that different people create every day, the inevitable question must follow: How else might other groups of people come to interpret transmediality in other cultures not dealt with in the pages of this book? And how else might transmediality begin to reshape cultural communities; to tell stories of political, social and heritage tradition; and indeed to fulfill any number of other cultural functions around the world? Only time will tell, but for now let's relish in the extensive, salient and wide-ranging insights of our contributors, beginning with a study of the UK before moving through chapters on Spain, Portugal, France, Estonia, the USA, Canada, Colombia, Brazil, Japan and, finally, Russia.

Bibliography

Alpert, David and Rick Jacobs. "Videogames and Licensing in the Hollywood Film Market." Paper presented at the *Korea Games Conference*, October 16, 2004.
Baltruschat, Doris. *Global Media Ecologies: Networked Production in Film and Television*. London: Routledge, 2010.

Bechmann Petersen, Anja. "Internet and Cross Media Production: Case Studies in Two Major Danish Media Organizations." *Australian Journal of Emerging Technology and* Society 4:2 (2006): 94–107.

Birkinbine, Benjamin J., Rodrigo Gómez, and Rodrigo Wasko (eds.). *Global Media Giants*. London: Routledge, 2017.

Dena, Christa. "Transmedia Adaptation: Revising the No Adaptation Rule." In *The Routledge Companion to Transmedia Studies*, edited by Matthew Freeman and Rampazzo Gambarato Renira. London and New York: Routledge, 2018.

Dulczewski, Zygmunt. Florian Znaniecki: życie i dzieło. *Poznań: Wydawnictwo Poznańskie*, 1984.

Evans, Elizabeth. *Transmedia Television: Audiences, New Media, and Daily Life*. New York: Routledge, 2011.

Evans, Elizabeth. "Building Digital Estates: Transmedia Television in Industry and Daily Life." Paper presented at the *ECREA TV in the Age of Transnationalisation and Transmediation Conference*, Roehampton University, June 22, 2015.

Freeman, Matthew. *Historicising Transmedia Storytelling: Early Twentieth-Century Transmedia Story Worlds*. London: Routledge, 2016a.

Freeman, Matthew. "Small Change – Big Difference: Tracking the Transmediality of Red Nose Day." *View: Journal of European Television History and Culture* 5:10 (2016b): 87–96.

Freeman, Matthew. "'Real' Transmedia: Cultures and Communities of Cross-Platform Media in Colombia." *Antenna: Responses to Media and Culture*. January 27, 2016c. Accessed 18 July 2017. http://blog.commarts.wisc.edu/2016/01/27/real-transmedia/.

Gambarato, Renira Rampazzo. "Transmedia Project Design: Theoretical and Analytical Considerations." *Baltic Screen Media Review* 1:80 (2013): 80–100.

Grainge, Paul, and Catherine Johnson. *Promotional Screen Industries*. London and New York: Routledge, 2015.

Gray, Jonathan. *Show Sold Separately: Promos, Spoilers, and Other Media Paratexts*. New York: New York University Press, 2010.

Halas, Elżbieta. *Towards the World Culture Society: Florian Znaniecki's Culturalism*. Bern: Peter Lang, 2010.

Harvey, Colin. *Fantastic Transmedia: Narrative, Play and Memory across Science Fiction and Fantasy Storyworlds*. Basingstoke: Palgrave Macmillan, 2015.

Hay, James, and Nick Couldry. "Rethinking Convergence/Culture: An Introduction." *Cultural Studies* 25:4 (2011): 473–486.

Holt, Jennifer, and Kevin Sanson (eds.). *Connected Viewing: Selling, Streaming and Sharing Media in the Digital Age*. London: Routledge, 2014.

Kinder, Marsha. *Playing with Power in Movies, Television, and Video Games: From Muppet Babies to Teenage Mutant Ninja Turtles*. Berkeley: University of California Press, 1991.

Jeffery-Poulter, Stephen. "Creating and Producing Digital Content across Multiple Platforms." *Journal of Media Practice* 3:3 (2003): 155–165.

Jenkins, Henry. *Convergence Culture: Where Old and New Media Collide*. New York: New York University Press, 2006.

Jenkins, Henry. "Transmedia 202: Further Reflections." *Confessions of an Aca-Fan: The Official Weblog of Henry Jenkins*. August 1, 2011. Accessed 2 November 2012. http://henryjenkins.org/2011/08/dening_transmedia_further_re.html.

Jenkins, Henry. "Transmedia What?" *Immerse*. November 15, 2016. Accessed 4 August 2017. https://immerse.news/transmedia-what-15edf6b61daa.

Johnson, Derek. *Media Franchising: Creative License and Collaboration in the Culture Industries*. New York: New York University Press, 2013.

Kushner, David. "Rebel Alliance: How a Small Band of Sci-Fi Geeks Is Leading Hollywood into a New Era." *Fast Company*. May 2008. Accessed 21 September 2013. www.fastcompany.com/798975/rebel-alliance.

Lemke, Jay. "Critical Analysis across Media: Games, Franchises, and the New Cultural Order." Paper presented at the *First International Conference on Critical Discourse Analysis*, Valencia, 2004.

Machin, David, and Theo van Leeuwen. *Global Media Discourse: A Critical Introduction*. London: Routledge, 2007.

Mayer, Vicki, Miranda J. Banks, and John Thornton Caldwell. *Production Studies: Cultural Studies of Media Industries*. London: Routledge, 2009.

Mirrlees, Tanner. *Global Entertainment Media: Between Cultural Imperialism and Cultural Globalization*. London: Routledge, 2013.

Mittell, Jason. *Complex TV: The Poetics of Contemporary Television Storytelling*. New York: New York University Press, 2015.

Ryan, Marie-Laure. "Ontological Rules". In *The Routledge Companion to Imaginary Worlds*, edited by Mark J.P. Wolf, 74–81. London and New York: Routledge, 2017.

Saint-Gelais, Richard. *Fictions Transfuges: Transfictionnalité et ses enjeux*. Seuil: Paris, 2011.

Scolari, Carlos A. "Media Evolution: Emergence, Dominance, Survival, and Extinction in the Media Ecology." *International Journal of Communication* 7 (2013): 1418–1441.

Scolari, Carlos A., Paolo Bertetti, and Matthew Freeman. *Transmedia Archaeology: Storytelling in the Borderlines of Science Fiction, Comics and Pulp Magazines*. Basingstoke: Palgrave Pivot, 2014.

Williams, Raymond. *Culture and Society 1780–1950*. London: Chatto and Windus, 1958.

Wolf, Mark J.P. *Building Imaginary Worlds: The History and Theory of Subcreation*. London and New York: Routledge, 2012.

Part I
European Transmediality

1 United Kingdom

The Justified Ancients of Mu Mu's 'Comeback' as a Transmedia Undertaking

Matt Hills

Work on transmediality, despite being concerned with intellectual properties moving across media, has tended to focus on film, television, comic books and video games. When introducing transmedia storytelling as a concept, Henry Jenkins discusses the *Matrix* franchise (2006, 101). And it is emblematic of the field that Jan-Noel Thon's (2016) *Transmedial Narratology and Contemporary Media Culture* focuses on films, graphic novels and video games. Such an orientation has assumed that some media are not well suited, or even especially relevant, to understanding transmediality. For instance, popular music has been largely occluded, despite the fact that

> transmedia can play an important role ... since the identification of special characteristics within a given case is not restricted to the sphere of musical sounds and structures, rather the overall phenomenological spectrum of popular music, including gesture, (moving) image or fashion, is factored in. It is very likely that this perspective captures the realities of popular music fans.
>
> (Jost 2015, 4)

Rather than using transmediality as a lens through which to understand pop music and its fans, music has instead been confined to a distinct 'media family', and one not concerned with narrative (Thon 2016, 72) or cross-media meanings. However, here I will focus on a highly successful UK pop music act from the 1980s and 1990s: the Justified Ancients of Mu Mu (The JAMs)/the KLF, made up of Bill Drummond and Jimmy Cauty. In the summer of 2017, Cauty and Drummond staged an unusual multiday happening in Liverpool entitled 'Welcome to the Dark Ages' ('WTTDA'), the city being linked to the duo's pop-cultural history. The title of the event related to diegetic incidents from Drummond and Cauty's novel *2023* (Justified Ancients of Mu Mu 2017), where the internet is catastrophically disrupted, leading to a new 'Dark Age' (Gell 2017).

I am interested in considering the 'transmedia aesthetics' (Long 2017, 140) of popular music. In fact, the KLF have been described by Jeremy Deller – a leading proponent of participatory art – as 'one of the great mythological bands of all time' (in Harrison 2017, 18). As a pop music act, the JAMs/KLF have crafted a significant mythos around and through their music (Fitzgerald and Hayward 2016), appropriating Robert Shea and Robert Anton Wilson's novel *The Illuminatus! Trilogy* along with aspects of Discordianism as a new religious movement. The KLF also deleted their entire back catalogue at the height of their fame and single sales, and burnt £1 million – income from their pop career – on the island of Jura in 1994.

But if pop has typically been excluded from transmedia theorizations, then so too have the JAMs/KLF been marginalized in academic work. They are frequently lauded in music criticism and journalism; Bob Stanley's history of pop posits that either The Beatles or The KLF would be 'a hard one to argue with', if 'you were forced to name your favorite group of all time' (2014, 646). In a similar vein, chapters have been devoted to The Jams/KLF in book-length pop criticism of the 1990s focusing on sampling (Beadle 1993), and in later histories of 'indie' music mavericks (King 2012), while multiple volumes have been produced about the KLF's exploits by writers and music journalists (Higgs 2012; Shirley 2017). In contrast to their pop-journalistic canonization, scholarship focusing on the band – including Drummond and Cauty's subsequent literary and artistic work – has been thin on the ground (see, for example, Fitzgerald and Hayward 2016; McLeod 2011; Wiseman-Trowse 2014). I am therefore aiming to belatedly focus academic attention both on this particular UK band and the relationship of their music to transmediality.

'WTTDA' was unusual for the manner in which it shifted between music, popular fiction, physical merchandise, film, multiple forms of participatory art, and the announcement that Drummond and Cauty – as aging former pop stars – had entered a new and wholly serious career phase as undertakers, with all of these aspects being framed in relation to 'the realities of popular music [JAMs/KLF] fans' who had aged alongside their idols. It was announced in advance on bidolito.co.uk – the JAMs' mythos encompassing a strong opposition to music industry norms – that 'The Justified Ancients of Mu Mu in any of their ... guises ... [would] not be performing music'. Instead, the event (officially running from 23–25 August 2017) was immediately preceded by the book launch of a novel by the JAMs, *2023: A Trilogy*, itself timed to coincide with the end of a self-imposed twenty-three-year moratorium on Drummond and Cauty discussing their burning of the £1 million.

But if there was to be no pop music reunion, *contra* what has been attacked as 'retromania' (Reynolds 2011) and taken seriously in pop music scholarship as 'repackaged' pop (Driessen 2017), then how could 'WTTDA' function transmedially (and locally/internationally) in relation to the band's mythology? I will consider how – despite the fact there was no traditional 'reunion' performance from the JAMs/KLF – in a series of ways, their 1980s/1990s pop music output – and its associated mythos – was honored, updated and transmedially extended into literature, merchandise, and even the funerary arrangements of 'mumufication'. In what follows, then, I will address the role(s) of fandom and place within the transmedia undertaking of 'WTTDA'.

'Where on Earth to Begin?': The Mythology of the JAMs/KLF as a Challenge to Conventions of the Pop Music Industry … and Fandom

Only 400 tickets (priced at £100) were available for 'WTTDA', and when they went on sale it was not entirely clear what the event would involve. Potential ticket purchasers were told via bidolito.co.uk: 'There are no guest lists. There are no press passes. Every one of the 400 ticket holders will be expected to be Volunteers'. By selling such a limited number of tickets for a one-off event, the JAMs secured a sense of exclusivity as well as challenging typical industry hierarchies (where 'guest lists' and 'press passes' would usually grant privileged access over and above fans' access to ticketing). At the same time, however, ticketholders were not positioned as standard consumers within the 'experience economy' (Pine and Gilmore 1999), given that they were also expected to carry out the role of a 'Volunteer'. An anonymized contributor to Liverpool's niche newspaper covering the city's music scene, *Bido Lito!*, who wrote up 'WTTDA', observed that:

> We paid £100 for a bit-part in [something]… We 400 had become the band. It trumps that bit, which is just entertainment, where the singer makes you yell you're having a good time to obscure the emptiness.
>
> (One of the 400 2017, 28)

Bido Lito! played a key role in promoting the happening, stressing how it was grounded in the city's pop music-derived identity, and in Drummond and Cauty's (but especially Drummond's) prior links to Liverpool. The music paper's editor, Christopher Torpey, used an editorial to discuss a previous 'Situationist event' overseen by Drummond in Liverpool in 1984, said to be 'pure Drummond in its theatrical flair, designed purely to mess with the audience's heads' (Torpey 2017a, 9). The mystery surrounding 'WTTDA' took on a similarly theatrical lure. In Torpey's terms, 'these gaps in our knowledge are the key, cavities … conjecture, folklore and character flood into. These are the things a city is built on' (Torpey 2017a, 9) – namely, the creations and accretions of pop music mythology. Once the dust had begun to settle, Torpey returned to his theme that Liverpool itself was a collection of ever-evolving mythologies and (trans)mediations:

> [During those] surreal days in August, 23 Roscoe Lane … became the hub for the Justified Ancients of Mu Mu's Discordian/Situationist/

absurd (delete as appropriate) Welcome to the Dark Ages event. It was a brief period when it seemed like Liverpool was the centre of the world; ...on [the] national news, and filled with people buzzing with excitement and ritualistic fervor.

(Torpey 2017b, 9)

Just like its 1984 forerunner 'A Crystal Day', this event, too, was rendered more permanent via the fragmentary transmedial archives of the national press and broadcasters, operating alongside fan-posted footage of surprise guest Jarvis Cocker performing a newly reinterpreted rendition of 'Justified and Ancient'. But impermanence also necessarily ghosted across the happening (Wiseman-Trowse 2014); left behind it were peeling fly posters, chalked expressions of fandom for the Volunteer-created band Badger Kull, spray-painted signs and fans' memories of 'being there' which would 'live long [for] those for whom the legend around the KLF is almost sacred' (Torpey 2017b, 9).

Connections between the JAMs and Liverpool are positioned by *Bido Lito!* as not just one master story but 'many stories, not an easily navigated narrative footpath but a labyrinth of art and ideas. So where on Earth to begin?' (Fairclough 2017, 13). Transmedia narrative in the guise of popular music mythology becomes sedimented into fans' 'imagined memories', with fans wishing they could have 'been there' at canonized/romanticized gigs and ordinary moments when scenes or bands first emerged into the pop-cultural limelight (Duffett 2013, 229). Indeed, given the prevalence of pop's transmediated and recirculated 'imagined memories' – with these key moments, for example the KLF's performance at the 1992 Brit Awards, being recounted again and again in media coverage and pop journalism – it could be argued that the fans who eagerly acquired tickets for 'WTTDA' were wagering on the future fan-cultural status of 'having been there' at this happening, anticipating and projecting *future memories* of fan exclusivity. Rather than merely assimilating live events into an experience economy of popular music and myth, this places the JAMs' mythos at the service of fans' personal (and communal) mythologizing.

There is a sense of 'Transmedia Earth' here in terms of Liverpool's hosting of the event, with narratives of the city and the JAMs/KLF providing a network of connections for fans to navigate metaphorically and literally, as well as the pre-event mystery (and post-event picking-over) facilitating a transmedial 'negative space' (Long 2017, 147) which could be filled by fans' speculations, critiques, photos and commentaries. But alongside the locality of the event and its transmedia array of meaning-making, the involvement of fans was significantly international. 'The 400' ticketholders used a shared map within their Facebook group – containing 370 members at the time of writing – to plot where attendees had travelled from. Although the predominant cluster was UK based, this geographical information showed that fans had also travelled from Ireland, North America, Norway, Sweden and Denmark, Austria,

Holland, Spain, Germany, Switzerland, Israel, the United Arab Emirates, Australia and New Zealand. Evidently, to participate in the event (and the Facebook group) fans needed a degree of proficiency in the English language. However, given the exclusivity of the happening, and its potential to create future memories indexed to high fan status, it is perhaps unsurprising that such an international fan cohort was called into being.

How did 'WTTDA' draw on the pop music mythology of the JAMs/ KLF? Dan Hassler-Forest has been one of the few scholars to explicitly discuss pop music as transmedia storytelling, arguing that pop can be 'far more loosely organized than the fantastic worlds in media more preoccupied by narrative, such as literature, film, comic books, or even videogames': while its 'albums, music videos, and stage performances [can] contain obvious narrative elements, they simultaneously remain open to a wide variety of alternative readings' (2016, 175). Pop music can thus work via what Aaron Delwiche terms 'soft' transmedia, where 'a shared fictional world unfolds across media channels but there are relatively few narrative links between the channels' (2017, 37). Additionally, Hassler-Forest observes that even specific pop music tracks, using sampled sonic effects, dialogue and/or lyrics, can convey heteroglossic narrative content (2016, 175). The JAMs, by appropriating material from cult novel *The Illuminatus! Trilogy*, position themselves with the book's 'Justified Ancients of Mummu' (Higgs 2012, 232) as agents of chaos opposed to rival repressive forces that are manipulating and using the record industry (Fitzgerald and Hayward 2016, 52). *The Illuminatus! Trilogy* posits two secret societies – the chaotic Discordians and the repressive Illuminati – who have clandestinely been at war. By inserting phrases from Shea and Wilson's novel into their music, and making use of the '23 Enigma' from Discordianism, where the number 23 is emphasized and granted a mystical status (Higgs 2012, 239, 242–243), the JAMs/KLF transmedially aligned themselves with a mythos of grandly elemental (but hidden) conflict played out through popular music.

At the same time, the high-selling singles at the commercial peak of the KLF's pop career were also narrated as part of a 'trilogy', being self-dubbed the 'Stadium House Trilogy'. These tracks – What Time is Love?, 3AM Eternal and Last Train to Trancentral – use recorded crowd noise as a type of world-building device, creating the (fictional) sense that they are occurring at raves:

> The 'stadium' aspect of their sound refers to the singles' dense sound mix, high dynamic range and the use of background crowd sounds to give the performances an epic quality (as if the artists were being cheered on by a massive crowd). They also featured frequent use of branding lyrics (such as 'KLF is gonna rock ya' and 'Ancients of Mu Mu').
>
> (Fitzgerald and Hayward 2016, 55)

This repeated 'brand assertion' (ibid) or self-reference – common across the JAMs/KLF musical oeuvre, as well as via their 'Blaster in the Pyramid' logo and consistent typeface – is therefore fused with production emphasizing 'sufficient crowd noise, a thumping bass line and a propulsive house beat so that ... the listener was transported and submerged in the disorientating euphoria of a rave in full swing' (King 2012, 391). By interweaving epic Discordian narrative and an 'epic quality' of sound and production via self-branding, the band engaged in an 'intermedia campaign ... steeped in excess' (Fauteux 2015, 60), creating 'a myth which ... [was] self-propagating, self-sufficient, self-consuming and self-recreating' (Beadle 1993, 223).

This insistent narrative excess and brand assertion has occurred across all their different pop guises, including the Tinelords, the K Fundation and K2. It is present – via sleeve imagery and the accompanying video – in the Timelords' use of a car, 'Ford Timelord', to front their single 'Doctorin' the Tardis' (Hayward and Fitzgerald 2013, 142). It is also felt in the K Foundation's subsequent burning of £1 million, and the KLF's deletion of their back catalogue – something that, as an independent, they were able to enact – as well as via K2's self-reflexive 'comeback' in 1997 with a brass band version of 'What Time is Love?' (Drummond 2001, 342–343). The catalogue deletion and money-burning created further transmedial 'negative space' (Long 2017, 147), inspiring bootlegging and fan-compiled catalogues of official releases along with attempts to understand and narrate the band's destruction of £1 million. The latter very much informed 'WTTDA', as a 'Hearing' at the end of Day One discussed the meaning of Drummond and Cauty's money-burning via a series of commentaries and eye-witness accounts. Meanwhile, the world-building 'Stadium House Trilogy', whereby raves could be imagined even if listeners did not actually attend them, was reflected in the 'pop' discourse (Frith 1996, 41–42) of Day Three's Graduation Ball with its performing DJs and fictional/imagined band, Badger Kull. Most of 'WTTDA' was far more focused on what Simon Frith has identified as 'folk' and 'art' discourses of popular music (1996, 39–41), revolving around a festival-like gathering of fans with the JAMs/KLF plus associates, and involving the activities of participatory art.

However, a 'pop' discourse was also integrated into the rites of Day Three. The KLF's commercially successful popular music was commemorated, and characteristically extended into a new self-branding narrative, by the live appearance of Jarvis Cocker who performed a re-imagined/'remixed' version of 'Justified and Ancient', continuing the JAMs/KLF tradition of reworking their own material multiple times with different vocalists (King 2012, 398). Lyric sheets were distributed to attendees, emphasizing the new Jarvis-specific reworking of Tammy Wynette's previous version, and despite requests that the performance should not be filmed by fans, it nonetheless circulated online.

Thus although the JAMs themselves did not perform, their back catalogue was nonetheless updated, not as an instance of 'retromania' (Reynolds 2011) where the musical past was nostalgically replayed, but rather in heteroglossic dialogue with the KLF's earlier selves (Earl 2010, 131) and fan memories (Harvey 2015, 38–39). Indeed, the recreation of 'Justified and Ancient' was highly emotional for many fans present. For those who were perhaps teenagers or pre-teens at the time of the JAMs/KLF's pop ascendancy (One of the 400 2017, 28), this allowed an individualized 'affective scene' – the relatively privatized or domestic consumption of KLF's music in the present day, where other fans might be imagined via Facebook groups and YouTube uploads rather than physically encountered (Bennett 2013, 60) – to be converted into a communal, shared experience of intensified affect.

How else did 'WTTDA' proceed? Those who formed the 'first-hand participants of the event' (Bishop 2012, 37) – including myself, given my interest in the event as a highly unusual fan gathering – were allocated tasks on Day One. Attendees chose a number from a set of eight (vague and absurdist) job options when they arrived, as well as being free to select 'none at all' (Robinson 2017), and names were then randomly selected for the many roles.

Every attendee received a job card; fans online subsequently sought to catalogue these, while others creatively photoshopped alternative versions, such as 'Dark Ages Cynic', 'Facebook Whinger' and 'Casual Onlooker', all of which parodied the responses of those not directly involved as Volunteers. The 'Dark Ages Cynic' was instructed to 'comment endlessly on social media … about how pointless and crap' the event was. 'You will say the JAMs were only out to make money from the 400 and promote their book, 2023. You will not be deterred by first hand experiences or testimony from anyone who was actually there'. Similarly, the 'Facebook Whinger' was commanded to 'join the KLF Facebook group and complain incessantly that the KLF are not doing what you want them to. Music is the only form of art that makes you happy – and your negative posts and comments will attest to this fact'. These humorous examples of fan creativity acknowledged actual tensions within KLF's online fans (with much of this activity being centered on Facebook groups). Sections of fandom were evidently opposed to 'WTTDA', seeing it as some kind of inauthentic sell-out, whereas other fans were opposed to it on the basis that, for them, the JAMs/KLF were purely a pop music act, rendering the post-KLF art-making activities of Drummond and Cauty irrelevant to their fandom along with 'WTTDA'.

As well as highlighting tensions and divisions within the interpretive community of online fandom, fan-created job cards also lampooned the 'Casual Onlooker', whose task was always to answer 'I'm not sure' when asked what was happening. The fan-generated job cards therefore have a tendency to privilege and authenticate first-hand experience of the event. Critical non-participants are depicted as having to ignore the pleasures and participations of 'the 400', while onlookers comedically lack knowledge of the event's inner workings.

However, 'WTTDA' was merely one part of a range of coordinated JAMs activities. A related array of merchandise was launched online simultaneously, and of course the novel *2023: A Trilogy* was also tied into the event, meaning that press coverage for the happening, and the JAMs' re-emergence, could also function as promotion for the book. As such, all of this can be read as textbook branding and transmedia strategy: 'Part of the conceptual breakthrough ... of theorising transmedia ... has been to comprehend it simultaneously as storytelling in and of itself and equally as promotion for further' branded products (Freeman 2016, 30; also see Meier 2017). Barbara Ellen's *Guardian* piece voiced the same scepticism in relation to some fans: 'Although the KLF would deny involvement in anything so pedestrian as a book launch, the novel is the focus of the ... event I'm attending ... on multiple sites around Liverpool' (Ellen 2017).

And yet, the way in which 'WTTDA' relates to *2023: A Trilogy* is far from 'pedestrian', instead self-reflexively critiquing popular music's fan-celebrity relations. Allocated jobs are mainly due to be performed on Day Three of the event, but ahead of that was the book launch ('The Ice Kream Van Kometh') at twenty-three seconds past midnight on Day One. The launch, hosted by Liverpool's radical bookstore News from Nowhere, appeared to correspond to fans' typical desire to get closer to their fan objects – in this case briefly meeting Drummond and Cauty. But rather than the book being signed and personalized or dedicated, the JAMs were rubber-stamping people's copies. The notion of receiving a personalized version of the book was preserved, but simultaneously undermined and questioned. Relatedly, the book stamping – parodying the usual expectations of such a promotional event – was hemmed in by a set of rules: '"When approaching the JAMs, do not try to engage them in idle conversation", ordered a poster taped to the [bookshop] window.... "Do not attempt to take a selfie with the JAMs. Or with anyone else, ever again"' (Hodgkinson 2017, 4). Additional rules focused on the fact that participants should not 'film or photograph the JAMs while they are working', assuring fans that 'If any historic memorabilia ... is produced for autographs Dead Perch Menace [the JAMs' security] will confiscate that object and destroy it' (Robinson 2017).

Rather than welcoming fans' desires and standardized industry expectations (of acquiring a selfie or a photo, as well as signed merchandise accompanied by a brief chat), this confronted fans with a disillusioning set of restrictions. In line with The KLF's mythology, then, the book launch set out 'to deconstruct conventional notions of celebrity, success, fan worship, and even authenticity itself, forcing their followers to confront their most cherished assumptions about the rules of popular music' (Barker and Taylor 2007, 329). The 'authentic' fans' moment of meeting a celebrity becomes mere 'work' for the JAMs, but at the same time as refusing to play by the usual rules of a signing, the JAMs intensify their own anti-establishment authenticity. Hence the initiation of the transmedia array of 'WTTDA' primed fans to reflect on how they would previously have been disciplined to behave as fans. This intense self-reflexivity continued on into the participatory art of Days Two and Three, and I will now move on to consider that 'soft' transmedia aspect of the happening.

'Between Contemplation and Use': Fandom and/as Participatory Art during 'WTTDA'

The second day's billed 'reading' was not, in fact, a reading of the new book by the JAMs (as would, again, be typical for a publishing industry promotional event). Instead, as another of 'the 400' noted in their *Uncut* magazine review:

> Drummond and Cauty assign the ... attendees a page from the book [each], then give them the day to come up with an artistic response. It seems an impossible task, but the results, presented in Liverpool's Burned-Out Church at dusk, are spectacular, involving fire, whisky, space operatics and an obscene rewriting of 'Feed The World'. The volunteers are now the act, not the audience, while The KLF themselves sit off to one side, loving the creativity they've unleashed. The entire event seems to be an anarchic deconstruction of the creative industries.
>
> (Duane 2017, 5)

In this instance, rather than positioning Drummond and Cauty as distant workers in the midst of a supposedly personalized, intimate book signing, their expected role (that of authorities on the book, perhaps performing a reading of it) is once more inverted. The fans 'are now the act', while Drummond and Cauty sit in the audience. Fan creativity is guided, as each of the 400 becomes a 'page keeper' – some carried out individualized acts of productivity while others interpreted the guidelines as calling for group/chapter-based art.

Transmedia theory and work surrounding participatory art have rarely collided. Nicolas Bourriaud's influential definition views it as 'art taking as its theoretical horizon the realm of human interactions and its social context, rather than the assertion of an independent and *private* symbolic space' (2002, 14), with any question of mediation – let alone transmedia – being displaced altogether. Instead,

> the figures of reference of the sphere of human relations have now become fully-fledged artistic 'forms'. Meetings, encounters, events, various types of collaboration between people, games, festivals, and

places of conviviality, in a word all manner of encounter and relational intervention thus represent, today, aesthetic objects likely to
be looked at as such.

(Bourriaud 2002, 28)

By contrast, Claire Bishop's work on participatory art not only allows a
role for mediation, but it actually prioritizes transmedia flows, archives
and versionings:

> participatory art ... is both an event in the world, and at one remove
> from it. As such, it has the capacity to communicate on two levels –
> to participants and to spectators – the paradoxes that are repressed
> in everyday discourse, and to elicit ... experiences that enlarge our
> capacity to imagine the world and our relations anew. But to reach
> the second level requires a mediating third term – an object, image,
> story, film, even a spectacle – that permits this experience to have a
> purchase on the public imaginary.

(Bishop 2012, 284)

Bishop thus applauds an artwork that has 'become the epitome of participatory art: *The Battle of Orgreave* (2001) by the British artist Jeremy
Deller' (2012, 30) for 'the way in which the work takes into account the
apparatus of mediation in relation to a live performance' (2012, 37). As
such, it has a transmedial identity or a 'multiple identity' that

> allows it to reach different circuits of audience: first-hand partici-
> pants of the event in 2001, and those watching them from the field
> (primarily Yorkshire locals); those who saw the television broadcast
> of Figgis' film of this work (Channel 4, 20 October 2002) or who
> bought the DVD; those who read the book and listen to the CD of
> interviews; and those who view the archive/installation in the Tate's
> collection.

(Bishop 2012, 37)

The participatory art of 'WTTDA' thus became similarly transmedial and
multiplied. Fans responded by creating and uploading videos, by distrib-
uting lyric sheets and by tweeting, while others aimed to archive or record
as much of the art and its presentation as possible, also using social media. In a sense, the novel *2023* can be seen as encouraging this transmedia
response, given that much of it focuses on fictionalized and refracted versions of the real-world JAMs and KLF, offering counterfactual accounts
of their actual pop music career. One version of the KLF comprises two
young Ukrainian women, Tat'jana and Kristina, with the (supposedly)
fictional 'Cauty' and 'Drummond' instead becoming undertakers: 'As for

Cauty and Drummond – 'The Undertakers to the Underworld' – it is not known if they have started work yet on *The Great Pyramid of the North*' (Justified Ancients of Mu Mu 2017, 376). In the *LA Review of Books*, Ron Hogan described the novel as 'a literary form of collage that mirrors the sampling techniques the JAMs employed in early releases like ... "Whitney Joins the JAMs"' (Hogan 2017). Thus the novel asks to be interpreted, by knowledgeable fan-readers, as a transmedial construct, drawing on the always-already transmedia pop 'mythos' of the band.

By setting up Day Two's 'reading', Drummond and Cauty enacted 'the grey *artistic* work of participatory art – deciding how much or how little scripting to enforce – rather than ... the *ethical* black-and-white of 'good' or 'bad' collaboration' (Bishop 2012, 33), furnishing guidelines for Volunteers via the pages of *2023*. But they also refused any position of authorial dominance, calling into question the typical power relations between celebrity producers and fans:

> Drummond seems keen to offer participants in his art the option of acting in nomadic ways that might subvert the very practices that he is engaging with.... Clearly Drummond is willing to evade the stratification of himself as the Artist to which an audience must surrender, a theme constant with other democratising ... texts authored or co-authored by him, such as *The Manual (How to Have a Number One the Easy Way)*.
>
> (Wiseman-Trowse 2014, 165; see Cauty and Drummond 1998)

Members of 'the 400' have themselves engaged in theorizing the experience, stressing the emergent autonomy of participants: '"Welcome To The Dark Ages" was a reaction by The K Foundation to the current cultural-political status quo and its unstated aim was the creation of not Art but Artists' (Gell 2017). Here, in a performance of fan authenticity, the KLF moniker is rejected – *contra* its prominent use in media coverage of the happening (Duane 2017; Ellen 2017; Harrison 2017) – and the post-KLF art world/money-burning group identity of Drummond and Cauty ('the K Foundation') is more precisely used. The media's reliance on The KLF as an identifier speaks to the fact that it was through popular music and an associated 'prankster' or trickster role (extended into their money-burning), that Drummond and Cauty's mythology arguably took on its strongest shape. By opposing this, fan knowledge can be displayed, but more importantly, the 400 also begin to self-mythologize here, acting as an emergent addition to the JAMs/KLF mythology. Indeed, the collective have established their very own Facebook group, producing a variety of archival and keenly analytical blog posts, a fanzine, and poetry and prose based around the Liverpool experience.

Events of 'WTTDA' Day Three, the 'Rites of Mumufication', involved a further deconstruction of the creative industries. In this 'gigantic human art installation made of many moving parts' (Ellen 2017), the Volunteers' allocated job roles coalesced into a productive sequence. As Nicolas Bourriaud has observed:

> Those artists proposing as artworks ... also sometimes use a relational context defined in advance so as to extract production principles from it. The exploration of relations existing between, for instance, the artist and his/her gallery owner may determine forms and a project.
> (Bourriaud 2002, 33)

But the most pressing 'relational context' already in play between attendees and the JAMs, alluded to in the book-stamping's rules, was not that of 'artist and ... gallery' but rather *pop music artist-fandom*. In the transmedia masterstroke of the event, fandom was integrated into the domain of participatory art, as a number of fans were called upon to (re-)perform fandom – not for the JAMs/KLF, but instead for an act named Badger Kull, itself composed of four bassists who were all Volunteers. The entire industry machinery of popular music was replicated around them via allocated job roles, so that Badger Kull also had their own superfans, a manager, roadies, stylist, social media producers, poster designers and so on. The band, who performed their only song at The Invisible Wind Factory club at the end of Day Three when they were only a day or two old, were hence entirely imagined and created through the 400's artful participatory culture, prompted by the structure of 'WTTDA'.

Badger Kull and their instantaneous 'meta' fandom parodied the '[p]articipatory consumption through social media' and authorization of 'the authentic' that characterize television programs like *The X Factor* (Cvetkovski 2015, 176). Here were 'celebrities' and 'pop stars' who, in stark reality, were unknown quantities of indeterminate talent, having been co-created by the participatory art of fans-performing-fandom and fans-performing-industry. Rather than singular pop music tracks being remixed via the creative 'postproduction' of sampling and its 'communism of forms' (Bourriaud 2005, 35), this transmedia storytelling involved the industrial apparatus of popular music being playfully remixed and re-narrated, with the alleged 'destiny' of pop music talent being reframed as pure contingency.

Badger Kull did not represent the only way that fandom was hybridized with participatory art, however. Nicolas Bourriaud's notion of 'operative' or 'operational realism' (2002, 35, 112) explores not 'existing types of relations', such as celebrity-fan, but instead:

> Other practices ... aimed at recreating socio-professional models and applying their production methods. Here, the artist works in

the real field of the production of goods and services, and aims to set up a certain ambiguity, within the space of his activity, between the utilitarian function of the objects he is presenting, and their aesthetic function.

(Bourriaud 2002, 35)

This 'wavering between contemplation and use' (ibid.) was exercised through the aestheticization of real goods in the form of JAMs merchandising. As former superfan Peter Robinson (2015) observed on the Pop Justice website, 'THERE IS DEFINITELY MERCH. (... everything costs £20.23 because the JAMs book is called 2023 ...)' (Robinson 2017). This disruptive move makes no sense when viewed from within the industrial standards of merchandise pricing: a T-shirt, mug, bag of nails and a poster would not be expected to occupy the same price point. Fans were bemused by the possibility of paying £20.23 for a mug, leading to jokes, such as 'Did you buy one or become one?' (Scaramanga Silk 2017). As one fan theorist also noted:

Clearly, the cost versus perceived value of each of these goods is very different. However, *place these in an art setting, with a strong fan base* and all of a sudden, pricing becomes very different. Did people buy these items? Virtually all are now sold out on the L-13 [producer-supplier's] website.

(Scaramanga Silk 2017, italics added)

The strand of 'art' discourse sometimes linked to popular music (Frith 1996, 39) was most strongly evoked by one specific piece of JAMs merchandise, though. This was a Starbucks paper cup where the corporate logo had undergone a Situationist subversion in line with narrative content from *2023*. In the novel, Yoko Ono enters into a co-branding arrangement with Starbucks, resulting in new slogans for the coffee company including 'War is Over' (Justified Ancients of Mu Mu 2017, 40). The merchandised cup thus acted as a physical manifestation and token of redesigned Starbucks mugs in the novel's diegesis. In this regard, it was unlike other merchandise which incorporated the book's title and pre-existing JAMs' logos and reworked slogans, but which did not fully represent 'tactile transmediality' for the reader-participant by 'bridging the gap between the virtual 'worlds' [of the fiction] and the lived material body' (Gilligan 2012, 25).

This 'tactile transmediality' was also rendered exceptional in relation to other available merchandise by being offered in a 'deluxe' version (for £60.69) including a display case and plinth, as befitting a valuable art object. To complicate matters yet further, the exact same Ono-styled cup was in functional use at the venue. For a few pounds you could drink coffee from a *2023* transmedia artefact – treating it as functional – or for £60.69 you could display the same item as a pristine artwork. Bourriaud's 'wavering between contemplation and use' was hence starkly dramatized for attendees:

> Coffee cup or work of art? Depends which cash register you faced … The KLF in their various guises have experienced endless boot-legging of their catalogue so are in touch with unofficial products. Starb**ks War Is Over is a theme within the novel *2023* and these cups acted as a physical souvenir of that storyline… Interestingly, a form of morality was enforced when a cease and desist letter arrived at L-13 recently… Starbucks response may only serve to make the cups more desirable.
>
> (Scaramanga Silk 2017)

Due to the enforced rarity occasioned by their discontinued production, the 'War is Over' cups have been offered on eBay for ever more extortionate prices. Tactile transmediality and participatory art converge here through L-13's provision of real merchandise targeted at fan consumers and yet re-contextualized as (liminal) aesthetic practice.

The transmedia undertaking of 'WTTDA' did not only take *2023* as its 'primary' text, even if the creativity of page keepers, L-13 merchandising and a twenty-three-minute triptych 'film of the book' would seem to convey this impression. In fact, the playful fragmentation of the real-world JAMs/KLF into multiple, counterfactual versions of the band in *2023* enabled the novel to hide in plain sight what would prove to be the most significant transmedia extension of meaning of the whole event:

> the undertakers Cauty and Drummond were … hoping to … start work on the building of their long-promised pyramid – The Great Pyramid of the North… Cauty and Drummond had made a name for themselves in the undertaking trade using the strapline 'The Undertakers to the Underworld'. In doing so they had made a … promise to all the families who had entrusted them with the funeral rites of their nearest and dearest, … [that] they would use some of the ashes of the said 'nearest and dearest' in the making of a brick, and each of these bricks would then be a part of a pyramid that Cauty and Drummond would build.
>
> (Justified Ancients of Mu Mu 2017, 1)

Rather than furnishing a quirky and fictional version of the JAMs, this narrative was carried over into the rituals (and commercial realities) of 'WTTDA', with Day Three featuring 'Claire and Rupert Callender from the Green Funeral Company… [T]hey announce they're going into business with the JAMs as 'Callender, Callender, Cauty and Drummond,

Undertakers to the Underworld'. It's not a joke' (Ellen 2017). Likewise, plans to build a pyramid in Toxteth were unveiled, along with 'mumufication'; fans could purchase £99 bricks into which 23 grams of their ashes would be fired after their cremation, with each brick then being added to the People's Pyramid. As Barbara Ellen (2017) notes, as well 'as a book launch, and a kind of community art installation, it seems this has all been a giant advertisement for the JAMs' new 'MuMufication' business initiative'. Novelist Adelle Stripe took a critical view of this in her review for *The Quietus*, arguing that 'the KLF are an exercise in design, propaganda and dogma ... Drummond and Cauty are having the last laugh ... [as] their music is irrelevant. It's the myth that counts' (Stripe 2017).

Yet this neat binary of music/myth fails to regard pop music as transmedial: the JAMs/KLF brand of 'soft' transmedia pop is precisely about both dimensions. It is a matter of how mythology and music intersect, and how loose narratives of music (and techniques of music production) can form aspects of 'self-referential' (Beadle 1993, 223) world-building and alluring 'negative space'. The Jarvis-and-members-of-the-400 version of 'Justified and Ancient' was, after all, a key part of the 'predictably unexpected announcement' (Duane 2017, 6) that the JAMs had become undertakers.

Importantly, this was not a pop music comeback in any conventional sense, purely marked by backward-looking nostalgia or retromania. If anything, it was ultimately opposed to any denial of passing time, problematizing an imaginative projection back into 1990s pop, and focusing on the inevitability of death for aging stars and fans alike. But even this narrative had self-referential roots in the established JAMS/KLF myth; the brickmakers H.G. Matthews, producers of the 'Mu Mu'-branded mumufication bricks, had previously manufactured The Brick that contains ashes from the K Foundation's burning of £1,000,000 of their own money. And as an anonymous member of the public observed during the K Foundation's tour: 'By having the ash, or the brick, you're just keeping it all going, aren't you?' (cited in Brook 1997, 244). Mumufication refracts and 'remixes' the KLF mythology, 'keeping it all going' by displacing a single brick containing ashes from £1 million with a multitude of bricks potentially containing the future ashes of KLF fans.

'WTTDA' can be thought of less as a comeback, then, and more as a self-reflexive transmedia undertaking (novel, merchandise, film, fan-created art, event), one that trades on and plays with the JAMs'/KLF's pop music legacy:

> No one would have been interested in the activities of The K Foundation and their other post KLF literary and artistic endeavours if they'd not recorded classics like *What Time is Love?*, *3AM Eternal*,

Last Train to Trancentral and *Justified and Ancient*.... It was the success of Bill Drummond and Jimmy Cauty in the music business that gave them the ...credibility to launch their post KLF careers.

(Shirley 2017, 10)

Conclusion: Accept the Contradictions

I have argued that transmedia studies can (and should) be extended beyond its typical limits, tackling pop music and, more specifically, the 'mythos' surrounding the work of Cauty and Drummond (Fitzgerald and Hayward 2016). Known under a variety of monikers, but most famously as the Justified Ancients of Mu Mu, the Timelords, the KLF and the K Foundation, these creatives went on to have careers in art and literature, following the infamy of their £1 million burning. Their popular music was marked by repeated 'brand assertion', and by rampant self-referentiality and auto-remixing, borrowing from *The Illuminatus! Trilogy* and Discordianism as a new religious movement. And their 'Stadium House Trilogy' (plus 'Justified and Ancient') used production techniques, along with pop-video imagery, that allowed fans to imagine the surreal world of the KLF. This popular music and its mythology can therefore be interpreted as 'soft' transmedia (Delwiche 2017), loosely tied together by narrative threads across media, and by a stylistically and philosophically coherent mode of absurdist world-building.

The 'WTTDA' event of summer 2017 drew an international group of 400 fans to Liverpool, while remaining grounded in Drummond and Cauty's links to the city, and a profound sense of mystery, or transmedia 'negative space' (Long 2017), which fan commentary and social media usage could occupy. Although the event was partly legible as a promotional enterprise – for both the novel *2023* and the Mumufication undertakers' business – it also stretched transmedially into various kinds of participatory art, performance, merchandising and an impressionistic film-of-the-novel, as well as featuring a newly arranged, guest-performed version of one of the KLF's hit singles. Above all, the happening asked fans to question their typical fan practices and to 'remix' these in unexpected contexts, for example by acting as fans of the invented band Badger Kull. And this posed questions of fan consumption through the aestheticization of merchandise as 'tactile transmediality' (Gilligan 2012). The outcome was a pop 'comeback' quite unlike any other, performing 'art' and 'folk' discourses far more than those of 'pop' (Frith 1996), and straining at the bounds of pop music nostalgia (Reynolds 2011) by compelling attendees to pay attention, however seriously, to their own mortality. Weaving (trans)media together in this bounded, ritualistic space and time, 'WTTDA' was both local and transnational; impermanent and textually traced; co-present and disseminated via social media;

subversive and promotionally on-brand. In this case, theorizing popular music and its mythologies as a form of transmedia undertaking means accepting the contradictions.

Bibliography

Barker, Hugh, and Yuval Taylor. *Faking It: The Quest for Authenticity in Popular Music*. London: Faber and Faber, 2007.

Beadle, Jeremy J. *Will Pop Eat Itself? Pop Music in the Soundbite Era*. London: Faber and Faber, 1993.

Bennett, Andy. *Music, Style and Aging: Growing Old Disgracefully?*. Philadelphia, PA: Temple University Press, 2013.

Bishop, Claire. *Artificial Hells: Participatory Art and the Politics of Spectatorship*. London: Verso, 2012.

Bourriaud, Nicolas. *Relational Aesthetics*. Dijon: Les Presses du Réel, 2002.

Bourriaud, Nicolas. *Postproduction: Culture as Screenplay – How Art Reprograms the World, Second Edition*. New York: Lucas and Sternberg, 2005.

Brook, Chris (ed.). *K Foundation Burn a Million Quid*. London: Ellipsis, 1997.

Cauty, Jimmy, and Bill Drummond. *The Manual [How to Have a Number One the Easy Way]*. London: Ellipsis, 1998.

Cvetkovski, Trajce. *The Pop Music Idol and the Spirit of Charisma: Reality Television Talent Shows in the Digital Economy of Hope*. Basingstoke: Palgrave Macmillan, 2015.

Delwiche, Aaron. "Still Searching for the Unicorn: Transmedia Storytelling and the Audience Question." In *The Rise of Transtexts: Challenges and Opportunities*, edited by Benjamin W.L. Derhy Kurtz and Melanie Bourdaa, 33–48. New York and London: Routledge, 2017.

Driessen, Simone. "The Affordances of Repackaged Popular Music from the Past." PhD Diss., Erasmus University, Rotterdam, 2017.

Drummond, Bill. *45*. London: Abacus, 2001.

Duane, Paul. "Mu Day Rising." *Uncut* (November 2017): 5–6.

Duffett, Mark. *Understanding Fandom*. London and New York: Bloomsbury Academic, 2013.

Earl, Benjamin. "The Reformer's Charter: Setting Bloom's *Anxiety of Influence* in the Context of Melodic Rock." *Popular Music* 29:1 (2010): 131–142.

Ellen, Barbara. "KLF Welcome to the Dark Ages Review – What Time Is Chaos?." *The Guardian*. August 26, 2017. Accessed 24 October 2017. www.theguardian.com/music/2017/aug/26/the-return-of-the-klf-what-time-is-chaos.

Fairclough, Damon. "Welcome to the Dark Ages." *Bido Lito!* 80 (August 2017): 12–14.

Fauteux, Brian. "Reflections of the Cosmopolitan City: Mapping Arcade Fire's *Reflektor* and its Intermedia Promotional Campaign." *Journal of Popular Music Studies* 27:1 (2015): 48–68.

Fitzgerald, Jon, and Philip Hayward. "Chart Mythos: The JAMs' and The KLF's Invocation of Mu." *Shima* 10:2 (2016): 50–67.

Freeman, Matthew. *Historicising Transmedia Storytelling: Early Twentieth-Century Transmedia Story Worlds*. New York and London: Routledge, 2016.

Frith, Simon. *Performing Rites: On the Value of Popular Music*. Oxford: Oxford University Press, 1996.

Gell, Andy. "Making Art to Make Artists to Make Art." *The Justified Ancients of Mu Mu Present Welcome to the Dark Ages by Page 130.* October 15, 2017. Accessed 25 October, 2017. https://welcometothedarkagespage130.com/2017/10/15/making-art-to-make-artists-to-make-art/.

Gilligan, Sarah. "Heaving Cleavages and Fantastic Frock Coats: Gender Fluidity, Celebrity and Tactile Transmediality in Contemporary Costume Cinema." *Film, Fashion & Consumption* 1:1 (2012): 7–38.

Harrison, Ian. "Return to Mu Mu Land." *Mojo.* November 2017 (288): 17–18.

Harvey, Colin B. *Fantastic Transmedia: Narrative, Play and Memory across Science Fiction and Fantasy Storyworlds.* Basingstoke: Palgrave Macmillan, 2015.

Hassler-Forest, Dan. *Science Fiction, Fantasy and Politics: Transmedia World-Building beyond Capitalism.* London: Rowman and Littlefield International, 2016.

Hayward, Philip, and Jon Fitzgerald. "Rematerialization: Musical Engagements with the British TV Series *Doctor Who.*" In *Music in Science Fiction Television: Tuned to the Future,* edited by K.J. Donnelly and Philip Hayward, 135–150. New York and London: Routledge, 2013.

Higgs, John. *The KLF: Chaos, Magic and the Band Who Burned a Million Pounds.* London: Orion Publishing, 2012.

Hodgkinson, Will. "Why Did the KLF Burn a Million Pounds? 'Because It Was Fun.'" *The Times 2: Arts.* August 25, 2017: 4–5.

Hogan, Ron "'Still No Master Plan": The Justified Ancients of Mu Mu's "2023: A Trilogy."' *LA Review of Books.* October 15, 2017. Accessed 25 October 2017. https://lareviewofbooks.org/article/still-no-master-plan-the-justified-ancients-of-mu-mus-2023-a-trilogy/.

Jenkins, Henry. *Convergence Culture: Where Old and New Media Collide.* New York: New York University Press, 2006.

Jost, Christofer. "Popular Music and Transmedia Aesthetics: On the Conceptual Relation of Sound, Audio-Vision and Live Performance." In *Reinventing Sound: Music and Audiovisual Culture,* edited by Enrique Encabo, 2–13. Newcastle upon Tyne: Cambridge Scholars Publishing, 2015.

"Justified Ancients of Mu Mu." *2023: A Trilogy.* London: Faber and Faber, 2017.

King, Richard. *How Soon Is Now? The Madmen and Mavericks Who Made Independent Music 1975–2005.* London: Faber and Faber, 2012.

Long, Geoffrey. "Creating Worlds in Which to Play: Using Transmedia Aesthetics to Grow Stories into Storyworlds." In *The Rise of Transtexts: Challenges and Opportunities,* edited by Benjamin W.L. Derhy Kurtz and Melanie Bourdaa, 139–152. New York and London: Routledge, 2017.

McLeod, Kembrew. "Crashing the Spectacle: A Forgotten History of Digital Sampling, Infringement, Copyright Liberation and the End of Recorded Music." In *Cutting Across Media: Appropriation Art, Interventionist Collage and Copyright Law,* edited by Kembrew McLeod and Rudolf Kuenzli, 164–177. Durham and London: Duke, 2011.

Meier, Leslie M. *Popular Music as Promotion: Music and Branding in the Digital Age.* Cambridge, MA and Malden, MA: Polity Press, 2017.

One of the 400. "What Became of the Dark Ages?." *Bido Lito!* 82 (October 2017): 28.

Pine, B. Joseph, and James H. Gilmore. *The Experience Economy.* Boston, MA: Harvard Business School Press, 1999.

Reynolds, Simon. *Retromania: Pop Culture's Addiction to Its Own Past.* London: Faber and Faber, 2011.

Robinson, Peter. "How Deep is Your Love: Fandom in the Twenty-First Century." i.D., February 19, 2015, Accessed 25 October 2017. https://i-d.vice.com/en_uk/article/wj5x89/how-deep-is-your-love-fandom-in-the-21st-century

Robinson, Peter. "Greetings from Liverpool, Where One of the World's Greatest Ever Bands Have Sort of Reformed." *Pop Justice.* August 22, 2017. Accessed 25 October 2017. www.popjustice.com/briefing/greetings-from-liverpool-where-one-of-the-worlds-greatest-ever-bands-have-sort-of-reformed/.

Scaramanga Silk. "A Scale of Value and Values." *Welcome to the Dark Ages.* 2017. Accessed 25 October 2017. www.welcometothedarkages.com/2017/10/19/a-scale-of-value-and-values/.

Shirley, Ian. *Turn Up the Strobe: The KLF, The JAMS, The Timelords – A History.* London: Cherry Red Books, 2017.

Stanley, Bob. *Yeah Yeah Yeah: The Story of Modern Pop.* London: Faber and Faber, 2014.

Stripe, Adelle. "Justified & Ancient Seems A Long Time Ago: The JAMs In Liverpool." *The Quietus.* August 29, 2017. Accessed 2 November 2017. http://thequietus.com/articles/23079-jams-liverpool-toxteth-day-of-the-dead-adelle-stripe-bill-drummond-jimmy-cauty-jarvis-cocker-jeremy-deller.

Thon, Jan-Noël. *Transmedial Narratology and Contemporary Media Culture.* Lincoln and London: University of Nebraska Press, 2016.

Torpey, Christopher. "Editorial." *Bido Lito!* 80 (August 2017a): 9.

Torpey, Christopher. "Editorial." *Bido Lito!* 82 (October 2017b): 9.

Wiseman-Trowse, Nathan. "'You Should Try Lying More': The Nomadic Impermanence of Sound and Text in the Work of Bill Drummond." In *Litpop: Writing and Popular Music,* edited by Rachel Carroll and Adam Hansen, 157–168. Farnham and Burlington: Ashgate, 2014.

2 Spain

Emergences, Strategies and Limitations of Spanish Transmedia Productions

Carlos A. Scolari, Mar Guerrero-Pico and María-José Establés

This chapter presents a state-of-the-art transmedia production in Spain in the area of fictional narratives. Like in many other societies, the concept of transmedia storytelling was introduced in Spainish media in the early 2000s and was adopted by professionals, corporations and researchers as a keyword for naming a new set of media strategies. Despite this explosion of transmediality, it can be argued that Spanish productions feature a series of limitations compared to projects from broader markets. For instance, there is an overall view in Spain that transmediality is a creative afterthought, particularly in the main media corporations of the country, though this view is lessened in the small production companies (Scolari, Jiménez and Guerrero 2012). This opposition between major and minor corporations reveals two different approaches to transmediality: on the one hand, a tactical perspective where transmedia expansion is developed along the way and, on the other hand, a strategic perspective where transmedia planning is at the very inception of the project.

Based on these two approaches, this chapter introduces and describes a first generation of transmedia productions in Spain – led by *Águila Roja* (TVE 2009–2016) – and reflects on the emergence of a more advanced second generation of transmedia fictions, such as *Isabel* (TVE 2012–2015) and *El Ministerio del Tiempo* (TVE 2015–2016). In both moments, public service broadcasting has been a prominent key player in the narrative and promotional expansion of these transmedia products, although commercial broadcasting can account for successful examples among these ventures, such as *El Barco* (Antena 3 2011–2013). Specific transmedia projects based on crowdfunding, such as *El Cosmonauta* (2013), are also included in this map of Spanish transmedia production along with some notes on Spanish fan culture. Finally, we reflect on the future of transmedia experiences and projects in the Spanish domestic market.

The (Critical) Emergence of Transmedia Strategies and Research in Spain

According to the *Report on the State of Culture in Spain 2016* produced by Fundación Alternativas (Bustamante 2016), the economic crisis and its social consequences produced some kind of disaffection for many citizens. Meanwhile, the request of more transparent, equal and participatory political processes opened many possibilities for improving the quality of the Spanish democracy. Between 2008 and 2013, the Spanish cultural market lost around 4,000 companies and more than 100,000 jobs, while, in the following five-year period (2009–2014), the cultural budget of the Spanish State was reduced by 44.21% (Bustamante 2016, 18). Thus, even as cinema production increased (more but cheaper films were produced) the audiences concentrated on a small number of productions (five movies accounted for the 82% of the total national film revenue). In television, the Spanish public radio–television service (RTVE) and other autonomous media companies were equally affected by these budget reductions.

Following the hard adjustment that television operators had to make to adapt to the substantial reduction of their advertising revenues, the market has balanced out. At first, production costs and labor costs were reduced. A concentration process led by government was then initiated. The final result has been the consolidation of two large television corporations (Mediaset and Atresmedia) that control about 90% of the advertising market. Throughout this process, national public television has been left with an unsustainable financing model, which has meant the slowdown of a system that had acted as the engine of audiovisual production (Álvarez Monzoncillo and López Villanueva 2016, 45).

Between 2008 and 2015, the investment in audiovisual production of all television channels has dropped from 474 to 328M Euros, which equates to a reduction of 30.8%. Since the dimension of the pay-per-view channels is not enough to support a continuous profitable production, Spanish television is supported mainly by the broadcasters, especially for fiction and entertainment. During the 'Great Depression' of the Spanish economy, the media corporations maintained the fixed costs of their structure (essentially, personnel) and reduced direct investment around 30%. To decrease the risk, they reduced the number of new programs being made and put an emphasis on 'secure' traditional formats – namely, reality television formats and talk shows (Álvarez Monzoncillo and López Villanueva 2016).

According to Bustamante, 'Spanish cultural activities have suffered since 2008 a serious setback in terms of market and economic profitability' (2016, 15). This date is important: in 2008, the Spanish version of Henry Jenkins' *Convergence Culture* was first published, the academic best-seller that popularized the concept of transmedia storytelling around the world. In other words, when transmedia development started in Spain, the national creative and cultural industry was focused on the economic crisis and the different stakeholders were planning survival strategies, rather than expansion strategies. And in that context, for most of the media agents, the production of transmedia works was considered largely to be an expensive 'luxury', on that was impossible to afford in such a critical and limited landscape.

However, even now that the crisis seems to be approaching an endpoint, the *Plan for the Promotion of Cultural and Creative Industries 2016* by the Spanish Ministry of Education, Culture and Sports (MECD) still does not include any direct reference to transmedia production. Though it mentions the need for new business models based on crowdfunding, digital streaming and new gamification strategies, the closest reference to transmedia strategies can be found when the *Plan* focuses on user-generated content, stating:

> Digitisation has led to changes on participation and consumption habits. Culture has passed from the social to the particular, and now can be enjoyed alone in front of a screen. The digital tools available have turned consumers into producers and generators of their own content, which has led to the emergence of new business models based on what is known as user-generated content or UGC. UGC cover all types of creation using digital technologies, including videos, blogs, forums, podcasts, social media, photography, wikis and ebooks.
>
> (MECD 2016, 13)

Beyond this difficult and transitory context, a number of transmedia initiatives have been developed in Spain in recent years. Media companies have developed transmedia projects from scratch (such as *Panzer Chocolate*) or, a more commonly, what started as original 'monomedia' productions (such as *El Cosmonauta* or *El Ministerio del Tiempo*) have since morphed into transmedia projects along the way. These transmedia productions developed during the crisis will be analyzed in the following sections. Furthermore, discussions about transmedia storytelling went beyond the Spanish audiovisual market. Areas or institutions far away from the traditional media industry, like museums, are now 'going transmedia':

> After suffering cuts in their budgets, museums and art centers ... began to consider strategies to allow their sustainability. These are based on the development of collaborative social networks around their activities, and the co-creation and commercialization of multimedia content through transmedia narratives.
>
> (Quijano 2014, 35)

Regarding academic research, the first scholars and researchers to initiate discussions about transmedia storytelling in Spain were those working on new media (Scolari 2009), education (Lacasa, Martínez-Borda and Méndez 2008) and communication studies (Hernández Pérez and Grandio 2011). The translation and publication of books such as Jenkins' *Convergence Culture* (2008) introduced the discussion about transmedia storytelling into the Spanish academic circuit and propelled the first research in this field. As local transmedia production was almost nonexistent at this time, researchers instead focused on international examples, such as *24* (Scolari 2009), *Battlestar Galactica* (Hernández Pérez and Grandío 2011) and *Fringe* (Belsunces Gonçalves 2011; Guerrero-Pico 2016). Then, in 2010, the Catalan Audio-visual Council supported one of the first exploratory studies about transmedia production in Barcelona (Scolari, Jiménez and Guerrero 2012; Scolari et al. 2011).

Since 2010, the Spanish media professionals and corporations have gradually introduced transmedia storytelling into their discourses and practices. Agencies like FCB promoted transmedia strategies in advertising; to date, their video *Cinderella 2.0: Transmedia Storytelling* (FCB Global 2013) is an exemplar of what a transmedia marketing production could be. Publication of texts beyond the academic circuit include Scolari (2013), and the implementation of professional courses on transmediality at Universidad Carlos III (Madrid).

In the following sections, we will describe and analyze a series of transmedia productions created in Spain in recent years: *Águila Roja* (2009–2016), *El Barco* (2011–2013), *Isabel* (2012–2014), *El Cosmonauta* (2013) and *El Ministerio del Tiempo* (2015–). These transmedia works, sometimes developed by public and private companies, or joint ventures between the public and private sectors, were selected because of their popularity and/or innovative traits.

Águila Roja (2009–2016)

Even if transmedia storytelling strategies have been incorporated in the Spanish media industry only in the last decade, there is already a corpus of paradigmatic works that should be taken into account. One of the first productions to 'go transmedia' was *Águila Roja*. Produced by Globomedia, *Águila Roja* has arguably been one of the flagships of RTVE, Spain's public broadcasting service, not only in terms of ratings but also in terms of its transmedia ambitions. Since the series' premiere in February 2009 on La 1's prime time, the series became a ratings hit throughout nine seasons for its unprecedented mix of period drama, adventure, fantasy, comedy, and a broad appeal based on a variety of characters and subplots. Set in 17th century Spain, during Habsburg King Philip IV's reign, the series focuses on the story of Gonzalo de Montalvo, a village teacher seeking revenge for his wife's murder under the mask of Águila Roja, a fearless ninja-skilled vigilante who becomes the champion of the poor and oppressed. *Águila Roja*'s transmedia universe comprises a film, a video game, a comic book, two novels, merchandise and user-generated content.

The video game *Mi Águila Roja* is a free multiplayer online platform that allows the users to manage their own 17th century Spanish village and set agreements and trade with them. The series' weekly episodes serve as guiding threads to the game's missions and several characters appear to help the players pass the different challenges. In addition, when the series was on hiatus, the game introduced new missions that expand the series' narrative world while the main plot – or 'mothership' (Jenkins, 2009) – remains untarnished and canonical. Meanwhile, the comic book *La Sociedad del Loto Blanco* (Ruiz Córdoba, Manuel and Sierra 2011), created by one of the series writers, expands the imaginary world historically and 'transtemporally' (Freeman 2016) to 16th century China. The film, titled *Águila Roja*, then follows the adventures of the eponymous character in another independent story, adding new characters. In two tie-in novels, *Águila Roja* and *La profecía de Lucrecia* ('Lucrecia's Prophecy') they directly address a portion of the series' floating enigmas related to the characters' past. In regard to merchandising, the series generated an array of products that include board games, card game sets and costumes. Finally, user-generated content has been profuse, veering mostly toward parody, a tendency that has been adopted by popular variety shows featuring their own comedy sketches based on the series.

Águila Roja exemplifies what Scolari, Jiménez and Guerrero (2012) refer to as 'tactic transmedia expansion', as the series' transmedia enlargement happened in a progressive manner, without a previous strategy. This approach differs to other transmedia projects that have their expansion mapped out from the start, defined as 'strategic transmedia expansion'. Tactic expansion constitutes the most common modality of transmedia development globally, and it can be found in a number of powerhouse franchises (Star Wars, Marvel, DC, etc.). In the case of *Águila Roja*, the project was primarily a television show from which the rest of the transmedia satellites were aligned via 'retroactive linkages' (Wolf, 2012; see also Scolari, Bertetti and Freeman 2014) with which the 'master-narrative', or 'mothership', stands as the transmedia anchor.

The series certainly set a milestone in Spain's transmedia sphere. On the one hand, it can be considered the first mainstream television show to fully undertake transmedia expansion, and, on the other hand, it also introduced an innovative style of producing and promoting RTVE's original fiction that was successfully consolidated in the following years (see *Amar en tiempos revueltos*, *Isabel*, *El Caso* and *Víctor Ros*, among others). Alongside the different media expansions, the project held a similarly strong online and social media presence. For instance, RTVE's online division deployed a website targeted at a variety of users (Guerrero 2014) and a consistently busy Twitter account that helped foster an engaged fan community.

El Barco (2011–2013)

El Barco is a teen science fiction series produced by Globomedia and aired on Antena 3 for three seasons (2011–2013). It features a similar combination of drama, action and *Lost*-like mystery seen in *El Internado* (2007–2010), the network's previous success in the same demographic. Set on a training ship called Estrella Polar, a massive storm leaves the ship and its crew stranded in the ocean with no working communication and the revelation that they might be the only survivors on Earth. *El Barco* is not the first Antena 3 series to develop transmedially. Like previous series, *El Internado* (2007–2010), *Física o Química* (2008–2011), *Los Protegidos* (2010–2012) (García Mirón 2014), *El Barco*'s narrative satellites include a mobile app, unofficial user-generated content and a video game. For the latter, an online multiplayer strategy game permits each user to become the captain of their own ship and to gather a crew and manage supplies. However, *El Barco* stands out for the introduction of two new transmedia units in the Spanish transmedia context – that is, Twitter episodes (or 'twittersodes in the digital vernacular') and a reality competition show aired on Antena 3.

The twittersodes transferred *El Barco*'s world to social media. Following a script penned by the show's writers, fourteen character accounts chatted for an hour before the airing of each episode on television, and provided narrative breadcrumbs for audiences to follow. The twittersodes proved to be a successful idea for the producers of the show: the last twittersode, #ElUltimoBarco ('The Last Ship'), was released in parallel with the series finale, and achieved a 97.34% social share, with more than 200,000 comments (Antoral 2013). In addition, other hashtags related to the show made it on national and international trending topic lists during the series finale (Mayor Mayor 2014). Alongside the social media content, the reality show *El Barco: Rumbo a lo desconocido* ('The Ship': Unknown destination') took place in the hiatus between the first and second seasons. Fourteen contestants were locked up for a month in an exact replica of the fictional ship where they took up challenges and were eliminated as they approached the end of the journey. Unlike the Twitter experience, the launch of the show turned into a ratings failure despite it being promoted as the first reality show based on a television series. In fact, the lack of a heavy promotion across other Antena 3 shows might be one of the potential causes for the failure, as not enough viewers other than the hardcore fans of the series would know about its ancillary reality show.

In terms of transmedia strategies, however, *El Barco* mirrors other successful international teen series, such as the British series *Skins* (E4 2007–2013), notably through its use of social media to expand the imaginary world as well as the viewers' experience and the desire to build a loyal community around its fictional brand (Grandío and Bonaut 2012).

In contrast to Jenkins original definition of transmedia storytelling (2003), the twittersodes were not vital expressions needed to follow the series' narrative, nor did they show a great degree of fan-character interaction beyond what was scripted. Nevertheless, by being present in a media venue populated by their teen target audience, and capitalizing on the increasingly popular habit of live-tweeting, they offered a fresh experience in Spanish transmedia storytelling.

Moreover, and despite the uneven audience performance of its reality show, *El Barco* was still a test case regarding the type of transmedia expressions chosen to further develop imaginary worlds across media platforms. Granted, such decision-making is subjected to multiple factors, such as the availability of sufficient budget and human resources, but those assets were effectively utilized as a way to deliver something pioneering at the time. Equally innovative was the fact that the transmedia deployment of the show took a 'strategic approach' since the beginning, specifically the twittersodes, which were already implemented in the series premiere (although the television series remained the mothership throughout).

Isabel (2012–2014)

Isabel is a series produced by the production company Diagonal TV for La 1 (RTVE). The series is based on real events and tells the tale of Queen Isabella I of Castile (known as the Catholic Queen) throughout 39 episodes across three seasons (2012–2014). Written by a team of writers led by the brothers Javier and Pablo Olivares, the first season features Princess Isabella's formative years, following her ascension to the throne in 1474. This season aims for historical fidelity thanks to the exhaustive documentation work by the writers (Salvador-Esteban 2016). Although writers took certain licenses when narrating the historical facts across the series, these are more palpable in only the last two seasons with the simplification, or even with the invention, of various episodes in the history of Spain (Ruiz Pleguezuelos 2016). The scripts of seasons two and three were coordinated by Jose Luis Martín, after the Olivares Brothers left their positions as script coordinators. The second season covers Isabella's life from the Castilian Civil War (1474) until the conquest of the Nasrid Kingdom of Granada (1492), and the third season starts with the discovery of America (1492) and concludes with Isabella's death (1504).

Although launching the series was fraught with various difficulties (due to the cancellation of its scheduled premiere in January 2011 and its postponement until September 2012 (Barrientos-Bueno 2013)), once the first season finally debuted, it quickly received accolades from both viewers and critics. Beyond the series, its transmedia universe expands through profiles on official social media, such as Twitter, Facebook and Instagram. Two spin-offs followed – one a feature film, *La Corona*

Partida – and another a television series, *Carlos, Rey Emperador*. Several books (three novels based on scripts, and academic and informative works explaining key aspects of both character and historical narratives) also followed, as did itinerant exhibitions of the costumes used in the show and a crossover in the fourth episode of *El Ministerio del Tiempo* featuring the Catholic Queen played by Michelle Jenner, the same actress who embodies her in *Isabel*.

Drawing on their previous experience with *Águila Roja*, the team in charge of the RTVE website began experimenting with different digital initiatives, and other additional contents (Molpeceres-Arnáiz and Rodríguez-Fidalgo 2014), even those created by fandom (Establés-Heras 2016). *Isabel*'s narrative universe expanded through the seasons. The websites RTVE.es and Lab.RTVE.es offer different content created with the aim of enhancing the informative and educational nature of the series. In addition to having access to all the episodes online, users can enjoy two interactive documentaries on the conquest of the Nasrid Kingdom and the surrender of Granada, narrated by the characters of Isabella and Boabdil. There are interactive infographics about the different royal families that appear in the series and additional information about characters, customs and curiosities of the period in which *Isabel* is set. Additionally, there was a special show called #*TantoMonta*, available only in RTVE.es, featuring detailed episode analysis and special interviews with the cast.

Similarly, viewers who watched the series live during the first season could access in real time the series app, *Más Isabel*, featuring additional content to learn in greater depth the themes and characters that were being depicted in the series (Barrientos-Bueno 2013). This double-screen strategy was gradually extended throughout the series, from viewers' searchers on the internet, to web portals, such as Wikipedia, in order to know the historical accuracy of the contents of the series. Apart from the series canon, we can add all the user-generated content created by *isabelinos* (the nickname by which the fans of the series are known). In this sense, we can highlight the Twitter accounts that imitate, in a parodic way, the way of speaking and the personality of the characters. The fan forum *La Corte de Castilla*, for example, where administrators developed a gamification strategy for users to gradually access all the content hosted in the site, features fanart, fanvids, and Tumblr gifs and memes subtitled in English to bring the series closer to foreign viewers (Establés-Heras 2016).

El Cosmonauta (2013)

El Cosmonauta is a science fiction feature film (premiered in May 2013) that included more than thirty web videos, a mockumentary, a book and a series of products, all of which construct the imaginary world. Considered as the first high-level audiovisual production in Spanish crowdfunding, *El Cosmonauta* received more than €400,000 from almost 5,000 partners around the world. The *El Cosmonauta* project was born in 2009 as a monomedia project but the dynamics of the production process opened it up to new spaces, affordances and practices. As *El Cosmonauta* transformed itself into a transmedia project, new content and pieces emerged. Many of them were never produced, for example an alternate reality game, or a series of 'mobisodes' linked with mini video games. The team created 15 specific episodes and during the editing process left about 30% of the images out of the final cut to transform them into new episodes. In this case, the transmedia content did not only expand the narrative universe, but the merchandising also played an important role in the diffusion and financing of the project. According to the producers, consumers have the right to decide when, how and where they watch the movie, to pay for it (or not), to share it, and/or to modify it in ways they see fit. The producers have also proposed a Partnership Program for the exhibition of the film and the creation of a whole media experience around the story.

El Cosmonauta generated a vast textual galaxy around it. Many of these expressions formed part of the overarching 'hyperdiegesis' (Hills 2002), such as the feature film, while other textual pieces should be considered paratexts (like the film trailer or *The Hummingbird*, a mockumentary). But like any transmedia project, *El Cosmonauta* did not finish with the feature film premiere. Inspired by projects such as *Memento in Chronological Order or Star Wars: Episode III.5: The Editor Strikes Back*, the team invited users to re-edit *El Cosmonauta* in June 2012. They released the raw videos and sound files online so that users could edit their own version of the movie, transform it into a short film, remix it, make a parody, or include the images in a brand new production (*Reedita El Cosmonauta* 2013).

El Cosmonauta was the first high-level audiovisual production in the Spanish crowdfunding movement that became transmedial, and in that sense should also be considered the first Spanish transmedia production based on a crowdfunding strategy. The creation of an international community of fans and the textual expansions positioned this production as one of the best examples of Spanish transmedia productions. Further, *El Cosmonauta* is one of the most interesting examples of transmedia storytelling coming from the margins of the media market: it was born as a bottom-up initiative long before media corporations started talking about transmediality. The producers were pioneers both in economic and cultural arenas.

El Ministerio del Tiempo (2015–)

This science fiction series was created by Javier and Pablo Olivares (*Isabel*), and produced by Cliffhanger and Onza Entertainment for La 1 of RTVE. It narrates the adventures of a group of agents based in a secret Department that controls a series of doors that allow them to travel through the history of Spain. The function of this Department is to keep historical events unchanged, but the agents soon discover that there are exceptions to the rule with double agents who bet on changing the history of the country. *El Ministerio del Tiempo* is a production packed with intertextual references, and explores all kind of television genres, from comedy to drama, through police procedural to thriller, science fiction or historical epic. It is one of the most well-known Spanish series internationally, and even if it was thought as a television show, *El Ministerio del Tiempo* became transmedial because of the emergence of a huge community of fans, known as the ministéricos, not only in Spain but also in Latin American countries. In particular, fan production related to the series is very prolific (Lacalle, Castro and Castro 2016): posters, role-playing games, cosplay, character profiles on social media, remixes, fan arts, fanfics, fan vids, etc. Some of these fanworks are even impacting different cultural arenas, such as education or tourism (Establés-Heras 2016).

Aiming to appease an emergent contingency of dedicated audiences, the producers of *El Ministerio del Tiempo* have further developed the transmedia experience beyond the streaming of the episodes on RTVE. es, the online show #*LaPuertaDelTiempo* or the social media profiles from the second season onward. In addition, Pablo Lara joined the production crew as a Transmedia Producer, and he was credited as such in each episode. As part of the expansion strategy, an official merchandising store was opened, selling products designed by fans, with profits divided between fans and producers. To promote product exclusivity, sales had a limited number of orders for a very short period of time. The profits were distributed between the producers and the fans participating in this initiative (Prensa RTVE 2016).

During the second season, a virtual reality special episode was filmed. 'El tiempo en tus manos' ('Time in your hands') was a pioneering production in the Spanish and international context: it is the first expansion of a television series to utilize immersive content that must be watched with 3D glasses. It is a production recorded with a stereoscopic system that allows audiences to visit the facilities of the Department and interact with the characters. At the same time, the absence of one of the actors for professional reasons (he was filming another series) led to the creation of a series of podcasts that kept open a parallel narrative thread set in the Philippine Revolution (1896–1898). The novel *El Tiempo es el que es* (*Time As It Is*) also expands the narrative world with three new adventures: one in the 8th century to rescue a lost agent, another in the 17th century set in Cartagena de Indias, and the third, to save a colleague who has been trapped by the Nazis during World War II. These initiatives were complemented by a strong presence on social media, a webseries where the character Angustias makes confessions in front of the camera and a separate website with dozens of extra content available that has to be accessed with different passwords every week. Before the beginning of the third season, producers bridged this third instalment and the two first seasons through the comic *Tiempo al Tiempo* (El Torres, Martínez and Molina 2017), in which the main characters of the series have to save the life of the Head of the Department of Time. In addition, there are new podcasts set in the 1960s so as to bring a character back to the series.

It can be said that *El Ministerio del Tiempo* is a production that clearly shows the tensions that emerge in the transition from a media ecology focused on broadcasting to another focused on network substantiations. In this sense, *El Ministerio del Tiempo* is one of the first Spanish works to be presented as an advocate of post-broadcasting, a phase in which a new model of production, circulation and consumption in the media industry is being formed.

Spanish (Trans)Media Fandom

El Ministerio del Tiempo also highlights a notable mixing of producer and fan practices, even in the context of a major television series. Broadly, Spanish media-based fan culture largely replicates the practices seen in long-running Western and Asian media fandoms. Indeed, the influence of American US and Japanese media fandom is notable either in the objects that inspire the Spanish fans and productions, or in the specific language used in their interactions.

As happens in other fan cultures, it is necessary in Spain to make a distinction between the development of fandom before the spread of the internet and after it. Before the proliferation of the internet and other digital affordances, and coinciding with the release of Hollywood's blockbusters in the late 1970s and early 1980s (*The Exorcist, Jaws, Star Wars, Blade Runner*, etc.), Spanish fan culture was initially anchored around the cinematic subgenres of fantasy, horror and science fiction, which were celebrated in fanzines and other amateur publications (Pujol 2013). In the mid-1980s, the arrival of anime shows on Spanish regional television channels, most notably the popular *Dragonball*, marked another turning point for fandom in Spain with the emergence of a thriving manga and anime community that would record anime shows, trace them on their television screens for its posterior distribution on paper or photocopy manga pages (Sánchez-Navarro 2013). Later on, the popularization of the internet in the mid-1990s would transform these production habits into archiving, subtitling and scanlation (scanning and translation of comic books). Normally, these activities took place on online forums and fansites which were also becoming locales of discussion and creation (fan fiction, fan art, etc.) for other Spanish-speaking media fandoms originating in movies (*Lord of the Rings*), television shows (*Buffy the Vampire Slayer*) and books (*Harry Potter*).

In regard to television fandom, there were already fans gathering around online forums like *TusSeries.com,* a big community resembling the extinct TelevisionWithoutPity.com for Spanish and Latin American fans, while the airing of ABC's *Lost* on Spain's public television during the summer of 2004 forever changed the landscape of fan culture in the Spanish context. A sort of 'Lostmania' spread among television fans and users who had never been familiar with fan practices were suddenly keen to discuss theories, chasing spoilers and news in the array of forums, websites and blogs dedicated to the series that ensued. One of the most popular sites was *Pardillos* – a wordplay between *Perdidos,* the Spanish translation of the series' title and the Spanish slang *pardillos,* losers – a parodic webcomic created by the fan Carlos Azaustre who, upon its success, published it as a comic book in 2008 (Scolari 2013).

Lost was the entrance point for transmedia fandom, with viewers now for stayed to watch television and discussing it in the following years across channels, which in turn coincided with a renewed splendor of television fiction (Cascajosa Virino 2016; Mittell 2015). Migration to social media, such as Twitter in the late 2000s, provided fans with different opportunities, to connect not only with other fans but, also, with the producers of their favorite shows who willingly engage in these conversations through their personal accounts (Proulx and Shepatin 2012). With fans embracing live-tweeting, social media has become another part of television programming, with shows and networks promoting the use of Twitter hashtags 'to channel user interaction with televised content' (Association of Internet Researchers 2014, 1). For fans, it marks another locale to become more visible and make their voices heard, especially in the case of low-rated shows like *El Ministerio del Tiempo.*

Transmedia Storytelling and New Business Models

Why, then, has transmedia storytelling been adopted by media corporations as a central communication and business strategy in the last fifteen years? Echoing the fan practice discussed above, the answer to this question can be found in the deep transformations of audiences following the arrival of the internet and the emergence of new interactive media experiences. As other scholars have attested, in the broadcasting era, audiences were seen to 'quiet' in front of the television screen; today, they are fragmented into millions of different and asynchronous consumer situations. The initial image of *The Simpsons* (the whole family, all together, in front of the television set) does not exist anymore: each member of the family is consuming different content on a different device. If cable or satellite television and VHS players introduced a first fragmentation of the audience in the 1970 and 1980s, the spread of online video platforms like YouTube or Vimeo, as well as the incorporation of video reproduction features in social media and the emergence of

Netflix or Amazon in the video market, have radically transformed media consumption practices. More than 'fragmentation', in other words, we should be talking about the 'atomization of audiences' (Scolari 2014).

The atomization of audiences, however, is producing a crisis in the traditional broadcasting business models in Spain. If the old model was based on selling peoples' attention spans to companies through the intermediation of advertising agencies, the new business models are more amorphous and experimental. Traditional advertising or subscription business models are often not enough to keep the media machine working in full force. The atomization of audiences and the crisis of traditional broadcasting business model have led to producers now testing new strategies and to develop new products. Transmedia storytelling is one of these new strategies, as is crowdfunding. Let's see a Spanish case to analyze their interaction.

Crowdfunding as a Transmedia Business Strategy

As explained previously, *El Cosmonauta* is a science fiction feature movie that became transmedial. According to Nicolás Alcalá, one of the creators of *El Cosmonauta*:

> in the early months [the project] was conceived only as a movie. However, I have notes in my notebook when I was writing the script, even though it was a short movie, where I wrote things like 'Fragmenting?', 'How do viewers watch today?', or 'transform it into a series?'. The change occurred when we visited Power To The Pixel (the second edition, I guess) and I heard Lance Weiler, Ted Hope and especially Mike Monello talk about that. I returned from this trip convinced that the project should be transmedia though I still didn't have any idea what this meant (and would not understand it until many months later, during the editing process, when today's transmedia project finally took shape).
>
> (Scolari and Roig-Telo 2015)

Many different strategies come under the name of crowdfunding, from platforms that treat funds as microdonations – Verkami or Goteo – to entrepreneurs that consider crowdfunding as a good way of securing investments. As *El Cosmonauta* transformed itself into a transmedia storytelling experience the distribution model also changed and adopted new features. Originally designed to be premiered at different moments, the production team finally opted for a simultaneous premiere in all release windows (cinema, web, television and DVD/USB) so that the user could choose the format that they want to watch the movie in.

The final cost of the project was €860,000. In November 2012, six months before the release of the feature movie, the team had brought in €399,000 via crowdfunding. For Alcalá, the crowdfunding demands

of *El Cosmonauta* represented a 'creative, wonderful and unique' production experience but which was also 'extremely exhausting'. From an
economic perspective it was 'very difficult to reconcile with other works'
and 'not profitable enough to fully compensate' the effort (Scolari and
Roig-Telo 2015). In effect, *El Cosmonauta* started as a monomedia project but the dynamics of crowdfunding had transformed it into a transmedia experience. This production shows that transmediality is not just
a storytelling strategy with the objective of consolidating a narrative-
centered audience of fans; it is also a financial strategy that aligns closely
with what Matthew Freeman terms 'commodity braiding' (2014). In this
case, crowdfunding created the necessity of producing new content for
contributors. However, crowdfunding is not necessarily a magic solution
to all of the financing problems that arise with transmedia production.
For small teams, the implementation of a funding strategy based on mi-
cropayments requires full-time dedication, making it difficult to develop
more than one project at a time or to exclusively focus on the audiovisual
creation process.

Conclusion

In the last decade or so, the growth of a fictional transmedia market in
Spain has been strongly impacted by the economic recession, which has
conditioned the way in which media projects are now produced and expanded. First, we can observe a prevalence of what we have called tactical
expansion vs. strategic expansion in practically all of our observed cases.
Projects without an initial transmedia plan entered transmedia production as they were consolidating their commercial success, giving rise to
the assumption that larger budgets are required to produce imaginary
transmedia worlds. Only now that the economic landscape is bouncing
back, Spanish media corporations are beginning to see transmediality as
a strategic and ingrained part in the narrative and commercial design of
their products. Outside of earlier discussed cases, such as *El Internado*
and *El Barco*, this shift toward transmedia strategy is especially notable in the private sector. To date, the private sector has been proverbi-
ally towed by the public one, which has been setting the standards both
creatively – with an open attitude toward transmediality despite the
economic situation – and aesthetically, regularly exploiting different moments of the country's history in productions of diverse genres.

Second, and in line with this direct relationship between transmedia
development and healthy budgets, we must highlight the strong presence
of television projects on the Spanish transmedia map, as evidenced in this
chapter. At the beginning, television companies were the most equipped
to take on transmedia development, although examples like *Panzer
Chocolate* or *El Cosmonauta* pose a challenge to this argument, and to
the fact that only those with enormous budgets can afford transmedia

experimentation and proliferation. In this sense, and as a third observation, *El Cosmonauta*'s complex journey to receive financing via crowdfunding remains an enlightening yet contradictory experience for future projects based on crowdfunding in Spain. Enlightening because it shows how loyal fans and audiences can support and help projects at different stages of production, and contradictory because crowdfunding is not enough to deal with financing issues, or the key to commercial success.

Even in the face of such financial issues, which are themselves heightened by the costly nature of transmediality, fan activity goes beyond the borders of the low-budget independent scene and often actively supports transmedia projects of this kind. As was shown earlier, *El Ministerio del Tiempo* is the typical monomedia production that, thanks to its fandom, started to conquer other media platforms, and was hence able to survive the dictatorship of broadcast ratings. This form of fanbase empowerment, and the increasing attention of media companies toward fannish forms of consumption and production, is ultimately indicative of how the post-broadcasting era is finally being taken over by fictional transmedia production in Spain.

Acknowledgements

This chapter was funded by the Spanish Ministry of Economy, Industry and Competitiveness through the Doctoral Training Grants 2015 program (Ref. BES-2015–071455).

Bibliography

Álvarez Monzoncillo, José. M., and Javier López Villanueva. "La producción audiovisual: promesas a través de la crisis." In *Informe sobre el estado de la cultura en España 2016: La cultura como motor de cambio*, edited by E. Bustamante, 43–52. Madrid: Fundación Alternativas, 2016.

Antoral, José Manuel. "El Barco se despide consiguiendo el 97% del share social." *Antena 3.com*. February 22, 2013. Accessed 25 March 2017. http://blogs.antena3.com/socializados/barco%ADdespide%ADcon%ADsiguiendo%ADshare%ADsocial_2013022200002.html.

Association of Internet Researchers. "Social TV: Quantifying the Intersections between Television and Social Media." In *Selected Papers of Internet Research 15: The 15th Annual Meeting of the Association of Internet Researchers*, 1–23. Daegu, Korea: Association of Internet Researchers, 2014.

Barrientos-Bueno, Mónica. "La convergencia y la segunda pantalla televisivas: el caso de Isabel (TVE)." In *Proceedings of I Congreso Internacional Comunicación y Sociedad*. Logroño: Universidad Internacional de La Rioja, 2013.

Belsunces Gonçalves, Andreu. "Producción, consumo y prácticas culturales en torno a los nuevos media en la cultura de la convergencia: el caso de Fringe como narración transmedia y lúdica." MA diss., Universitat Oberta de Catalunya, 2011.

Bustamante, Enrique. *Informe sobre el estado de la cultura en España 2016. La cultura como motor de cambio*. Madrid: Fundación Alternativas, 2016.

Cascajosa Virino, Concepción. *La Cultura de las Series*. Barcelona: Laertes, 2016.

El Torres, Desireé Bressend, Jaime Martínez, and Sandra Molina. *Tiempo al Tiempo*. Girona: Aleta Ediciones, 2017.

Establés-Heras, María-José. "Entre fans anda el juego: audiencias creativas, series de televisión y narrativas Transmedia." *Opción* 11 (2016): 476–497.

FCB Global. "Cinderella 2.0: Transmedia Storytelling (video)". *YouTube*. May 20, 2013. Accessed 25 March 2017. www.youtube.com/watch?v=CP-zOCl5md0.

Freeman, Matthew. "The Wondergul Game of Oz and Tarzan Jigsaws: Commodifying Transmedia in Early Twentieth Century Consumer Culture." *Intensities: The Journal of Cult Media* 7 (2014): 44–54.

Freeman, Matthew. *Historicising Transmedia Storytelling: Early Twentieth Century Transmedia Story Worlds*. London: Routledge, 2016.

García Mirón, Silvia. "La aplicación de posibilidades transmedia e interactivas en las producciones seriadas de ficción de Antena 3: Análisis de la etapa Planeta." *Communication Papers* 3:4 (2014): 23–36.

Grandío, María del Mar, and Joseba Bonaut. "Transmedia Audiences and Television Fiction: A Comparative Approach between Skins (UK) and El Barco (Spain)." *Participations: Journal of Audience & Reception Studies* 9:2 (2012). www.participations.org/Volume%209/Issue%202/30%20Grandio%20 Bonaut.pdf.

Guerrero, Mar. "Webs televisivas y sus usuarios: un lugar para la narrativa transmedia. Los casos de Águila Roja y Juego de Tronos en España." *Comunicación y Sociedad* 21 (2014): 239–267.

Guerrero-Pico, Mar. "Dimensional Expansions and Shiftings: Fan Fiction and Transmedia Storytelling in the Fringeverse." *Series: International Journal of TV Serial Narratives* 2:2 (2016): 73–85.

Hernández Pérez, Manuel, and María del Mar Grandío. "Narrativa crossmedia en el discurso de ciencia ficción: Estudio de Battlestar Galactica (2003–2010)." *Área Abierta* 28 (2011): 1–20.

Hills, Matt. *Fan Cultures*. London: Routledge, 2002.

Jenkins, Henry. "Transmedia Storytelling. Moving Characters from Books to Films to Video Games Can Make Them Stronger and More Compelling." *MIT Technology Review*. January 15, 2003. Accessed 25 March 2017. www. technologyreview.com/s/401760/transmedia-storytelling/.

Jenkins, Henry. *Convergence Culture. La Cultura de la Convergencia de los Medios de Comunicación*. Barcelona: Paidós, 2008.

Jenkins, Henry. "The Revenge of the Origami Unicorn: Seven Principles of Transmedia Storytelling (Well, Two Actually). Five More on Friday." *Confessions of an Aca-Fan: The Official Weblog of Henry Jenkins*. December 12, 2009. Accessed 14 July 2017. http://henryjenkins.org/blog/2009/12/the_ revenge_of_the_origami_uni.html.

Lacalle, Charo, Deborah Castro, and Mariluz Castro. "España. Innovación y tradición." In *OBITEL 2016: (Re)invención de géneros y formatos de la ficción televisiva*, edited by Guillermo Orozco Gómez and Maria Immacolata Vasallo de Lopes, 295–333. Porto Alegre: OBITEL, 2016.

Lacasa, Pilar, Rut Martínez-Borda, and Laura Méndez. "Developing New Literacies Using Commercial Videogames as Educational Tools." *Lingüistics and Education* 19:2 (2008): 85–106.

Mayor Mayor, Francesc. "Transmedia Storytelling desde la ficción serial española: El caso de Antena 3." *Cuadernos de la Información y la Comunicación* 19 (2014): 69–85.

Ministerio de Educación Cultura y Deporte. *Plan de fomento de las Industrias culturales y creativas*. Madrid: Ministerio de Educación, Cultura y Deporte, 2016.

Mittell, Jason. *Complex TV: The Poetics of Contemporary Television Storytelling*. New York: New York University Press, 2015.

Molpeceres-Arnáiz, Sara, and María Isabel Rodríguez-Fidalgo. "La inserción del discurso del receptor en la narrativa transmedia: el ejemplo de las series de televisión de ficción." *Historia y Comunicación Social* 19 (2014): 31–42.

Prensa RTVE. "'El Ministerio del Tiempo' lanza la primera tienda de 'merchandising' oficial con productos diseñados por los fans". *Web RTVE.es*. 2016. Accessed 25 March 2017. www.rtve.es/rtve/20160304/ministerio-del-tiempo-lanza-primera-tienda-merchandising-oficial-productos-disenados-fans/1312903.shtml.

Proulx, Mark, and Stacey Shepatin. *Social TV: How Marketers Can Reach and Engage Audiences by connecting Television to the Web, Social Media and Mobile*. Hoboken, NJ: John Wiley, 2012.

Pujol, Cristina. "Amiguetes Entertainment: el club social del fanatismo de turno." In *Fanáticos: La cultura fan*, edited by Antoni Roig, Daniel Aranda, and Jordi Sánchez-Navarro, 251–278. Barcelona: UOC Press, 2013.

Quijano, Mario. "Los museos y centros de arte: necesaria y urgente adaptación al entorno digital." In *Informe sobre el estado de la cultura en España. La salida digital*, edited by Enrique Bustamante, and Fernando Rueda, 35–44. Madrid: Fundación Alternativas, 2014.

Ruiz Córdoba, Juan Manuel, and Àlex Sierra. *Águila Roja: La Sociedad del Loto Blanco*. Barcelona: Glénat, 2011.

Ruiz Pleguezuelos, María Rocío. "Adaptaciones (in) necesarias en las series históricas recientes." *Index Comunicación* 6:2 (2016): 319–336.

Salvador-Esteban, Lucía. "Historia y ficción televisiva. La representación del pasado en 'Isabel'." *Index Comunicación* 6:2 (2016): 151–171.

Sánchez-Navarro, Jordi. "Fantasías animadas: el estudio de los fans occidentales del anime como subcultura." In *Fanáticos: La cultura fan*, edited by Antoni Roig, Daniel Aranda, and Jordi Sánchez-Navarro, 45–68. Barcelona: UOC Press, 2013.

Schaaff, Anaïs, and Javier Pascual. *El tiempo es el que es*. Barcelona: Plaza & Janés, 2016.

Scolari, Carlos A. "Transmedia Storytelling: Implicit Consumers, Narrative Worlds, and Branding in Contemporary Media Production." *International Journal of Communication* 3 (2009): 586–606.

Scolari, Carlos, A., Sara Fernández de Azcárate, Manuel Garín, Mar Guerrero, Manel Jiménez, Aitor Martos, Matilde Obradors, Mercè Oliva, Óliver Pérez, and Eva Pujadas. "Narratives Transmediàtiques, Convergência Audiovisual i noves Estratègies de Comunicació." *Quaderns del CAC* 38 (2011): 75–85.

Scolari, Carlos A., Manel Jiménez, and Mar Guerrero. "Narrativas Transmediáticas en España: Cuatro Ficciones en busca de un destino cross-media." *Comunicación y Sociedad* 25:1 (2012): 137–164.

Scolari, Carlos A. *Narrativas Transmedia: Cuando todos los medios cuentan*. Barcelona: Deusto, 2013.

Scolari, Carlos A. Narrativas Transmedia: Nuevas formas de Comunicar en la era Digital. *Anuario AC/E de Cultural Digital 2014*, 71–81 (2014). http://unica.upf.edu/es/node/2261.

Scolari, Carlos A., Paolo Bertetti, and Matthew Freeman. *Transmedia Archaeology. Storytelling iin the Borderlines of Science Fiction, Comics and Pulp Magazines.* Basingstoke: Palgrave Macmillan, 2014.

Scolari, Carlos A., and María-José Establés. "El Ministerio Transmedia. Expansiones Narrativas y Culturas Participativas." *Palabra Clave* (Special Issue: Fandom), 2017.

Scolari, Carlos A., and Antoni Roig-Telo. "Crowdfunding and Transmedia Storytelling: A Tale of Two Spanish Projects." In *Crowdfunding the Future. Media Industries, Ethics and Digital Society,* edited by Lucy Bennett, Bertha Chin, and Bethan Jones, 207–226. New York: Peter Lang, 2015.

Wolf, Mark J.P. *Building Imaginary Worlds: The Theory and History of Subcreation.* London and New York: Routledge, 2012.

3 Portugal

Transmedia Brand Narratives, Cultural Intermediaries and Port Wine

Matthew Freeman and
Ana Margarida Meira

Currently, transmedia narratives blend cultures and markets into inseparable entities, with global markets converting products by bringing them together as parts of multiplatform phenomena. Meanwhile, cultural intermediaries transform products and brands even further, shaping their perception and bridging gaps between producers and consumers. But how does transmediality intermingle with the work of cultural intermediaries to convert the relationship between consumers, producers and items of old and new non-media products and brands?

In Portugal, few products are so deeply rooted in the tradition and culture of the country as port wine. As well as representing a significant proportion of the country's exports, port is also a piece of history and a part of the memory of a country that has a profound bond with remembrances. This chapter looks at the brand narratives surrounding one of the oldest port wines in Portugal – Kopke – and a more recent brand of port – Vasques de Carvalho – so to understand the relationship between cultural heritage and brand narratives across platforms. We argue that the brand messages of these two port wines, though communicated differently, are underpinned by the same conceptual categories, which has ultimately helped to imbed port wine into the fabric of Portugal's cultural heritage. We will demonstrate this argument via the lens of cultural intermediaries – drawing on a set of five interviews with practitioners – so as to showcase how the communication of cultural intermediaries' narratives leads to the building of links between Portugal's cultural heritage and the products the country promotes.

Branding and Cultural Intermediaries

Narrative production, transmitted through multiple media platforms, is a practice that has growing relevance to today's brand strategies and consumer perceptions. Consumers are increasingly demanding knowledge of the multiple realities around them. It is not enough anymore for brands to merely offer quality products with a functional and economic value. Today, products must be more than a tangible response to a priority; consumers now seek emotional attachments to their brands, each with unique experiences and a sense of empathy for the inheritance of a product that revives pleasant and authentic memories (Holt 2004).

Concepts of branding have of course defined the engagement of consumers for decades (Lury 2004). But in a media context, John T. Caldwell argues that 'branding has emerged as a central concern … in the age of digital convergence' (2004, 305). Catherine Johnson shows how television programs, in particular, are 'now being constructed as brands designed to encourage audience loyalty and engagement with the text beyond the act of television viewing' (2012, 1). Considerations of branding in this context work to evoke what Henry Jenkins calls brand extension, 'the idea that successful brands are built by exploiting multiple contacts between the brand and the consumer' (2006, 69). For Jenkins, this, too, 'should not be contained within a single media platform, but should extend across multiple media. Brand extension builds on audience interest in certain content to bring them into contact again and again with an associated brand' (ibid.). Following this logic, we can understand the link between brand extension and transmediality, since the latter is similarly conceptualized according to its extension of clearly defined or branded content across as different media.

Furthermore, given that both brand extension and transmediality are really about extending communication across an array of channels by bringing those channels closer together, it is possible to understand the relationship between these phenomena and cultural intermediaries. Very much describing an in-between sector, cultural intermediaries refer to 'the taste-makers defining what counts as good taste in today's marketplace' (Maguire and Matthews 2014, 1); they have a critical, if rather under-scrutinized, value in the contemporary media and cultural landscape by operating with, between, through and around the media and cultural landscape. If transmedia narratives are built by brands to tell the stories that define the essence and identity of their products, then cultural intermediaries bring together groups of experts with consumers, acting as storytellers and opinion influencers. These experts work to transform transmedia narratives into a social and cultural phenomenon since they construct a bridge between the tangibility of the products, producers and brands and an intangible dimension enclosed by emotions, inheritances and collective memories of consumers. These narratives are ultimately reinterpreted by cultural intermediaries and transmitted to other consumers in order to influence tastes, lifestyles and experiences – thus traversing multiple media forms.

Historically, though, the term cultural intermediaries had its origin in the lines written by Pierre Bourdieu in 1984. The author was referring to a group that he called new petite bourgeoisie, which represented a part of the working middle class that grew in size and influence since the mid-20th century. The concept of the cultural intermediary has subsequently been used by several authors and applied to several chronological moments. Cultural intermediaries are, therefore, people with an experience, a set of attitudes and a specific knowledge about certain products or areas that gives them, for a group of consumers, legitimacy and authority.

They are people who have acquired experiences over the course of their lives that have given them an accurate view of the market, brands and products. In addition to being knowledgeable about the tangible and intangible characteristics of particular products or categories, they are also consumers and are therefore placed on a level of proximity that allows for deeper and more personal forms of communication – typically narrative based.

According to Maguire and Matthews (2012), there are three dimensions to the work of the cultural intermediary: context, knowledge and impact. First, all cultural intermediaries are themselves reflective of a set of *contexts*, dynamics and circumstances; the narratives that are constructed by these practitioners are undoubtedly influenced by their own social and historical contexts, the social circuits in which they act, their occupations and the dominant interests of their group. Our chapter attempts to understand the weight of the Portuguese context in relation to the narratives of port wine built by cultural intermediaries. Second, this ability to understand the market, the result of its context, experiences and memories, is contingent on the *knowledge* of a cultural intermediary. In addition to technical knowledge about products, these practitioners carry with them an experience that feeds into their shaping of narratives that help to contextualize and ascribe value to a product in the minds and hearts of consumers. Third, it is assumed that since cultural intermediaries work to transform products into cultural products, framing them, contextualizing them with brand narratives, this practice ultimately influences consumers' opinions about a brand: it makes an *impact*, often via the media, which influences beliefs and our emotional connections to products.

Keith Negus (2002) raises questions about the presumed special significance of cultural intermediaries within the production/consumption relations of contemporary capitalism, focusing on the ways in which cultural intermediaries recreate as well as bridge the sense of distance between production and consumption. Anne M. Cronin (2004), meanwhile, explores the status of advertising practitioners as cultural intermediaries and uses that analysis to think through the contested relationship between consumption and production, and culture and economy. Based on the UK context, Cronin argues that

> the role of advertising practitioners should not be understood solely in terms of a mediation between producer and consumer; instead, their role should be conceived in terms of a negotiation between multiple "regimes of mediation", including that of the relationship between advertising agencies and their clients.
>
> (2004, 1)

This chapter will explore this negotiation further – between the regimes of brand narratives, cultural heritage in Portugal, and the role of transmedia storytelling within this.

Brand narratives, indeed, are key work for today's cultural intermediaries, and shape how non-media products can be understood as transmedia narratives. Many of today's brands are opting to create narratives for and around their products as a way of engaging and sustaining the engagement of consumers. In coined 'cultural branding', the idea is for brands to utilize cultural trends emerging in society in order to build brand strategies that reflect those trends (Holt 2004). In reference to the l'Occitane brand, for example, Luca Massimiliano Visconti argues that 'when companies adopt a narrative approach to branding they can establish a stronger dialogue with customers and defend their competitive advantage more effectively' (2010, 231). With brand narratives, the identity of the brand cannot easily be imitated since it is carved from and imbedded into the specific cultural climate of a given country and time.

Brands, then, must master the art of storytelling – of building an imaginary world that many people wish to enter – much like the art of transmedia storytelling (Jenkins 2006) because today it is essential for brands to have the ability to 'produce dreams for public consumption where imagination, emotions and dreams are central' (Jensen 2001, 2). And yet a difficulty for today's brands is to achieve a balance between communicating the quality of the product, including its functional characteristics, and the construction of narratives that engage and sustain interest from consumers as if it were a story or piece of entertainment. The functional dimension of the product will only serve the needs and expectations of people as consumers; it will not necessarily engage their imaginations, emotions and dreams. Ironically, it is the influence on emotions that best conquers, bonds and influences our personal decisions.

Thinking more culturally, brand narratives have the potential to speak to cultural identities, past or present, and thus – when formed via or in dialogue with cultural intermediaries – can inform the cultural heritage of a country. Broadly, cultural heritage is an expression of the ways of living developed by a community that are passed on from generation to generation. In other words, it is a cultural practice contingent on narratives and practices of storytelling, be those narratives based on people or brands, and in one medium or across several media. The affective and emotional connection that is shaped between consumers and products goes through the interpretation of narratives that are connected with the collective memories of a heritage. Narratives combine relevant moments of the past, the present and the future of the brand, the product and the history. The phenomenon of narrative production by cultural intermediaries ties consumers to a moment of sharing individual and collective memories, transforming this complex dialogue into an intangible dimension formed by cultural spaces. How, then, do cultural intermediaries in Portugal work to build and extend brand narratives for port wines as a means of reconstructing a sense of cultural heritage transmedially?

Port Wine and Methodological Approach

The main focus of this chapter is to analyze the dynamic process of narrative production in the context of a non-media based product, and to understand the relationships between these multiplatform brand narratives and ideas of cultural heritage in Portugal. Specifically, we focus on port wine as the chosen object of study. In addition to being a product with history, memories and identity, port is a product that is screaming for a renewal in the new brand-consumer reality. Port wine is

> an object of great history, nomadic, that lives on a river by which it is transported by boats, which remains for years in kites and when is tasted caresses the palate. But [people] are generally unaware of the hours of work, the number of people involved, the liters of sweat and the tons of matter involves.
>
> (Búzio and Lencastre 2010, 50)

Historically, port wine is a product that results from 'work, knowledge and techniques that a particular human group has developed over time' (Pereira 1996, 179). For with this product, which reflects the knowledge acquired by successive generations, tradition has acquired such prominence, at least in Portugal, that it sometimes conflicts with any sense of evolution and innovation. Port, in order words, is associated with tradition and is part of the country's sense of cultural heritage: 'it is that no wine is given by nature' (Pereira 1996, 179). Port wine is very much the result of a system of relationships between vine growers and merchants. Its production has greatly affected the Douro region in that the production of port wine is now dependent on this region, in turn building Douro as the epicenter of 'an active process of communication' across Portugal and resulting in its regional identity (Parkhurst 2004, 3). As Manuel Novaes Cabral, one of the cultural intermediaries interviewed, explains further:

> UNESCO recognised the Douro vineyard as a World Heritage Site in 2001. It recognized, as the classification itself indicates, the vineyard Douro, wine and vineyards and the interaction of Man with Nature itself. It is a landscape carved by generations and generations of people who have passed by. Port wine already has a great international projection, but this recognition of UNESCO has highlighted the importance of this region that unites people and nature with mastery.

As was indicated more generally earlier, narratives are essential elements for understanding and analyzing port wine as well as the relationships between port wine and how its narratives are constructed by cultural intermediaries to form the Portuguese country's identity and memory. As well as being an object with several prisms to explore and which can bring diverse perspectives on the theme of cultural transmediality, the port wine narratives are under-explored areas of investigation, despite bringing significant advances for how we might understand the communication of brands and related consumer behaviors, which in this case bring us 'open, rich, detailed and often personal perspectives' (Hyvärinen 2008, 447). Knowing that brands have to transport their products into an emotional, experiential and cultural dimension, how does this storytelling practice compare across old and new products? In particular, how do the brand narratives surrounding Kopke – the oldest port wine in Portugal – compare with those of Vasques de Carvalho – a recent brand of port?

To approach this question, we return to cultural intermediaries. Five practitioners from this sector in Portugal were interviewed: Otília Lage, who specializes in knowledge of Douro and its cultural narratives over the years; Manuel Pintão, an educator by trade and producer of port wines; João Paulo Martins, a journalist by profession; Gaspar Martins Pereira, the author of several biographies and official histories of the Port Wine Houses; and Manuel Novais Cabral, who is president of the Institute of Douro and Port Wines. Our main aim with these interviews was to understand how transmedia narratives about two different port wines in Portugal transform the relationship between consumers and products in the cultural spaces of Portugal. Our open interview approach allowed these interviewees to share their experiences, recollections and perspectives on port wine and for us to analyze if, during the creation of these brand narratives, there are common elements that have led to the construction of a relationship between the product and the consumers, through spaces that become cultural. Let's begin, then, by introducing the first of the port wines – Kopke, the oldest of the two.

Kopke

Established in 1638 by Christiano Kopke and his son, Nicolau Kopke (coming to Portugal as representatives of the Hanseatic League), the House of Kopke is the oldest port wine export firm. Through many generations, the company was run by several representatives of the Kopke family, obtaining an excellent reputation for its wines over the years. Some of its members were deeply involved with the Oporto trade, mainly in the 19th century, when Joaquim Kopke, known as 'Barão de Massarelos', took part in numerous economic actions. Meanwhile, the company was sold to the Bohane family at the end of the 19th century, who tried to run it from London, where they had most of their economic interests. However, the distance between the UK and Portugal, not to mention the two World Wars, prevented the full control of the company and they therefore opted to sell it. Then, in 1953, and after some negotiations, the Barros family, whose leader was Manuel Barros, bought the House of Kopke and since then it has belonged to this family group. In fact, Manuel Barros was connected with the export and commercialization of port wines since his youth. After becoming a partner of Barros, Almeida & Co., he bought other firms, such as Hutcheson, Feuerheerd, Feist – all of which are old port wine exporters. Manuel Barros and his sons, João and Manuel, ran the company until the middle of the 1970s, trying to build the brand image even more by developing an important agricultural unity in the Douro district. Today, Kopke, the oldest port wine brand, is the assumed leader in the 'Porto Colheita' category – translated simply as 'Port of the Vintage' and which connotes tradition, prestige and quality.

Looking across an array of media texts, including television advertisements, billboards and the product website, one can identify six elements that make up the brand message of Kopke. These six brand elements comprise: *history*, communicated namely via the product tagline 'It's part of our legacy'; *age*, as in the website message that 'the House of Kopke is the eldest Porto wine export firm'; *family*, such as the regularly reinforced public message that, through many generations, the company was run by several representatives of the Kopke family; *reputation*, as in reviews stating the brand's 'excellent reputation'; *Douro*, such as cultural understandings that the brand tries to develop an agricultural unity in the Douro district; and *quality and prestige*, as in related and aforementioned cultural messages that 'nowadays Kopke is the oldest Porto wine and is the assumed leader in the Porto Colheita category'.

Kopke's brand narrative emphasizes the importance of the brand in terms of the history of Portugal as a whole – communicating its sense of identity collectively as 'our' identity. The television advertisement, for example, goes through several moments in the history of the brand and the family that gave it its name: the Kopke family. The advertisement emphasizes the family as a synonym for reputation, for antiquity and, consequently, for legitimacy. Across media, this narrative goes on to reveal the importance of updating in a territory that is essential for its identity: Douro. The acquisition of the brand by the Sogevinus Group brought new tools and perspectives to Kopke, placing it in the market as the oldest brand of port wine, reinforcing a sustained sense of longevity that is sustained across print and broadcast media.

According to the cultural intermediary practitioners interviewed for this chapter, all of these six brand narratives were very deliberate, with each intended as a way to infuse Kopke into the cultural heritage and memory of the Portuguese culture. With regard to history, for instance, Manuel Pintão discusses how 'in addition to the sublime quality, port wine carries within itself the weight of history, the value of an inheritance that was built by our ancestors with an impressive succession of human effort. Communicating that history is crucial'. João Paul Martins, similarly, explains how this idea of history is crucial to consumer products, noting that 'when people drink Kopke they are drinking history; they are drinking all of the information that comes from that history and which makes wine much more than a drink: it is something that carries incredible strength'. João Paulo Martins, further, suggests that the communication of the brand's history is 'more ceremonial: I think the fact that it is a wine with so much history, it makes you want to talk about it'. In terms of age, moreover, Gaspar Martins Pereira notes how 'Kopke has several associations, beginning with antiquity. It is important to communicate this status as a pioneer in the history of denominations of origin, tying the brand to Portugal and its own history'. As for family, Otília Lage explained how a key concern has been to reinforce the familial manual labor that goes into the making of Kopke, particularly in the past: 'In the 1940s, they worked in Douro from sun up to sun down and ate a malt of broth or took home bread – those fortunate enough to have it. This inscrutable hard work is now caught up in the narratives of the brand, as is the central idea that the brand is about a family listening to people' – which in turn fuels cultural messages of Kopke's reputation, quality, as well as its ties to the region of Douro. Indeed, for Otília Lage, that particular regional tie is significant: 'the history of Douro and the history of port wine is a story of crises – socially, commercial, politically – which all build Kopke's significance'. How, though, do these brand messages compare to Vasques de Carvalho – the newer brand?

Vasques de Carvalho

As was indicated in our introduction, what is crucial to articulate at this stage is the fact that, despite the age difference between the two studied brands of port wine, in actual fact both Kopke and Vasques de Carvalho are underpinned by much the same conceptual categories. And this similarity is surely the reason why port wine as a product is now linked so profoundly to the cultural heritage of Portugal. Before demonstrating this specifically, allow us first to outline a brief history of Vasques de Carvalho so as to articulate its difference to Kopke.

The history of the Vasques de Carvalho family has strong roots, and is often mistaken for the history of the Douro. Its origins date back to the middle of the 19th century and the family wine company, which has always transformed its production into generous wine, selling partly to the exporting houses and aging another part, adding value to it. In 1880, José Vasques de Carvalho, great grandfather of the company's current managing partner António Fernando Lopes, decided to age the wine for decades and carefully store it in the family warehouses up to the present day. In the middle of the 20th century, the family then began acting as merchants of wine, acquiring grapes from third parties. This strategic change, taken by Maria Amélia Pereira

Lopes, allowed the company to increase its stock. By the 1970s, Maria
Amélia had acquired the status of Port Wine Bottling Producer. In
2000, the company Vasques de Carvalho was officially formed. In
2012, the heirs of Maria Amélia shared the assets inherited from her
mother, with the company's current managing partner staying with
the company Vasques de Carvalho, as well as sharing the stocks of
wines. In order to add value to the Vasques de Carvalho port wine
in what is a crowded and sophisticated market, the company joined
forces with Kurtpace SA, affording the acquisition of high quality
grapes and wines for the production of diversified port wines of special, innovative categories.

Again looking across an array of media texts, namely newspaper advertisements, billboards and the product website, it seems that the same
six elements can be argued to make up the brand message of Vasques de
Carvalho, albeit are communicated in different ways. In this case, these six
brand elements are communicated thusly: *history*, such as the tagline that
'There is always a single story that hides behind a wine'; *age*, as in the description on the website that 'this wine has been aged and carefully stored
in family warehouses to this day'; *family*, as in the same website's affir-
mation that 'the history of the Vasques de Carvalho family has roots as
strong as a vine'; *reputation*, such as popular reviews of how the company
'allows the acquisition of high quality grapes and wines'; *Douro*, such as
the aforementioned point about the history of the company often being
confused with the history of the Douro; and *quality and prestige*, such as
discussions found in newspapers about 'the production of the first Vínica
Velha DOC Douro' and its exporting houses all working to 'add value'.

Much like that of Kopke, the narrative constructed by Vasques de
Carvalho emphasizes the importance of history behind the wine. The
element of history is relevant here, despite being a new company, since
it leads to the interconnection of several elements by the passage of time
across media: visualized as the history of port itself, the history of the
family, and the history of Douro. Linked to each of these cultural histories, the brand relates its identity closely with the Douro, in particular,
which as has been shown is intertwined with the cultural associations
of port wine in Portugal. Even though Vasques de Carvalho is a newly
marketed brand, it is thus perceived as part of the history of port itself –
a perception that is helped and further reinforced by the fact that the
Vasques de Carvalho wine does technically date back to the 19th century, thus contributing to the antiquity and quality of the brand.

Precisely how, though, has Vasques de Carvalho managed to achieve
this status in such a short period of time? In the words of the cultural
intermediaries interviewed, imbedding the cultural heritage of Portugal
into the brand narratives of Vasques de Carvalho was an even more
strategic and difficult task, on account of the comparative newness of
this brand. As has been established, port wine's relationship with history

and with the dynamics of the Portuguese community make it a product whose value is passed down from generation to generation, preserving the essential characteristics of the culture through time. Far more than just a product, port wine must become a cultural product in the minds of the people, one that is associated with certain moments, places and rituals (Santos and Ribeiro 2012, 17). As Manuel Novaes Cabral elaborates in relation to Vasques de Carvalho more specifically:

> Because port wine is history – part of its identity, its quality – above all, it was important with Vasques de Carvalho that we communicated a sense of the way it makes us feel after drinking it. That the brand is diverse, more complex, that it is part of the country's individual and collective memories, which then builds our identity.

For Gaspar Martins Pereira, this sense of identity building in relation to Vasques de Carvalho was about acknowledging the sense of tradition associated with port wine rather that its age:

> Almost all companies are keen to refer to their age, since affirming the antiquity of the brand is a form of connection with the wine tradition. But in this case tradition is associated with antiquity, on the one hand, but on the other hand with distinction. Not everyone can have 40-year-old wines. Tradition has a touch of distinction because it is experience, the knowledge of the experience made, the traditional wisdom, the collective memories certainly.

For Pereira, building a brand narrative of the product's age was therefore about tapping into cultural ideas of the longevity of port wine itself, working to bring people together around Vasques de Carvalho: 'port wine unties tongues, you know? We wanted to suggest that drinking our port wine was about drinking in company, not drinking alone – drinking together with all ages, all generations'. Indeed, with regard to the message of family, Gaspar Martins Pereira indicates that articulating this particular brand message was much easier, discussing how Vasques de Carvalho was able to emphasize the long, family-led work process involved in getting the brand to market: 'knowing that it was all done by hand, and the very work of land clearing that existed, is impressive. This side of the work is still a long way off, and gives the brand a distinction of family'. According to Manuel Pintão, what was fundamental to the brand narrative of Vasques de Carvalho was the idea that its makers were 'born in a family related to port wine'. In terms of reputation, Manuel Novaes Cabral explains how Vasques de Carvalho sought primarily to balance brand narratives of tradition with messages of innovation in order to distinguish it while still embedding the product in the cultural history of Portugal: 'port wine is a tradition-bound wine, but today it has to adapt to innovations, needs and contexts. Our wine related to the tradition, culture and history of Portugal, without a doubt'. Says Cabral: 'the stories about port wine are endless because they are linked to our history, our legacy. We must maintain them with our brand, but we must innovate too'. And for Cabral, this brand narrative of tradition and innovation is about reminding consumers of the brand's link to Douro while highlighting the diversity of people involved in the making of the product:

> the Douro results from the enormous effort of generations, of people, of entire families who worked there and who have been succeeding in time. We try to remind people with our brand that we must not forget the enormous number of Spaniards who worked there and this symbiosis results in an important civilizational meeting.

This brand narrative of Vasques de Carvalho as important civilizational meeting is one that traverses multiple sites of media in Portugal, and which in turn helps to build this particular port wine as a product of perceived quality and prestige in the eyes of consumers.

Looking across Kopke and Vasques de Carvalho, then, there are indeed common structural elements to the brand narratives of both port wines, even though they are separated by age. For both brands, the story is extremely important and it is this narrative element that initiates the cultural meanings. Narrative works to build a connection with the passage of time, with the creation of memories, and with the identity of the country. Contextualizing both brands in relevant periods of the history of the country confers a sense of historical parallelism that is essential for the image of antiquity, longevity and stability that is important for all port wine brands. They both do this, in fact, by contextualizing the necessity of the brands with the economic and financial crises of that particular period. Kopke's narrative, in particular, uses the element of antiquity as a synonym for prestige and the reputation already built; Vasques de Carvalho, meanwhile, speaks of temporal antiquity. Importantly, seniority in the port wine market is recognized if the brand is seen to be part of the collective and individual memory of the country, if it has shared the relevant cultural, social, economic and political moments with its consumers over time – something that both Kopke and Vasques de Carvalho achieve.

In other words, there is the ability for both port wines to forge strong relationships with the memory of the country. By constructing the aforementioned brand narratives of history, age, family, reputation, Douro, quality and prestige constructed and maintained transmedially across multiple sites of media, such as television, print, radio and so on – both Kopke and Vasques de Carvalho are seen to embody the traditions, values and histories of Portugal. In short, both port wines have become part of the memory of the country, ingrained into its culture. In an era where the need to build known, stable brand universes is commonplace, memory plays a decisive role in consumer decisions. The space that port wine products occupy in individual and collective memories is crucial, at least in this cultural context, for creating emotional affinities with consumers. With port wine, in fact, memory is an essential element, which is built collectively and transmedially through inheritance, legacy and reality.

Conclusion

In this chapter, our objective was, first, to understand if there are any common elements between the narratives of the two studied port brands, and second, in turn, to understand whether the brand narratives of Kopke and Vasques de Carvalho correlate with ideas of cultural heritage in Portugal. Through an analysis of said brand narratives as well as those communicated through interviews with cultural intermediary practitioners, we have shown the great national and economic importance of port wine in Portugal, one that is thoroughly reflected in the very fabric of the country's political, social, economic and cultural identity.

In doing so, we have demonstrated how the construction of these kinds of cultural formations is correlated closely to the telling of brand stories about products across multiple media. In the case of Kopke and Vasques de Carvalho, the creation of narrativized and participatory brand meanings is a cultural-making phenomenon, one that leads to a change in cultural systems, perceptions and attitudes. We have examined the processes via which raw media materials become transformed into cultural products and cultural myths, establishing how this process of cultural transformation is led by narrative production and reinforced by transmedia storytelling. Above all else, this chapter clarifies precisely why it is so important to study narrative through the eyes of branding, but also cultural heritage and cultural intermediaries.

In short, and in the case of Portuguese port wines, the work of cultural intermediaries has contributed to an understanding of the country's cultural heritage by articulating remarkably consistent brand categories about different products, each produced at different times. In doing so, a sense of tradition and meaning has become associated with port wine, with different brands working to keep the cultural memory of port wine alive in different ways, reminding people of what is so important about the wine by emphasizing different strands of its history in different ways via different images. Branding and transmedia storytelling thus become a means of uniting people together in the cultural memory of what is most important. For as we have showcased repeatedly throughout this chapter in relation to two differing yet clearly – and importantly – overlapping port wines, and as Gaspar Martins Pereira concludes:

> It is undeniable that there is a relationship between port wine and our identity as a country, starting with the name. If we go to the foundation of this connection or the strength of this connection, we find a thousand arguments. Not only is it a sound, it is something that is a

sonority that becomes an association of ideas – a wine from a region, a wine with a history, a wine about certain people and certain processes, a wine, above all, that binds us together and which tells us all something very significant about our sense of time and place.

Bibliography

Bourdieu, Pierre. *Distinction: A Social Critique of the Judgement of Taste.* Cambridge, MA: Harvard University Press, 1984.

Búzio, Christina, and Chris Lencastre. "5 Sentidos-Tawny 40 anos." In *Lote 265: Para Uma Geografia do Douro*, edited by Graham Machado and Rosaline dos Santos, 40–55. Lisbon: University of Port, 2012.

Cronin, Anne M. "Regimes of Mediation: Advertising Practitioners as Cultural Intermediaries?" *Consumption Markets & Culture* 7:4 (2004): 349–369.

Holt, Douglas. *How Brands Become Icons: The Principles of Cultural Branding.* Boston, MA: Harvard Business School Press, 2004.

Hyvärinen, Matti. "Analyzing Narratives and Storytelling". In *The SAGE Handbook of Social Research Methods*, edited by Pertti Alasuutari, Leonard Bickman, and Julia Brannen, 447–460. London: SAGE, 2008.

Jenkins, Henry. *Convergence Culture: Where Old and New Media Collide.* New York: New York University Press, 2006.

Jensen, Rolf. *The Dream Society: How the Coming Shift from Information to Imagination Will Transform Your Business.* London: McGraw-Hill Education, 2001.

Johnson, Catherine. *Branding Television.* London and New York: Routledge, 2012.

Lury, Celia. *Brands: The Logos of the Global Economy.* London and New York: Routledge, 2004.

Maguire, Jennifer Smith, and Julian Matthews. "Are We All Cultural Intermediaries Now? An Introduction to Cultural Intermediaries in Context." *European Journal of Cultural Studies* 15:5 (2012): 551–562.

Maguire, Jennifer Smith, and Julian Matthews (eds.) *The Cultural Intermediaries Reader.* London: Sage, 2014.

Negus, Keith. "The Work of cultural Intermediaries and the Enduring Distance between Production and Consumption". *Cultural Studies* 16:4 (2002): 501–515.

Parkhurst, Shawn. "Identidade e contextos de identificação regional na zona do vinho do Porto." *VIII Congresso Luso-Afro-Brasileiro de Ciências Sociais.* 2004. Accessed 14 June 2016. www.ces.uc.pt/lab2004/inscricao/propostas.html.

Pereira, Graham Michael. "A Região do Vinho do Porto: Origem e Evolução de Uma Demarcação Pioneira." *Douro: Estudos and Documentos* 1:1 (1996): 177–194.

Santos, Jose Freitas, and Jose Cadima Ribeiro. "Estratégias Empresariais de base Territorial: O Caso Symington e a Produção de Vinho do Porto." *DRd-Desenvolvimento Regional em Debate* 2:1 (2012): 134–155.

Visconti, Luca Massimiliano. "Authentic Brand Narratives: Co-Constructed Mediterraneaness for l'Occitane Brand." *Research in Consumer Behavior* 12 (2010): 231–260.

4 France

Telling Tales of Cultural Heritage using Transmedia Storytelling

Mélanie Bourdaa

Transmedia storytelling is a narrative strategy often used to enhance and augment storytelling for audio-visual productions, such as television series or movies (see Jenkins 2006; Bourdaa and Kurtz 2016; Scolari 2013), as well as other media, and has long been studied and analyzed as a symptom of the entertainment industry (Freeman 2016). Like many of the other chapters in this book, this chapter aims to go beyond the field of entertainment – and, in this case, seeks to understand how strategies of transmediality can be applied to cultural heritage.

I will analyze the current transmedia productions in the field of cultural heritage in France and explore the beginning of the design and creative process of an exemplary project that I have been involved with myself. The chapter asks: What types of stories told on multiple media platforms can be used to valorize forms of cultural heritage? What kind of media platforms are being deployed to attract specific audiences and, in particular, young audiences – a question often raised by cultural institutions and museums? As will be demonstrated, particular transmedia strategies, far from being restricted to Hollywood entertainment, have made their way into museums and cultural institutions, which are just as eager to engage audiences and immerse participants in factual storyworlds. But here is the paradox: most of what we know about transmedia storytelling has been developed by observing Hollywood franchises and other popular entertainment, based on fictional narrative worlds. Therefore, engagement in a fictional storyworld is the epitome of transmedia storytelling. How, then, can we approach transmedia productions designed to convey historical facts and maintain a cultural function? How do you design a transmedia strategy for said facts when the canonical definition, and many of the renowned productions of the field, are linked with fiction?

To approach this question, first I define the context in which transmedia storytelling is evolving outside of the entertainment industries, and spreading across multiple sectors. Mutations have changed the media and cultural landscape and favored the rise of transmedia strategies, even if they have a history and roots in past practices (Freeman 2016). I will also define what transmedia storytelling is, as the academic term is often in tension with actual professional practices. Finally, I will analyze

French projects in order to draw up a typology of strategies, which can be used to understand how cultural heritage is narrated on multiple media platforms. Finally, I will explain our methodology for creating our own transmedia storytelling strategy in the 'MediaNum' (Digital Media for Patrimony and Cultural Heritage) project, which seeks to valorize the cultural heritage of the Nouvelle Aquitaine.

Changes and Mutations: The Rise of Transmedia Storytelling

In order to understand the issues around the valorization of cultural heritage, it is essential to identify the stakes around transmedia storytelling. Technological, narrative and participatory changes have paved the way for the development and success of transmedia strategies in multiple sectors, be it entertainment, pedagogy, or culture, relying on different media platforms, interactions with audiences and an acknowledgement of expert (fan) audiences. The introduction of new technologies in media practices has favored the expansion of transmedia storytelling. Several social, economic and cultural factors have led to the development and implementation of this narrative strategy in recent decades, with changes in the economy of production having brought media consolidations. Even if strategies of transmedia storytelling have been created in the past, as Matthew Freeman (2016) analyzes with examples of the *Superman* franchise or L. Frank Baum's *The Wonderful Wizard of Oz*, it can also be said that tectonic contemporary shifts have amplified this narrative form.

First of all, these shifts comprise: digital technologies are part of production strategies in different sectors of activity, be they the entertainment industry with the phenomenon of 'must-click TV' (Gillan 2010) and enhanced television (Ross 2008); the cultural sector with the use of social networks to interact with audiences; or the use of augmented realities to present museum collections or virtually reconstruct historic places and monuments (otherwise known as 'locative media/narrative'). For example, the city of Bordeaux proposes a walk in the city where tourists can use IPad technology to discover historical facts about Bordeaux in the 18th century. They are guided by a local historic figure, Monsieur de Tourny, which is recreated virtually for the project. Tourists and local people can discover new aspects of the city, learn historical facts and compare the city now with the city three centuries ago. Then, the narrative becomes more complex (Mittell 2006). This complexity is especially true when it comes to television shows, for example, where seriality amplifies the story arcs, as well as the augmentation of the stories scattered on multiple media platforms. But this narrative turn is also present in the way that producers tell stories around heritage and culture. The notion of world-building is therefore a central one as it allows the creation of storyworlds inhabited with characters, places and events that later will be diffused and scattered on different platforms in a coherent and unified way. Finally, audiences are more and more willing to participate, create, share content and play. Fan culture is infused with all those aspects of participatory culture (Booth 2010; Bourdaa 2015), and cultural institutions try to re-enact forms of invitation to interact in an attempt to draw young audiences to their collections, places and interests. In Bordeaux, for instance, CapSciences, the museum of science, launched an initiative to attract young audiences by deploying social networks around their exhibitions. They created Facebook pages, Twitter accounts, Instagram profiles and Snapchat stories to tell the narratives of the collections, or temporary exhibits.

These same questions are at the center of the MediaNum project, a transmedia strategy centered on an actual historic figure. MediaNum is a research program funded by the Region of Aquitaine in France and the Ministry of Culture. The project aims specifically to analyze the potential of transmedia storytelling to valorize patrimony and cultural heritage. The team is interdisciplinary and brings together academics from media studies, youth culture, museum studies, narratology, design and history, and with companies working in animation production and marketing. Each member of the team brings his/her own specificities to the project and thus a new point-of-view, which enriches its development. Moreover, MediaNum confronts academic thinking with professional pragmatism.

The project is divided into three stages: first, we created a map of existing productions worldwide, mixing cultural heritage and transmedia storytelling, and compiled this collection on a Tumblr page and on a wiki. The Tumblr page allowed a linear presentation of the listed projects, and people could only scroll down through posts and projects on these platforms. The advantage here was the visibility and indeed the usability of the platform, which was also linked to a Twitter account in order to share the content and interact with followers. The wiki, on the other hand, was designed to cross-reference the projects and allow research to be done on the platforms for a given project, cross-referencing the target audience and the type of stories or the types of funding (private or public), for example.

The second phase consisted of building our own transmedia strategy to emphasize the cultural heritage of the city of Bordeaux and its region. We chose to focus our strategy around the historic figure of Aliénor d'Aquitaine, mainly because she symbolizes the political and geographical reunification of the Nouvelle Aquitaine as it was during her reign as duchess and queen of France. She also travelled a lot during those times, visiting several places in the region, allowing us to use actual historic places in our strategy. Progress was documented in a research blog, itself a behind-the-scenes look at our methodology and the way we worked with the companies. Finally, we will test this strategy with 11-year-old students, who study Aliénor d'Aquitaine in their history program so as to understand what works or does not work. The education department will choose three classes in the region to run the tests and co-design a better strategy or a better story with them. Still, a question emerges: what kind of stories are we going to be able to tell in such a scenario without rejecting all of the facts? In the context of cultural heritage, it seems that a carefully orchestrated balance between fiction and fact is essential to building a strong narrative universe, to immerse audiences in the stories, and to be able to convey history and pedagogical elements, as will be demonstrated via the following France-based projects.

Transmedia Storytelling and Cultural Heritage: Some France-based Projects

Telling stories about cultural heritage is one of the missions that have been assigned to cultural institutions and museums in France in order to emphasize history in dialogue with audiences. Forms of augmented narration, such as transmedia storytelling, are combined with traditional forms of mediation, in museums particularly, such as guided tours, mobile applications or interactive objects. What is fundamental is the creation of a story to tell aspects of history and cultural heritage, a way to introduce elements of fictions and characters, to build a narrative universe in order to attract audience and encourage them to 'play with the storyworld' (Long 2016). But this new way of promoting mediation has also led 'to strategies of opposition, adaptation and inventiveness among museum mediators who try to adapt technological devices which do not correspond to their conception of cultural mediation' (Sandi 2016, 72). Indeed, theories of transmedia storytelling sometimes collide with rather archaic mediation practices, and the need for adjustment, especially with regards to technology, is necessary.

In France, such adjustment takes the form of transmedia storytelling specifically, which is developed in cultural and patrimonial projects, with three main objectives in mind: to appeal to young audiences; to develop projects using digital technologies with more traditional tools and devices; and to improve processes of mediation and encourage bottom-up creations. In doing so, French projects tend to valorize diverse heritages: historic monuments and places, immaterial heritage (folklore, legends, etc.), and history (historic figures, time periods, etc.).

Transmedia Storytelling to Re-Build Monuments

By way of example, in France two huge projects used transmedia storytelling and were focused on two iconic monuments: the Cathedral of Strasbourg and the Pantheon in Paris. Both of these projects built a narrative universe scattered across multiple media platforms and asked audiences to co-construct the story and the project with them.

Le Défi des Cathédrales (The Challenge of the Cathedrals), the first of these projects, allowed audiences to take part in the construction of the missing tower of the Cathedral of Strasbourg by becoming an architect in a (virtual) professional team. The project is composed of several media platforms, which favored the deployment of 'augmented storytelling' (Bourdaa 2012) and a process of collaboration and participation. The strategy began with an interactive web documentary, filmed with a subjective point-of-view that places the user in an active role as an integral part of the process. In this video, the user is hired by a team of architects to draw plans in order to build the Cathedral's missing tower. What follows is an investigation whereby the user becomes a detective/player and 'meets' in the documentary-game with people gathering insights into the history of the cathedral, its construction, specific technics and tools. When they have all the information they need, players use a new interactive tool, 'the tower builder', designed for the game, in order to construct the tower themselves. The gameplay mechanisms of the web documentary place the players in an active role and immerse them in a fictional narrative universe (a team of architects need help building the missing tower), where they meet actual historians, architects and priests. The project was reinforced by an in situ element where visitors could unlock additional informative content on the cathedral via scanning QR codes with mobile phone technology. Visitors could share their knowledge on social media and networks and tag their pictures, spreading content and creations even further. Finally, a social collaborative game on mobile devices and computers place the players 'in the past' when the cathedral was being built and required a collaborative effort to erect the structure collaboratively.

The Pantheon project, meanwhile, the second of the two, was launched during the renovation of the dome of the monument. The building works were extensive and required the installation of a canvas, which hid the roof of the building and was not aesthetically pleasing enough for such an iconic Parisian monument. The Center of National Monuments, in charge of more than one hundred monuments across France, decided to create a narrative universe in order to tell the story of the Pantheon and encourage visitors, local people and tourists to take part in the process. These groups of people all worked with the artist JR to create a collaborative work of art, a collage of portraits taken by people outside of specific monuments in France in order to cover the canvas. During the time of the project, from the pictures to the launching of the art piece, the Center used its social platforms, mainly Twitter and Instagram, to tell the story of the construction of the work of art and engage people in what would hopefully become a collaborative piece of art. The Center also created a game on Twitter, asking their followers to take a picture of themselves near the name of a historic figure buried in the Pantheon. This game was collaborative, informative and pedagogical, since the followers could discover characters from the Pantheon.

Both of these projects are important in terms of how they transmediated cultural heritage in three ways: first, they offered a pedagogical perspective on periods of French history while re-inventing mediation by using strategies of transmedia storytelling. Production teams created a narrative universe to immerse audiences in a storyworld while delivering historic information of the monuments. Second, they also used traditional tools, like pictures, *in situ* visits, and collages linked with digital equivalents such as interactive games, social networks and mobile applications. Third, they favored the participation of the audiences to build both the story and the piece of art, introducing new ways of collaboration and involvement, while inviting the audience to participate in projects of cultural heritage. These projects symbolize a type of participatory culture, a form of collaboration between audience and producers in the creation of art productions and a narrative universe. A participatory culture

> is a culture with relatively low barriers to artistic expression and civic engagement, strong support for creating and sharing one's creations, and some type of informal mentorship whereby what is known to the most experienced is passed along to novices. A participatory culture is also one in which members believe their contributions matter, and feel some degree of social connection with one another (at the least they care what other people think about what they created).
>
> (Jenkins, Mimi and Danah 2016 m 4)

In a similar participatory sense, albeit in a less mediatized context, monuments are part of the lives of inhabitants and tourists and are places they can visit. These two projects, therefore, use the reputation of both of those monuments in order to create momentum and co-creation with audiences. The creative acts performed by the audience acted as a cultural agenda for the institution, since production teams wanted a clear co-construction of the monument.

Tales of History with Transmedia Historic Figures

Historic figures have been the center of transmedia strategies in order to highlight a specific period of French history. In this case, the narrative universe is built using 'accurate' historic facts. Designed to promote an exhibition at the Château de Versailles, *Le Roi Est Mort* tells us more about the last days of King Louis XIV before his death. A dedicated website featured interviews with experts, while social networks were used to promote the exhibition and the participating museums, even before the exhibition itself took place. In all appearances, it was a very factual, didactic and nonfictional transmedia production designed to promote cultural heritage along with the institutions that keep it alive. The twist lies in the way the production was deployed: it was mainly promoted on Twitter, with a live-tweet of King Louis XIV during his last weeks on Earth, exactly three hundred years before. Every day, the Château de Versailles Twitter account detailed the King's activities and the evolution of his illness, just as contemporary reporters would 'live-tweet' the sudden illness of a world leader or the Queen of England. Just like any suspenseful narrative, it begins with a seemingly innocuous event: on 17 August, 1715 (2015 in the real, Twitter world), the King complains about a sharp pain in his left leg. The story was suspenseful in the sense that news of the upcoming exhibition and its ominous title was already buzzing, and that anyone curious enough to google Louis XIV would quickly understand that the story will not end well.

This is a tragic, factual story, but while a factual narrative would simply give us the main information right away (the King died on 1 September), the live-tweet used fictionalization mechanisms (characters, settings, cliffhangers, for example) to immerse participants in the storyworld: multiple points-of-view are used throughout, notably from those of the doctors, who are unable to understand the king's illness; famous people are quoted, with illustrations allowing us to picture them. Relentlessly, the live-tweet foreshadows a tragic end without actually announcing it before its time. It was only on 1 September, the date of the exhibition's opening, and the 300th anniversary of the King's death, that the live-tweet finally reached its tragic conclusion, with the hashtag #LeRoiEstMort. The denouement of this serialized story told over multiple tweets allowed the hashtag greater visibility: audiences felt more engaged by the story, and tweeted along with the hashtag, sometimes even adding new information to the story themselves. While the production was a huge success in promoting the exhibition, it also works to reveal the difference between history and fiction in a transmedia scenario: after the death of the King, the Twitter account continued to tell, sporadically, the aftermath of this historical event, without a clear sense that it was leading to another its conclusion. This strategy required a huge amount of historic documentation, because tweets were enriched with pictures, texts, paintings and quotes from historic figures.

Another transmedia project to center around historic French figures is *The Last Gaulois*, an animated documentary broadcast on France 2 (a French public service channel), which dealt with the lives of the people during the conquest of Gaule by the Roman Empire. This docu-fiction is centered on Apator, a fictional character, who interacts with two actual historic figures: Vercingetorix and Jules Cesar. Historic facts are intertwined with fictional details in order to create an immersive narrative universe for the audiences, and, in particular, for intended young audiences. The narration was augmented by an interactive online comic book, which acted like a prequel, introducing the fictional character of Apator and his life in a Gaulois village. The comic book was enriched by voice-over and sounds that placed the user in a specific ambiance. A historian collaborated on the project to ensure the viability of the historic and scientific facts and to give the best approach to what life was like during those particular times. Pedagogical modules composed of videos, games and index cards are also proposed to students to help improve their knowledge of this period.

These two projects thus mixed historic facts and fiction to create stories and give information on historic figures (Louis XIV, Jules César, Vercingétorix), places (The Versailles Castle, Alésia, Rome) and times (the death of King Louis XIV, the Conquest of the Gaule by the Roman Empire). But what chimes the most in those two projects is the absence of invitations to participate. The strategies here are all notably top-down, with the productions delivering the facts and the historic knowledge, and thereby not allowing audiences many latitudes to participate, almost as if historical figures are too sacred to be tempered by opportunities for collaboration and participation from the audience. This is all the more surprising in the first project, *The King is Dead*, since it makes use of a social platform, Twitter, which is itself based on interactions and dialogues, to tell its story. This project managed to build a narrative on the social media platform but allowed re-tweets to spread the content only, not the interactions with audiences. The cultural mediation on offer here is thus rather traditional, since the use of digital devices and forms of transmedia storytelling only operate as a pretext to expand the storylines, building momentum or providing further information regarding a character. These approaches are similar to what US television shows achieve via their transmedia strategies – that is, expanding the stories on multiple media platforms and using strategies of seriality, such as the cliffhanger, to envelop audiences into the narrative universe they have created for them. In transmedia strategies around television shows, further, comic books are often used to tell a character's past, itself commonly referred to as an 'origin story'. As M. J. Clarke argues, 'origins (incidentally, the title of a *Heroes* spin-off that was shelved due to the 2007 WGA strike) are Ur-stories that encapsulate everything a reader needs to know about a character' (Clarke 2013, 54). This tradition of telling origin stories was arguably born in the comics-associated superhero genre, where issues are centered on traumatic events leading to the birth of the superhero (see Batman, for example). Le Dernier Gaulois took some inspiration from this particular narrative technique while Le Chateau de Versailles also created daily cliffhangers to ensure audiences would follow their story.

Immaterial Culture Getting Tangible with Transmedia Storytelling

The final aspect to discuss of the permeation of transmedia storytelling strategies in cultural heritage projects concerns immaterial culture, such as folklore, traditions, languages or legends. These cultural objects are indeed not tangible, disappearing through times or sometimes losing their prominence from one generation to the next, especially if relying on oral tradition alone. Strategies of transmedia storytelling have helped these immaterial forms become less abstract and more material-based, and have acted as an archive, leaving traces of the immaterial cultural heritage in a state of transmission and re-appropriation by different audiences, both local and non-local. In their creation of a transmedia narrative around tales from the Corsican Island, for example, Agata Nicoli and Don-Mathieu Santini argue that:

> if transmedia storytelling seemed to be the tool adapted to the technological habits of the hyper-connected youth, the experience should be thought and designed in order to incite an interest for a central object, by favoring an act of participation more than consumption, and a will to appropriate traditional tales in a contemporary environment.
> (Nicoli and Santini 2017)

In this case, transmedia storytelling was thus the solution to a problem: the disappearing of, and indeed the lack of, interest in an oral heritage by a young audience. *La Chasse aux Légendes* (*The Hunt for the Legends*) is a project with a similar problem, but centered on legends from the Bask country in the south west of France. The aim of this transmedia project is to give life to some Bask legends in a story designed for children and families. Centered around a smartphone app, it starts by recounting an 'origin story' through an interactive comic, called a turbomedia, before sending young players and their families on actual locations across touristic areas of the Bask Country in order to hunt the fantastic creature at the heart of the tale, be it a dragon, a mermaid or a Cyclops, that must be 'captured' through the device's camera. The game is similar to the Pokémon Go application, where young players hunt for Pokémons and capture them in their phone. But *La Chasse aux Légendes* goes even further than Pokémon Go, framing these local legends through another, that of the Laminak, which are nature spirits from the same area. One of them, the young Gillen, guardian of the Temple, accidentally broke the Moon Stone that kept the legends trapped, after which every legend returned to its point of origin. The hunt is thus motivated by this framing narrative: the player must learn about the legends not for the sake of it, but because s/he must help Gillen to re-capture them. The audience is thus placed in a very active role, searching for the legends in order to help Gillen, and going to specific places in the Bask Country in doing so. An audio tale was also part of the transmedia strategy, telling the legends of the Bask Country used in the narrative universe, which was later edited into a book. Finally, the application contains a module of augmented reality, which allows the legends to appear in 3D when the child scans a code. Children can then choose to print it, to have an action figure of the legends and to collect concrete objects from the experience.

Likewise, *Forêt Océane* is a project intended to valorize the region of the Landes, also located in the south of France, via a transmedia narrative, this time based on a comic book. The objective is to unravel the invisible heritage of this region, what lies underneath the visible, to the local people and tourists. The 'mothership' (Jenkins 2006) of this transmedia experience is an interactive comic book, augmented with QR codes in its pages, which reveal video documents on the history of the region, its culture and its folklore. Eight periods in time are represented to see the evolution of the region. Importantly, this project is the result of a collaboration between different members of the team (the producer, the author, the artist, the technical staff, the transmedia architect, etc.) and also a collaboration between this team and the local people to build the narrative. The production team led meetings, collaborating with the local people to ensure that they were part of the creative process and that they could give insights and anecdotes into the culture and folklore. As the producer remarked in interview, the narrative needed to be rooted in the local network. To reinforce this aspect, tourist offices and local museums acted as a point of reference, selling the comics in their stores and giving information on how the strategy functioned in terms of local legends.

When strategies of valorization are focused on immaterial objects, then, they arguably need to be based on a strong narrative, on a story-world, with characters and places that will support the structure. This process of world-building is one of the key principles of transmedia storytelling, according to Henry Jenkins:

> This concept of world building is closely linked to what Janet Murray has called the 'encyclopedic' impulse behind contemporary interactive fictions – the desire of audiences to map and master as much as they can know about such universes, often through the production of charts, maps, and concordances.
>
> (Jenkins 2009)

Jenkins emphasizes the bottom-up reception and creativity of audiences and, in particular, fans who will use interactive and collaborative platforms such as Wikis to collect and share their information. But, of course, production teams and companies design complex narrative universes with great detail and then scatter chunks of the story on multiple media platforms. Television showrunners create a transmedia 'Bible' (that is, documents that contain details on character motivations and backstories, places, plots, narrative arcs, tone, etc., which helps producers and writers to build storylines that cohere with one another). When it comes to intangible culture, however, like the examples analyzed previously, producers of transmedia strategies use 'the art of world-building' (Long 2007) to immerse the audience in a tangible environment, something that they will relate to with places, characters and plots. This approach allows for the unraveling and valorization of folklores, legends and languages. *La Chasse aux Légences*, for example, based its storyworld on legends and a magical character, guardian of the Moon Stone. This character led the narrative and allowed audiences to interact with the stories, follow the unfolding of the narrative and identify with it. The world-building of Forêt Océane is rooted in the territory, with its culture, its traditions, its people, and so on. Both projects mixed actual historic facts, supervised by experts and scientists, with a fictional story in order to transport the audience into their universe, and at the same time provide information and pedagogical elements.

All of these French-based projects used strategies of transmedia storytelling to valorize cultural heritage, monuments, historic figures or folklore and traditions. But they also developed a different focus in their projects. Strategies around the valorization of monuments favor a bottom-up participation and collaboration, letting people create, share and discuss on social networks. Monuments are tangible objects, part of the audiences' lives, something that they can touch, visit and appropriate. It seems logical to include them in a strategy of valorization as they are part of the 'life' of the monuments and are proud of what the monument represents in the outside world. Historic figures, on the other hand, possess a sacred aura that is hard to play around with, as with Jenkins' 'silly putty' (1992, 156). It therefore seems impossible to introduce 'fictional facts' when the strategy is centered on a strong historic figure, such as King Louis XIV or Julius Caesar From this perspective, and akin to fictional world-building, fidelity to a (historical) canon is vitally important. The research process and documentation are always part of the justifications of the production team, giving depth to their valorization. In this context, the strategy is completely designed by the production team, the narrative closed, refusing any open collaboration from the audience. The objectives are thus informational and pedagogical, but in a more traditional way, even if the narrative form is original. Yet a strong narrative universe – a detailed storyworld – is still essential when it comes to the valorization of intangible cultural heritage.

The Creation of Our Own Strategy: A Work in Progress

What, then, of our own approach to applying transmedia storytelling strategies to a cultural heritage project? The first phase in our research program, the cartography of extant global projects of cultural heritage with transmedia narratives, allowed us to assess the impact of such strategies, to see what kinds of stories are told and on which media platforms. Those results were then collected on the Wiki and the Tumblr, and we started brainstorming possibilities for our own strategy of valorizing the cultural heritage of the Nouvelle Aquitaine. As was stated earlier in the chapter, we decided to center the narrative of this project on the historic figure of Queen Aliénor d'Aquitaine. This focus raised the same questions as with the Chateau de Versailles' *The King is Dead*, namely: which historic facts should be injected into the narrative universe, and which should not? And which degree of fiction will be deployed to create our storyworld?

To ensure a scientific and pedagogical value to the project, we asked an expert in Medieval History to supervise the project and to give us the History of Aliénor in order for our narrative to rely on historical facts.

We adopted an editorial angle that allowed us to mix historic facts with fiction while giving some pedagogic and informative details on the lives during the Middle Age. We were inspired by the projects created by the Versailles Castle on the death of King Louis XIV and by the project on *Le Dernier Gaulois*. With the help of an expert, we have selected five key moments of Aliénor's life (her childhood, her first marriage with King Louis VII, her reign as Queen of France, her captivity in England, and her end of life as a strategic political woman of influence) to reflect on life in general during the Middle Ages (education, the royal court, religion, political intrigues). For each personal and intimate event linked to Aliénor, a more general aspect of the Middle Ages will be told in a more journalistic way. Thanks to this editorial point-of-view, we can underline the extraordinary life of Aliénor d'Aquitaine while telling more fictional stories about the people, traditions and events of the Middle Ages.

As for the transmedia architecture, as it were, during an initial meeting with the whole team we listed all of the media platforms that we thought would fit into the strategy coherently: a tangible map, card games, a mobile application, a turbomedia (an animated online comic book), an escape game, a website, social media, board games and a diary were chosen. We then noted collaborative ideas on post-it notes with an assigned color code, each one representing one media platform, the moment in history, the journalistic tone or the intimate one, and the rabbit holes and bridges between the storylines. By doing so, we had the strategy mapped out, with the stories we wanted to tell and with the coherence of the editorial focus we defined earlier, as well as with the different media platforms we wanted to use to support pieces of the global storyworld. Finally, and using a free virtual online tool called Padlet, we re-created our strategy online in order to share it publicly and post it on our research blog. This was also a way to materialize the strategy for the whole team and to modify some key elements afterward, with each team member having access and administration rights.

Our transmedia architecture included a number of 'rabbit holes', as in strategic opportunities for audiences to follow content pieces. The first 'rabbit hole' is intended for students, teachers and families and will be sent to specific classrooms in the Nouvelle Aquitaine, and later to museums so to reach a wider audience. This first rabbit hole will contain a welcome kit with a map to illustrate the territory and the many travels of Aliénor d'Aquitaine: cards à la Pokémon to represent the characters that audiences will follow in the narrative universe, the rules of the strategy and the link to download the mobile application that will support different aspects of the stories. Essentially, this kit will be the entry point in the narrative universe and provide objects that audiences can keep and manipulate, as they wish.

In turn, a troubadour, a singer and music player, who told tales to the courts and Kings and Queens during the Middle Ages, will be the master of the game, leading audiences from one platform to the next and introducing the various intimate and journalistic storylines. For the five key moments we chose from Aliénor's life, we will deploy specific media platforms: an escape game to deliver her from her captivity; a diary in which Aliénor will recall her two weddings and the birth of her children (specifically Richard and Jean), an augmented travel guide with details of her trips, and a mobile application with a turbomedia and modules of augmented reality to view in 3D the monuments linked to her life and fate. The website will be more traditional, offering authentic documents and scientific and pedagogic information on Alinéor or the Middle Ages in general.

Conclusion

The MediaNum research project highlights a number of features, namely how transmedia storytelling, a narrative strategy usually used to enrich and augment entertainment productions, can valorize projects of cultural heritage. Of course, narrativizing monuments, historic figures, folklores and traditions is the mission of all museums and cultural heritage institutions. But transmedia storytelling aims to immerse audiences in story-worlds and narrative universes, giving them extra-details about characters (backstories, for example), places (*in situ* or virtually re-created) and historic facts (pedagogic value). Deploying stories across multiple media platforms is thus also a way to reach diverse audiences and to make them play an active part in the creative process, and participate in spreading content.

When looking at French-based projects specifically, like the ones analyzed in this chapter, one can sense hierarchies in the use of transmedia storytelling by cultural institutions. Museums and cultural institutions need to find ways to attract audiences – especially young audiences – to their narrative and material universes, but they are often constrained by a lack of capital or by a rather traditional view on how cultural heritage should be presented and valued. There is a paradox here, a difference of perception in the ideal use of how transmedia strategies should be deployed. There is still a long way to go in terms of fully embracing the potentials of transmedia storytelling within the cultural heritage sector. Even with the projects discussed in this chapter, transmedia storytelling is seldom applied to cultural heritage, partly because key aspects of the transmedia design process remain lacking, be it the collaboration of the audience, the creation of back stories or simply the use of multiple media platforms.

Bibliography

Booth, Paul. *Digital Fandom: New Media Studies*. New York: Peter Lang, 2010.
Bourdaa, Mélanie. "Transmedia: Between Augmented Storytelling and Immersive Practices." *InaGlobal*. September 6, 2012. Accessed 2 April 2015.

www.inaglobal.fr/en/digital-tech/article/transmedia-between-augmented-storytelling-and-immersive-practices.

Bourdaa, Mélanie. "Les fan Studies en question: perspectives et enjeux." *Revue Française des Sciences de l'Information et de la Communication* 7 (2015). http://journals.openedition.org/rfsic/1644

Bourdaa, Mélanie, and Derhy Kurtz, Benjamin (eds.). *The Rise of Transtexts: Challenges and Opportunities.* London and New York: Routledge, 2016.

Clarke, M. J. *Transmedia Television: New Trends in Network Serial Production.* New York: Bloomsbury, 2013.

Freeman, Matthew. *Historicising Transmedia Storytelling. Early Twentieth-Century Transmedia Story Worlds.* London and New York: Routledge, 2016.

Gillan, Jennifer. *Television and New Media: Must-Click TV.* London and New York: Routledge, 2011.

Jenkins, Henry. 2006. *Convergence Culture: Where Old and New Media Collide.* New York: New York University Press.

Jenkins, Henry. "The Revenge of the Origami Unicorn: Seven Principles of Transmedia Storytelling." *Confessions of an Aca-Fan: The Official Weblog of Henry Jenkins.* December 12, 2009. Accessed 20 February 2012. http://henryjenkins.org/2009/12/the_revenge_of_the_origami_uni.html.

Jenkins, Henry, Ito Mimi, and Boyd Danah. *Participatory Culture in a Networked Era.* New York: Polity, 2016.

Long, Geoffrey. "Transmedia Storytelling, Business, Aesthetics and Production at the Jim Henson Company." MA diss., Massachusetts Institute of Technology, 2007.

Long, Geoffrey. "Creating Worlds in Which We Play: Using Transmedia Aesthetics to Grow Stories in Storyworlds." In *The Rise of Transtexts: Challenges and Opportunities*, edited by Mélanie Bourdaa and Benjamin Derhy Kurtz, 139–154. London and New York: Routledge, 2016.

Mittell, Jason. "Narrative Complexity in Contemporary American Television." *The Velvet Light Trap* 58 (2006): 29–40.

Nicoli, Agata, and Santini Don-Mathieu. "Valorisation d'un objet du patrimoine immatérielpar l'outil transmedia: design d'une experience participative." *Revue Française des Sciences de l'Information et de la Communication* 10 (2017). http://journals.openedition.org/rfsic/2612

Ross, Sharon Marie. *Beyond The Box: Television and the Internet.* New York: Blackwell, 2008.

Sandi, Eva. "Les ajustements des professionnels de la mediation au musée face aux enjeux de la culture numérique." *Etudes de Communication* 46 (2016): 71–86.

Scolari, Carlos A. *Narrativas Transmedia: Cuando Todos los Medios Cuentan.* Barcelona: Duesto, 2013.

5 Estonia

Transmedial Disruptions and Converging Conceptualizations in a Small Country

Indrek Ibrus and Maarja Ojamaa

When the concepts of transmediality and transmedia storytelling first emerged, they were made to refer to practices in very large markets and to media products with a global reach. Both Marsha Kinder, with her (1991) critical approach to 'transmedia intertextuality', and later Henry Jenkins, with his (2003) approach to 'transmedia storytelling', discussed major global franchises and blockbusters produced by Hollywood or US network television companies. These were all hugely profitable with expensive productions for multiple platforms and global armies of dedicated fans. That is to say that, at its first stage of development, the transmedia concept evolved into an analytic instrument for large industry operations and the related sociocultural processes of the internet era. It was within such large-scale scenarios when both the economies of scale and scope logics of media markets that lay the groundwork for transmedia phenomena were of their most exemplary salience.

Estonia, in contrast, is a very small country. With 1.3 million inhabitants and an even smaller number of Estonian speakers (there is a significant Russian-speaking minority, approximately one-quarter of the population), it is one of the smallest media markets in the world defined by a distinct language. This means entirely different operational models for its media, its markets and its industries, as well as for its media and cultural policymaking. As the market scales are so much smaller in comparison to the global franchises that have dominated transmedia scholarship to date, there are much fewer resources and, therefore, more limits to innovation, including to multiplatform productions. Let us illustrate this with a few figures: the whole of Estonia's annual advertising market was worth €93 million in 2015; the annual budgets of its most popular television channels total about €10 million; most films produced in the country have budgets of less than €1 million. In most years there are about four to six feature-length fiction films produced. Most of these are financed by public grants so the film industry leans toward art house. At the same time, it is theatre that tends to be the most popular art form – Estonia is second only to Iceland in the number of theatre visits per inhabitant per year. Estonia is also the country with the most museums in Europe (19.6 per 100,000 inhabitants). These museums were visited 3.3 million times in 2015.

These statistics may reflect the specificity of media and culture production in a small northeastern European country where cheaper, but perhaps more immediate, interactionist forms of arts and culture dominate. On the other hand, this may also condition what kinds of transmedia projects could emerge in such circumstances. If there are very few genre films produced, if broadcasters' budgets are extremely limited and if the most popular art forms are different to those in the US, then what kinds of transmedia projects could emerge in such circumstances? These are the questions that this chapter aims to seek answers to.

However, there are more specific socio-economic and cultural factors that Estonia exemplifies as a case study of a specific type of country: the small peripheral European Union (EU) member state. Small size and little exporting power means that such countries tend to be on the receiving end of global cultural flows and policymaking trends in Europe. One of the arguments this chapter makes is that the emergence of transmedia concepts and practices in Estonia was not due to inherent evolution and new needs in the converging media sectors and other cultural fields. Instead, 'transmedia' as a strategy was proposed by policymakers and, even more so, was supported by regional policymakers outside of Estonia. In other words, transmedia strategies that are effectively forms of convergent media as well as other arts and Information and Communications Technology (ICT) or online service sectors have been enforced within the framework of creative industry policies in the EU (Ibrus and Ojamaa 2014). 'Creative industries', effectively a policy concept part of the strategies to facilitate the growth of business-oriented culture production, has become the dominant theme in cultural policymaking in the EU. The focus of creative industries' policies is not so much cultural as it is economic: to contribute to local or regional economic growth mainly by increasing exports. In relation to this, transmediality – notably as an opportunity for new kinds of exportable products and services, especially as supported by different EU funding measures – has been an extremely attractive proposition for Estonian policymakers and media and cultural industries at large. This chapter will demonstrate how this effectively externally and top-down-driven concept was applied in practice, given the specific cultural and economic circumstances of a very small country.

However, there is more of a local specificity to the circumstances in which Estonia has received and then molded the transmedia concept. While the creative industries rationale can be said to have been externally driven, the conceptual development within the academic domain known as cultural semiotics has been growing internally. While this theoretical approach is widely known and has been developed also elsewhere (most notably in Russia, but also in Italy, Spanish-language academia and Germany), its original home and core site of development is Estonia.

Originally developed mostly by Juri Lotman (1990, 2009, 2013), his cultural semiotics is unique in addressing how change happens in culture: in his view, conditioned by interrelationships between dialogic and autopoietic communication resulting in either stable or 'explosive' evolutionary phases in different domains of culture. Regarding the 'dialogic' relationships between different media and other cultural domains, it is forms of intersemiotic translations between these that, according to the cultural semiotic approach, lead to the emergence of new forms of culture, such as multimodal or transmedial texts and related cultural practices. In other words, cultural semiotics as a broader theory of cultural dynamics has been long ripe for absorbing and working with concepts such as transmediality (Ibrus and Torop 2015).

In the following pages, we will explain how the cultural semiotic take on transmediality has evolved in Estonia. But what is important is that cultural semiotics focuses on all of the cultural and creative practices and is not limited to industry strategies only. For this reason, it is probably unavoidable that the dialogues between the two approaches – one evolving endogenously in Estonia and the other relatively recently pushed by external forces (EU and local policymakers) – have been scarce to date. However, we point in this context to a new potential: using transmedia logic when planning the repurposing of digitized cultural heritage. Estonia is planning to digitize most of its heritage content, and these plans are motivated by both rationales for new kinds of business models for heritage repurposing and by rationales for facilitating new kinds of cultural dialogues, new forms of learning and reflecting on cultural histories and new forms of citizen-driven creativity. In other words, these different rationales are about to force the different conceptualizations and discourses of transmediality into dialogue in Estonia for the very first time.

Juri Lotman and the 'Invisible College' of Cultural Semiotics

The father of cultural semiotics, Juri Mikhailovich Lotman (1922–1993), was born and educated in Saint Petersburg, but moved to Tartu, Estonia because he could not take on an academic position in his home university (Leningrad State University) due to the local anti-Semitic stand. He started working as a lecturer at the department of Russian language and literature of Tartu University in 1954 and gradually broadened the scope of his research from studies of literary texts to analyses of texts in other sign systems, such as film, theatre, painting, history and so on. Out of his empirical studies grew a perception of universal principles of cultural sign systems that led him and other authors of the Tartu-Moscow school to a holistic and systemic approach to culture from the semiotic perspective.

The Tartu-Moscow semiotic school has been described as an 'invisible college' (Salupere and Torop 2013, 15) led by Lotman from Tartu, while most of the other members worked in Moscow. Their theory developed in dialogue with a relatively diverse range of authors, including Russian formalists, the Prague linguistic circle (Jakobson, Lévi-Strauss, Barthes, Wiener and others). In 1973 five of the key members of the school wrote a manifesto titled 'Theses on the Semiotic Study of Cultures (as Applied to Slavic Texts)' (Lotman et al. 2013), which can be considered the landmark of the beginning of cultural semiotics as a distinct approach, and which is primarily aimed at 'the study of the functional correlation of different sign systems [and] the hierarchical structure of the languages of culture' (Theses 1.0.0). New generations of Estonian scholars have continued the development of this approach.

The innovativeness of the cultural semiotic approach to culture is already manifested at the level of defining and delineating the object of study. First, the basic operational notions of text and semiosphere are used to conceptualize the object on different but isomorphic levels of culture. The latter refers to the view that an individual mind and a collection of minds (i.e. culture) as well as an individual text and a system of texts (e.g. a transmedial story) function in accordance with the same or at least very similar mechanisms. Thereby, the object of study (e.g. a transmedial story) appears simultaneously uniform and internally diverse. Also, its structural and synchronic aspects are balanced with the processual and diachronic dimensions. This means that a text can be described both from a more static viewpoint, concentrating on its composition and relations between its internal subparts, and from a more dynamic one, concentrating on its functioning within a larger intertextual and intercommunicational system. In relation to this, and in view of cultural semiotics, all texts are unavoidably part of more than one cultural subdomain and are therefore coded by different cultural codes. For instance, a prayer is structured according to the logic of verbal language, but also by a symbolic message of a particular religion and its specific organizing conventions that have evolved over time. While in the case of more traditional forms of culture such forms of multiple coding have only implicitly been present, in the light of the contemporary (digital) communicative environment with new text types (e.g. transmedia stories) and narrative and reception practices (e.g. seriality), this characteristic and its underlying mechanisms become explicitly visible. A transmedia textual universe consisting of multiple texts in different modalities that form parts of different cultural subdomains is a complex entity coded in a number of ways and as such calls for a cultural semiotic analysis.

Transmediality as the Epitome of Cultural Dynamics

The notion of transmediality itself first entered the Tartu cultural semiotics with David Herman's (2004) paper on transmedial narratology. It was realized that Herman's analysis of narrative texts had implicit parallels with Lotman's concepts pertaining to the more general level of culture as a whole. Thus 'transmediality' was adopted to describe a spontaneous and unpredictable pulverization of potentially any text (regardless of its mode or medium) across the space of culture. While within the Henry Jenkins-inspired discourse about transmediality it is possible and even important to designate whether or not one or another text or textual system can be labelled as 'transmedia', within the cultural semiotic paradigm any text can be described as transmedial on a generalizing level. In effect, any text is a transformation of previous texts in different media and any text continues its existence in culture in different forms of media. This cultural semiotics approach has been applied to make sense of the mechanisms of cultural dynamics, including the processes of both change and continuity.

The threshold of transmediality within cultural semiotics is the concept of translation: more precisely intersemiotic translation. The term itself was first introduced by Roman Jakobson (1971) to describe the parallel between the processes of rewording (intralingual translation), common translation from one natural language to another (interlingual translation) and the transfer of content from a verbal sign system to a nonverbal one (intersemiotic translation). Later, the latter has been applied to conceptualize transfers between any two sign systems: verbal or nonverbal. Intersemiotic translation is the building principle of transmedia storytelling projects as well. Their starting point is most commonly a verbalized story bible, which is later materialized in different sign systems all of which model the storyworld in accordance with the specific affordances and constraints of their mode and medium. The source of creativity of intersemiotic translations is the absence of semantic equivalents between the signifiers of different media as sign systems. Such a relationship, termed untranslatability by Lotman, implies inevitable and significant alterations of meaning (Lotman 2001, 36–38), which work to render the translation process as simultaneously inexact and nontrivial – that is, with a creative, innovative potential (ibid., 137).

When one text or a part of it is translated into another sign system (such as a novel translated into a film), the two together – in fact all the different medial versions of a text – converge into a mental/abstract whole both in the individual and in cultural memory. At the same time, it is often impossible to distinguish which aspects of this mental text originate in which version, especially in the narrative domain. Such a converged memorized story or storyworld is what unifies the coordinated transmedia projects and non-coordinated translations across different spatial and temporal layers of culture. This communicational particularity has led cultural semiotician Peeter Torop to define transmediality as the mental aspect of a text's being in culture (Sütiste and Torop 2007, 203). The new meaningful whole (a mental/abstract text) is not an occasional sum of the parts, but possesses an internal hierarchy, which is in accordance with the hierarchy of sign systems in a given culture at a given time. For example, we can describe the dominance of visual sign systems in the contemporary culture, which is reflected in the way we memorize different kinds of content, but also in how visual form plays a part in meaning-making in the process of reading verbal texts. This can be traced in different instances from the characteristics of the page (size, type, color of font and page, etc.) to the marketing of the book (covers, trailers, etc.). However, this has not always been the case. Cultural history also knows periods when audible and tactile aspects have dominated over others. Overall, the memorized whole balances the medium-specific variability with a sense of invariance that renders different texts/textual fragments recognizable as part of the given textual network.

The Dialogic Boundary between Text and Culture

The above is in turn related to a fundamental notion of boundary in cultural semiotics. Surrounding a text externally (that is, the beginning and ending of a narrative, or the frame of a painting, for example) serves the function of dialogue, separating the text from everything else into an individual entity, but at the same time linking the text with the surrounding texts. In other words, via its dialogic boundary, any text is simultaneously a whole and a part (of a larger intercommunicational whole). This same idea is evident in transmedia storytelling projects, but functions just the same in more sublime and implicit interrelations between texts (via common elements on the level of content, such as a shared topic, as well as on the level of form, such as a narrative device). Such an approach means that, for example, a film can be described as an autonomous text, but also as a sequence of audiovisual texts that possess all the characteristics of a whole and, third, as part of a transmedial text. Also, it allows us to conceptualize all of the individual medial representations of a historic event or a cultural motif as one transmedial text (Ojamaa 2018). On the most abstract level one might methodologically regard the whole of human culture as one multilingual text or message from humanity to itself (Lotman 2001, 33).

Therefore, transmediality is an inherent characteristic not only of a text, but also of the semiosphere at large, the two levels being regarded as isomorphic. The idea of the semiosphere (Lotman 2005) is used to conceptualize the sphere of meaning-making on both the micro and macro level – from the communication between two minds to the communication between all minds in culture. It is a spatial approach comprising concepts like boundary and core and periphery, but the space is of course abstract. The applicability of spatial metaphors on the conceptualization of textual and cultural transmediality was investigated by Saldre and Torop (2012).

The Lotmanian approach to dialogue as 'the elementary mechanism of translating' (2001, 143), presuming asymmetry of participants and the fundamentality of dialogic situation preceding even the language for holding a real dialogue, implies that unity is preceded by separation. In our context mediality is somewhat paradoxically preceded by transmediality. Therefore, complex meaningful systems are not built up from atomic particles (as could be interpreted from the individual sign-based semiotics of Peirce or Saussure), but rather the complexity is primary and individual elements are only analytically extractable from it. The reason for this is that an individual text or individual language is incapable of functioning without a larger semiotic environment.

A text or a semiosphere is not only surrounded by an external boundary, it is also crisscrossed with internal boundaries. This means that the aforementioned asymmetry intrinsic to dialogue partners is also a defining internal feature of any meaningful entity itself. Thus, the sign systems that a semiosphere consists of are defined by their boundaries, which on the one hand ensure their individuality, but on the other hand render them unavoidably interrelated to other sign systems. So, we can say that the language of literature is part of film language, which is in turn part of the language of video games, and so on. Any text is also a text in another medium and a reader in culture is always a polyglot. The activity of translation between its sign systems is thus culture's mechanism for supporting dynamics, the diversity of meanings and interpretations, which could be considered the source of vitality of culture.

Transmediality as a Mechanism of Cultural Memory

Notwithstanding the above, supporting innovation is not the only function of transmediality. It also enforces coherence and continuity in culture. The model of translation implies not only diversity, but also a sense of invariance: the existence of a repeated element that renders the new text recognizable from the previous one. With each translation of a text into another medium, its peculiarity, the invariant core that is shared by all the medium-specific variants, is clarified and its understanding is increased. While translations function as new texts on the level of communication, they can also be seen as self-reflective repetition from the viewpoint of cultural autocommunication, such as culture's own communication to itself. In this way the creative function of transmediality is coupled with the storing activity. The transmedial memory of culture is thus dynamic memory, enabling the meaningful growth of a text in culture. This growth is being facilitated by a repository of meaningfulness, which is immanent in any text and is realized in contacts with other texts. Translating the canonical texts that have functioned as the nodal points of cultural identity into contemporary media (and reception practices) so that they can retain their position within active cultural memory is the key means for ensuring cultural continuity and sustainability. In fact, it is a growing tendency to first read these texts not in their original form, but through a visual or multimodal version, which renders transmediality also a crucial topic from a pedagogical perspective.

With the appearance of a new translation the mnemonic whole is (re)transformed anew, which means that each additional version of a text or its fragment influences the ways in which we understand and remember the source text itself. This re-stresses the reflexive and self-organizing potential of transmediality on the level of culture, as in the case of cultural heritage texts the restructuring of textual memory may bring with it new ways of cultural self-description and hence restructuring of the system itself. This balancing of textual and cultural dynamics between the forces of heterogeneity and homogeneity (Theses 9.0.0) is of course a principle as old as human culture. But contemporary communication technologies coupled with new practices of creation and reception render these principles more visible and analyzable (Ojamaa and Torop 2015). Overall, then, within the last half decade of Estonian cultural semiotics the concept of transmediality has been adopted to make sense of some universal mechanisms of cultural dynamics via unpredictable and non-coordinated dialogues between texts of different sign systems.

Transmedia as the Epitome of 'Creative Industries'

Beyond the cultural semiotics perspective, the second and probably more popular way to think and talk about transmediality in Estonia is more practice oriented, but derives originally from policy discourse. This second perspective has its roots not only in the general processes of media convergence, but also in the emergence of the policy discourse on 'creative industries'. The formation of this discourse is generally perceived as part of the broader neoliberalization of cultural management and policy in the information-driven economy.

As is widely known, the creative industries approach emerged in the UK as part of Tony Blair's New Labour government's ideological framework in 2007–2008. The UK Department for Culture, Media and Sport created a task force that in 1998 published the *Creative Industries Mapping Document* that linked all 'industries' that build on individual creativity and generate wealth by exploiting intellectual property. The document named 13 different industry sectors that would together form the 'creative industries'. Among others, these included advertising, publishing, television and radio, film and video games. These fields of practice were expected to converge to an extent, which was relevant for the later conceptualization of transmedia storytelling and 'convergence culture' by Jenkins (2003). In other words, the convergence of these fields of practice was not only to happen in evolutionary ways, deriving from their own operational rationales, but would also be determined by policy means. The motivation for these policies was derived from the relative growth and exporting success of the IT industries; that is, from their demonstrated potential for scalable growth in the international markets. Therefore, the rationale for convergence was to combine the economies of scale logics of media and IT services markets and to turn the European subsidy-based media and other arts into the exporting industries of the information age. In other words, it is the service economy logic and its increasingly global scope, characteristic of the 'information society', that establishes the broad frame for the emergence of the creative industries as a policy discourse, as well as for its neoliberal underpinning.

While this approach most visibly emerged in the UK it quickly spread across Europe and the world, supported, first, by British cultural diplomacy and especially its worldwide British Council network. But for the member states of the EU it was the new EU policy frameworks that quickly acquired the central role. After the Lisbon Treaty was accepted in 2007, cultural policy was included among the EU's areas of responsibility. Since the core objective of the EU is the development of its common market, the emphasis was placed on increasing the international competitiveness and productivity of its creative industries. In practical terms this has led to several specific funding measures for the convergent creative industries (including the introduction of the Creative Europe program in 2015, measures in the EU Interreg programs for regional development, and specific calls in the research and development program Horizon 2020). Additionally, many member states have used their structural funds (funding targeted toward the structural development of especially the poorer member states) to support the development of their own creative industries.

In Estonia, all of these developments have resulted in a similar focus on the economic productivity of its cultural institutions and of all forms of culture production. But, different from some larger markets in the EU, the small domestic market for Estonian producers has meant that the core rationale for the creative industries is exports. With this realization we arrive at the specific nature of the rationales that are used to make 'transmedia' as a practice happen in smaller EU countries. Academic 'transmedia discourse' usually celebrates certain bottom-up dynamics of culture production, together with being optimistic about the extent of market-driven transmedia practices. Such accounts usually discuss the operations of big players in large markets. However, in smaller European countries the evolution of this practice may often be driven from the top, by various local and national authorities that seek cross-sector spillovers between the arts and ICT sectors. Therein is the expectation for scalable growth that would spill over and generate local growth. Businesses that exploit transmedia logic are seen as fulfilling these rationales and are therefore popular with authorities and their funding schemes for 'creative industries', 'innovation', or similar. Transmediality is therefore, to quite an extent, steered from the top, driven by expectations that market dynamics will happen after coordination by the states, cities, or other authorities.

EU Funding for Study Programs and Related Initiatives

In the previous section we described the general circumstances that could be seen as having conditioned the emergence of transmedia story-telling as a practice in Estonia. However, the story of its arrival is more concrete. In 2009, the Estonian Film Foundation (now the Estonian Film Institute) and Tallinn University's Baltic Film and Media School (BFM) joined a consortium (of mostly local film funds around the Baltic Sea) that applied for support from the EU Baltic Sea Region Interreg program to work on how the local audiovisual industry SMEs use crossmedia logic to advance their operational and business models in the digital era. Crossmedia was at the time the main industry term for multiplatform content development and provision. The application, which used many of the typical arguments described above, was successful and the First Motion consortium began its work. While reports of the consortium's work in the rest of northern Europe are available, its effects on the evolution of the transmedia scene in Estonia have been visible and significant.

It worked in two ways. First, BFM used the funding to develop and launch an MA level curriculum and later a BA level curriculum, both titled Crossmedia Production. For both levels courses on transmedia storytelling formed the backbone of the curriculum. What is of relevance for this chapter is that the ideas that were used at the initial stage of the MA curriculum development regarding what crossmedia or transmediality are and what they mean for culture were derived, to some extent, from the cultural semiotic approach described previously. The design of the curriculum departed somewhat from the idea that linking representative modes, remixing and translating from one mode to another, would be good not only for dynamics and innovation in culture, but also for facilitating dialogues and resulting sustainable coherence in culture. However, these ideas needed to be 'remixed' with the standard creative industry rationales described above, especially because BFM applied for more external funding: this time from a specific EU structural funds program aimed at advancing the Estonian educational sector. As the core aim of the measure was to develop practical MA programs building on cooperation with the industry, the curriculum had to be business friendly. It therefore put equal emphasis on understanding the cultural logics of transmediality or transmedia storytelling techniques and on technology and business management. The specific nature of external EU funding, for opening new kinds of creative industry study programs, directly affected what a study program on transmediality could teach in a small and relatively poor peripheral EU country.

After five years the MA and BA programs have produced fifty graduates, which for a country of only 1.3 million inhabitants and a film and television industry of approximately 2000 is a significant number. And it is growing. We have argued elsewhere (Ibrus 2016; Ibrus and Ojamaa 2014) that the emergence of this class of experts has had multiple effects on the media industry. First, there is the word-of-mouth diffusion of the concept among the professional class, spreading knowledge regarding not only the terminology, but also the tricks of the new trade. This spreading of knowledge has been further supported by a number of graduate projects having been co-produced with larger film or television producers and other kinds of cultural institutions, thereby increasing their visibility domestically and internationally. Some projects have even won awards from festivals, such as Filmteractive in Poland and Cross-Video Days in France. Another development has been the creation of a small sub-fund at the Estonian Film Institute to support the production of transmedia film extensions. The availability of funding and people with relevant skills spreading across media industries has had the aggregate effect of transmediality/crossmedia becoming accepted terms in these industries. We have also observed that the arrival of these skilled professionals has relieved the occasional frustration felt by film professionals, in particular, toward the need to develop transmedia solutions (documentary films commissioned by public service television channels now often need to have compulsory transmedia extensions, for example). Overall, this new breed of professional has generally been welcomed by the rest of the industry.

Lack of Steady Policy Framework

However, while the initial knowledge spread quickly across the industry and the practice was generally well received, the rapid development of the field has stalled due to lack of public funding for production. The aforementioned small grant system by the Estonian Film Institute was the only one remaining and funds have been too limited for larger projects to take off. In recent years the focus of this funding has been explicitly on film marketing and not on transmedia storytelling as a self-sufficient artistic practice. The Estonian Public Broadcaster (ERR), while receptive to the idea, has not contributed funds for the commissioning of transmedia projects. There is no dedicated public fund for digital or convergent arts. For this reason, the newly trained transmedia producers find themselves increasingly working in advertising or marketing industries instead of in the creative arts.

What can be deduced from this trend is that while the initial development was conditioned by top-down policy and more specifically by EU regional policy frameworks, the national policy frameworks either failed to support the further development of the emergent practice, or transmedia content production was expected to operate as a fully market-driven practice. Indeed, it has to an extent: audiovisual industries, especially when working with advertising, do tend to work on increasingly innovative and transmedia-like solutions. But, to make the connection to the cultural semiotic approach the cultural potential of transmediality regarding the facilitation of sustainable innovation and dynamics in a culture is not fulfilled in this way.

Transmedial Uses of Cultural Heritage

Although the two key ways of talking about transmediality in Estonia have so far existed rather like separate islands, it does seem that a bridge is being built. We are referring here to the digitization of cultural heritage that is taking place all over world, including in Estonia. There are now plans to digitize most of the country's heritage content in different modalities (including films, videos, photos, books, music, etc.). This process will be a huge undertaking, both in terms of cost and the amount of digitized material itself. Crucial from the transmedia perspective is that the heritage objects in diverse media not only need to be processed by digital technology, they also have to be systematized on the content level.

The expected value of the digitization projects lies both in securing the heritage and in the democratic provision of access to knowledge and past culture for all. This goal is in line with the preservative function of cultural memory. In small and relatively compact cultures such as Estonia there is the fascinating possibility of digitizing rapidly almost all of the heritage, which will allow for the creation of truly comprehensive descriptions of the entire culture, in its tangible and intangible forms, in verbal, visual, audiovisual and other modes. However, even in Estonia, where the cultural whole seems relatively perceptible, the corpus is still enormous and meaningful interaction with it by anyone will not be simple or self-evident. Therefore, the outcome of the technical digitization work will only ever be raw material that needs further cultural analysis and curation of its contents. The online collections, both public service databases such as Europeana or the archives of the ERR and commercial ones such as YouTube or Spotify, appear as gateways to access the heritage, but users will need further support to orient themselves through the material. For this purpose, then, the techniques of transmedia storytelling are expected to be enormously useful.

The second justification for the huge investment in digitizing Estonian cultural heritage is that digitized heritage is in turn expected to serve as a resource for the creative industries (see Oomen et al. 2009). Creative repurposing could lead to the emergence of new value propositions and contribute to general economic growth, not only through job creation, but also by its potential spillover effects into ICT innovation (Council of the European Union 2012). This growth could lead to political and financial support to reuse the heritage in transmedial ways. Content that originated in earlier times may appear elliptical in the present context and thus in need of additional comments or co-texts so that it can be understood.

Therefore, modally different peripheral texts will be needed to accompany heritage content that together will translate into a complex transmedial whole. Heritage content can be included in strictly curated thematic wholes, such as interactive textbooks, learning games, augmented reality applications, and so on. This all means that transmedia storytelling could become a fruitful strategy for immersing audiences deeper into new multimodal worlds that incorporate cultural heritage content and for supporting their meaningful dialogue with heritage in this era of media pluralization, market saturation and attention economy (Goldhaber 1997). Moreover, it could equally be used as a mechanism to create entertaining experiences for different audiences, as well as to enforce broad cultural dynamics by facilitating deep learning (Haggis 2003) in both formal and informal educational settings.

These two rationales for the digitization of cultural heritage illustrate quite clearly the complementarity of the preservative and creative functions of cultural memory. To preserve and to keep alive the riches of past culture means to keep them in active memory; that is, to relate culture's diachrony to its synchrony (Lotman 2001, 127). However, given the constant dynamics of cultural environment and the perpetual change of the communicational hierarchy of its sign systems, such preservation inevitably means transformation (and indeed transmediation). This transformation, for example, could take the form of translating a folkloric tale into a digital multimodal reading environment, archived personal letters from World War II into an experimental film, a medieval townscape into an alternative reality game and so on. Educating transmedia professionals who understand the balance between invariant aspects and medium-specifics of content in different sign systems and who can create coherent mental images of the past through new means of meaning-making could thus have a strong positive effect on the cultural identity. Strong identity presumes both knowledge of a shared past and literacy of present systems of communication, while the aim of strengthening the simultaneous coherence and diversity of cultural identities is generally perceived as extremely valuable both on the Estonian national level and on the European international level.

In practical terms, the work toward combining the rationales of creative industries and cultural semiotics for digitizing and enabling access to heritage content has already begun. This work includes developing business cases for heritage repurposing. The latter has comprised hackathons as well as acceleration and incubation services for start-up companies willing to work on new solutions and business models for heritage. The related policy work has focused not only on solving the legal issues of heritage reuse, but also on how to equip heritage content with good-quality metadata for various purposes, especially for facilitating uses in education. This has also resulted in humanities-based work on the related processes of cultural learning and intercultural dialogues and on the effects of service design on broader cultural processes. In other words, new dialogues between semioticians, entrepreneurs and policy-makers are evolving, creating a foundation for wholly new conceptualizations of transmediality based on the specific *genius loci* of Estonia.

Conclusion

This chapter has demonstrated the very particular conditioning factors that have shaped the further evolution of the transmedia concept in Estonia as a very small country accommodating a distinct scholarly approach to cultural analysis. In effect, using a concept derived from cultural semiotics – the complex dialogues between different discursive constellations, some having evolved within the country, some having been 'injected' into the country by various kinds of authorities – has resulted in further unique uses of the transmedia concept both in analytical and development work. The absorption of the concept has also depended on the socioeconomic set-up of the country: the small domestic market has conditioned what kinds of cultural institutions and in what markets effective transmedia strategies can be devised. Estonia's publicly funded film industry that leans toward art house has not generally seen much need for a multiplatform afterlife for its products. The limited budgets of television channels tie their hands, too. However, museums are plentiful in the country and some prominent institutions have been designing new profound and innovative transmedial outputs. This again links to the momentum of heritage content digitization as it seems to facilitate the convergence of creative industries and cultural semiotics-driven frameworks for the transmedia concept. As evidenced in the work of Hartley and Potts (2014), this kind of combination is not entirely unprecedented. However, this chapter has shown how structural and circumstantial aspects in a very small country condition not only the convergence of practices, but also the ways in which they are being understood.

Bibliography

Council of the European Union. "Council Conclusions on the Digitisation and Online Accessibility of Cultural Material and Digital Preservation." *Youth Education, Culture and Sport Council*, Brussels, 2012.

Goldhaber, Michael H. "The Attention Economy and the Net." *First Monday* 2:4 (1997). http://journals.uic.edu/ojs/index.php/fm/article/view/519/440.

Haggis, Tamsin. "Constructing Images of Ourselves? A Critical Investigation into Approaches to Learning Research in Higher Education." *British Educational Research Journal* 29:1 (2003): 89–104.

Hartley, John, and Jason Potts. *Cultural Science: A Natural History of Stories, Demes, Knowledge and Innovation.* London: Bloomsbury Academic, 2014.

Herman, David. "Toward a Transmedial Narratology." In *Narrative across Media: The Languages of Storytelling*, edited by Marie-Laure Ryan. Lincoln: University of Nebraska Press, 2004.

Ibrus, Indrek. "Micro-studios Meet Convergence Culture: Crossmedia, Clustering, Dialogues, Auto-communication." In *Media Convergence Handbook*, vol. 2, edited by Artur Lugmayr and Cinzia Dal Zotto. Heidelberg: Springer, 2016.

Ibrus, Indrek, and Maarja Ojamaa. "What Is the Cultural Function and Value of European Transmedia Independents?" *International Journal of Communication* 8 (2014): 2283–2300.

Ibrus, Indre, and Peeter Torop. "Remembering and Reinventing Juri Lotman for the Digital Age." *International Journal of Cultural Studies* 18:1 (2015): 3–9.

Jakobson, Roman. *On Linguistic Aspects of Translation. Selected Writings. II, Word and Language.* The Hague, Paris: Mouton, 1971.

Jenkins, Henry, "Transmedia Storytelling." *MIT Technology Review.* January 15, 2003. Accessed 4 February 2013. www.technologyreview.com/news/401760/transmedia-storytelling/.

Kinder, Marsha. *Playing with Power in Movies, Television, and Video Games: From Muppet Babies to Teenage Mutant Ninja Turtles.* Berkeley: University of California Press, 1991.

Lotman, Juri. "On the Semiosphere." *Sign Systems Studies* 33:1 (2005): 205–229.

Lotman, Juri. *Culture and Explosion.* Berlin: Mouton de Gruyter, 2009.

Lotman, Juri. *The Unpredictable Workings of Culture.* Tallinn: Tallinn University Press, 2013.

Lotman, Yuri. *Universe of the Mind: A Semiotic Theory of Culture.* Bloomington and Indianapolis: Indiana University Press, 2001 [1990].

Ojamaa, Maarja, and Peeter Torop. "Transmediality of Cultural Autocommunication." *International Journal of Cultural Studies* 18:1 (2015): 61–78.

Saldre, Maarja and Peeter Torop. "Transmedia Space." In *Crossmedia Innovations: Texts, Markets, Institutions*, edited by Indrek Ibrus and Carlos Scolari, 25–44. Frankfurt: Peter Lang, 2012.

Salupere, Silvi, and Peeter Torop. "On the Beginnings of the Semiotics of Culture in the Light of the Theses of Tartu-Moscow School." In *Beginnings of the Semiotics of Culture*, edited by Silvi Salupere, Peeter Torop, and Kalevi Kull, 15–37. Tartu: Tartu University Press, 2013.

Sütiste, Elin, and Peeter Torop. "Processual Boundaries of Translation: Semiotics and Translation Studies." *Semiotica* 163:1/4 (2007): 187–207.

Part II
North and South American Transmediality

6 United States

Trans-Worldbuilding in the Stephen King Multiverse

William Proctor

I don't really map anything out. I just let it happen
(King, in Breznican, 2017: 17)

There are other worlds than these
(King, 1982)

Since the publication of *Carrie* in 1974 – or, more accurately, since Brian De Palma adapted the novel for film two years later – Stephen King has grown into a transmedia powerhouse, an author not only responsible for writing over fifty novels and ten collections of short fiction, but also a dizzying array of transmedia expressions developed and deployed across various platforms over the past four decades or so. King has written comics (for example, *American Vampire*, *Road Rage*); screenplays based on his own work (*Pet Sematary*, *Silver Bullet*); original screenplays for film and television (*Kingdom Hospital*, *Rose Red*); work-for-hire (*Tales of the Darkside*, *The X-Files*); a serialized novel released in instalments, inspired by the spirit of Charles Dickens (*The Green Mile*); nonfiction books (*Danse Macabre*, *On Writing*); collaborations (Peter Straub, Richard Chizmar); music (*Ghostbrothers of Darkland County* with John Mellencamp; Michael Jackson's *Ghosts*); as well as essays, reviews and a steady stream of praise for popular authors, usually proudly displayed on the front cover of novels (commonly known as 'blurb'). For someone who claims that he writes 2,000 words every day, including birthdays and holidays, it is hardly surprising that King is one of the most prolific authors in recent memory. But even this is only the tip of the iceberg 'Tower.'

At various points in his career, King has experimented with new media technologies, often in innovative ways, often ahead of the curve. At the turn of the millennium, King published the first online e-book, *Riding the Bullet* (2000), which heralded a seismic shift in the publishing world, accruing downloads of over 400,000 during the first twenty-four hours of release – averaging 4.62 copies per second – and jamming Soft-Lock's servers in the process. The following year, King experimented with online self-publishing with a planned full-length novel released in instalments. At the time of writing, King has all but abandoned *The Plant*, but not because it was a commercial flop. In fact, King himself states that he made over half a million dollars in downloads, an enormous figure considering that users could access the document without financial cost, a system that has since become known as PWYW (pay what you want).[1] Although sales tapered off quite rapidly – down from 120,000 for the first instalment to 40,000 for the next – users cottoned onto the fact that they could download each instalment *gratis*, and King pulled the plug to focus on other projects. By 2017, King has yet to return to *The Plant*.

King's new media excursions include embracing Amazon's Kindle platform at a time when authors and publishers feared for the continued relevance of 'the book' and treated e-book readers as evidence that the devil's minions were hard at work making detritus out of print media. In early 2009, King published a novella, *UR*, to launch the second iteration of Amazon's Kindle e-book reader. The story functions both as an 'episode' in King's magnum opus, 'The Dark Tower', and as an extended commercial for the Kindle platform – the technology is featured as an element of the story itself, with the device being able to access a bevy of alternate realities. At various moments, King has debuted his short fiction on the e-book platform, such as *A Face in the Crowd* (2012), a collaboration with Stewart O'Nan (which, at the time of writing, remains available on Kindle and audio book only) and a novella, *In the Tall Grass*, written with his son, novelist and comic book writer, Joe Hill, which was first published in two parts in *Esquire* magazine, then crossed transmedially to Kindle and audio book. King also experimented with key shifts in mobile phone technology, such as adapting the (then) unpublished story, *N.*, which was delivered to users' mobile phones as 'a ground-breaking series of 25 original video episodes', 'the first comic-style book adaptation especially developed and produced for viewing on today's most popular small screen platforms' (Powers 2008).

King is also, of course, a stellar Hollywood film and television brand (Browning 2009, 2011; Magistrale 2003, 2008). Over sixty adaptations bear the author's signature, the majority of which are based on his novels and short fiction, but also branded on texts that the author played no part in creating, many of them extensions licensed by industry contracts,[2] including *The Rage: Carrie 2* (1999), *Firestarter 2: Rekindled* (2002), *Pet Sematary 2* (1992), *Sometimes They Come Back...Again* (1996), *The Mangler 2* (2002) and ten instalments in the 'Children of the Corn' film series, which has been ongoing for over thirty years – quite remarkable considering the short story of which the films are supposedly based upon only runs for thirty pages.

Taking all of this into account, then, it is not too much of a stretch to view King's output as transmedially significant in comparison to other living authors.[3] However, despite scholarly work on King continuing to grow apace (for example, see Hoppenstand 2010; Magistrale 2010; McAlfeer 2009; Wood 2011), academics have yet to turn their attention to the author's expansive oeuvre as a valuable case study in world-building. As Matt Hills explains in this volume, '[w]ork on transmediality, despite being concerned with intellectual properties moving across media, has tended to focus on film, television, comic books and video games' (2018). Given the prevalence of 'connected universes' across the present-day Hollywood blockbuster scene, where the likes of Marvel, DC and Star Wars – as well as less successful attempts, such as the Dark Universe – dominate the multiplexes, it is fair to claim that world-building rules the commercial roost in contemporary American cinema. And yet considering that 'literary fiction is probably the most active experimental laboratory of the world-constructing enterprise' (Doležel 1998: ix), the fact that literature (novels, novellas and short stories) has been hitherto excluded from world-building and transmedia studies requires redressing. It is this gap I want to focus on in this chapter, considering the ways in which King's imaginary world has been developed, not with coherent world-building in mind and design, but via a recalibration of the world's ontological rules – that is, 'what can and cannot exist, what is and isn't possible in a particular type of storyworld' (Ryan 2017, 74) – at various junctures in order to retroactively subsume various sub-worlds into an overarching 'hyperdiegesis' (Hills 2002). From such a viewpoint, this chapter demonstrates that King's imaginary world should be considered diachronically, that is, 'a gradual, discontinuous creation' which has 'no singular "big bang"' but, rather, 'has coalesced over time' (Hills 2017). Thus, the Stephen King multiverse is an example of what I would describe, in deference to Henry Jenkins and John Tulloch (1995), as 'an unfolding world'.

With this in mind, I want to illustrate that the narrative mechanics of the King world developed *transfictionally* (Saint-Gelais 2005, 2011), before moving onto the way in which later instalments in The Dark Tower series radically alter the world's ontological rules, allowing for 'retroactive linkages' to function as a form of *transfictional bridging* so as to pull disparate sub-worlds into a shared universe – or, 'multiverse', a common science fiction novum (see Proctor 2017). I will then explore the way that the world's ontological rules permit further extensions across platforms, such as comics and film, resulting in a kind of *reflexive transmedia storytelling*. In so doing, this chapter challenges the current fetishization of transmedia storytelling in academic and production quarters; especially the idea that forms of adaptation should be barred from transmedia storytelling paradigms (see Dena 2018). I will show how comics based on The Dark Tower novels can function as both adaptation *and* transmedia storytelling, thus complicating conceptual and cultural distinctions between the two.

Transfictional Storytelling and Compossible Texts

Coined by Richard Saint-Gelais, the concept of transfictionality describes a process whereby characters, locations and events inhabit and
share the same narrative space. In other words, 'two (or more) texts
exhibit a trans-fictional relationship when they share elements, such as
characters, imaginary locations or fictional worlds' (Saint-Gelais 2005,
612). Although transfictionality is conceptually heterogeneous and may
be activated in various different ways, the concepts of *croisement* and
annexions – crossings and incorporations – are of particular interest
for this chapter regarding King's world-building operations as the join-
ing together of 'two (or more) fictions which the reader had hitherto
every reason to consider unrelated, and which now find themselves con-
joined in a third text' (84). In order to differentiate between the various
operations of transfictionality, the concept of 'compossibility' (Doležel
1998) is necessary to demarcate which texts form the building blocks of
the imaginary world. To illustrate, I consider the transfictional bridges
between several of King's novels that subsume purportedly isolated texts
into a unified narrative terrain. I explain these *world-bridges* conceptually as comprising character, event and geography. The following examples provide outline and illustration (but not exhaustion).

King's mammoth novel, *IT* (1986), for instance, includes several
transfictional bridges that subsume and interconnect a variety of King
novels into a shared universe paradigm.[4] More than this, however, is
that transfictional expressions begin to variously build a network of connections that function as (world) building blocks, feeding into a shared
narrative terrain whereby a welter of crossings and incorporations provide substantive connections between fictions. I will now use *IT* as an
example of transfictional bridge(s), either emanating from, or pointing
toward, the text.

Midway through *IT*, the character Mike Hanlon recounts a story once
told by his father about a tragic fire at the Black Spot, a local nightclub
primarily for soldiers of color. This nested story within a story is less
important than the way in which the narrative provides a transfictional
bridge with King's third novel, *The Shining* (1977), through the character of Dick Halloran. In *The Shining*, Halloran is the caretaker of
the Overlook Hotel, the central location for the novel's action. In *IT*,
Halloran is featured some three decades prior to his introduction in *The
Shining*, and the character's inclusion serves as a 'flashback', 'a backward continuation meant to work its way upstream' (Genette 1997,
177). Such a brief appearance (a transfictional cameo, so to speak), operates to substantiate and concretize the King imaginary world as existing
within the same narrative space and, thus, pulls *The Shining* into *IT*'s
narrative orbit (and vice versa). In so doing, both novels become 'compossible' through transfictional relationships. Or, to explain it another

way, *The Shining* and *IT* novels are compossible texts, which means that they exist within the same imaginary space. On the other hand, however, the film adaptations of *The Shining* and *IT* are narratively *non-*compossible with their source texts (at least at the narrative level). Given that transfictionality covers a wide ambit and could feasibly include, say, characters crossing over fictions that do not chronological 'fit', such as the panoply of Sherlock Holmes' 'versions' that inhabit discrete story worlds (Lapoint 2017). To differentiate between generalized instances of transfictionality, we can describe compossibility within a particular storyworld as an example of *canonical compossibility*, which refers to all of the texts written directly by King.

At another point in the *IT* novel, Beverley Marsh – like Hanlon, a member of *IT's* 'The Loser's Club' – refers to Frank Dodd, 'that crazy cop who killed all those women in Castle Rock, Maine', a seemingly throwaway statement perhaps for casual King readers, but which nevertheless (hyperdiegetically) incorporates and subsumes *The Dead Zone* (1979) into *IT's* narrative and, by extension, *The Shining*. As a result, an 'event' in one novel can become a transfictional bridge when referred to in another, so that Frank Dodd's murderous spree also appears in the opening paragraph to *Cujo* (1983), along with John Smith, the reluctant psychic-protagonist of *The Dead Zone*:

> Once upon a time, not so long ago, a monster came to the small town of Castle Rock, Maine... He was not werewolf, vampire, ghoul or unnameable creature from the enchanted forest or from the snowy wastes; he was only a cop named Frank Dodd with mental and sexual problems. A good man named John Smith uncovered his name by a kind of magic, but before he could be captured – perhaps it was just as well – Frank Dodd killed himself.
>
> (King 1981, 3)

In essence, King's opening gambit summarizes *The Dead Zone* in a nutshell. Recounting the plot so directly, however brief, as well as demonstrating that the 'small town of Castle Rock' is also transfictional (which I shall turn to momentarily), characters, events and locations often 'crossover' from one novel into another and, thus, 'thicken' the parameters of the imaginary world through *repetitive association*. Put simply, the more that (trans) associations breach the borders of the literary text and puncture the diegetic wall separating one sub-world from another – a wall which is always-already porous and unstable – then the 'thicker' the world becomes 'and the greater the illusion of ontological weight that it has' (Wolf 2012, 247). As a transfictional event, then, the Dodd 'episode' in *The Dead Zone* bears the footprint of that novel and stamps its mark across several books, thus providing a sequence of transfictional bridges that establish multiple connections in one fell swoop, working as a type of *continuity cascading*, with each node in the network activating narrative interconnectivity even further. Beverley Marsh's comment may link *IT* with *The Dead Zone*, but doing so is only the beginning of a much more complex interrelationship between canonically compossible texts.

Trans-fictional events often occur in conjunction with transfictional characters, such as Sheriff Bannerman, the law enforcement officer in *The Dead Zone* who recruited Johnny Smith to assist with the spate of murders in Castle Rock due to rumors about his psychic abilities. At this point in the novel, Bannerman seeks out Johnny because he has made no progress in the case of the 'Castle Rock Strangler' (Dodd, it turns out, is a fellow police officer). Bannerman turns up in *Cujo* and meets a grisly end at the jaws of the rabid St. Bernard, while in *The Dark Half* (1989), we meet Alan Pangborn, the newly elected Sheriff of Castle Rock following Bannerman's death. Pangborn re-appears in *Needful Things*, 'the last Castle Rock story'.[5] In *Pet Sematary* (1983, 20), a novel that King claims almost did not see the light of day due to its nihilistic cynicism, Jud Crandall explains that there has been a rising tide 'of rabies in Maine now. There was a big old St. Bernard went rabid downstate a couple of years ago and killed four people.' Whether through the titular canine or his unfortunate victims, *Cujo* is invoked in several novels, establishing multiple world-bridges between various texts.

So, then, what we have here is a series of transfictional border crossings, of character and event, with each reference leading King's 'Constant Readers' (the author's affectionate mode for addressing his most dedicated fans) to another in a complex chain of signification, each ricocheting and reverberating endlessly across the texts of King's multiverse, ontologically thickening the world through repetitive association. However, transfictional characters and events are also thickened by the reoccurrence of environments that form the basis for King's version of Maine and provide the settings for many novels. In *IT*, for example, King sketches out a history of the fictional town of Derry in detail (1986, 196–198), as well as developing the more *outré* mythos of Pennywise, 'the apotheosis of all monsters' (6). More than this, however, is the way in which the locale of Derry (as with Castle Rock) serves as the central environment for multiple novels and, in this way, becomes a kind of *transfictional geography*. So, for example, in the 'Derry novel', *Dreamcatcher* (2001), a piece of graffiti proclaiming 'Pennywise Lives', sets off a chain of associations that leads directly back to *IT*, while in the process also referencing other Derry novels, such as *Insomnia* (1995) – which features the re-appearance of Mike Hanlon post-*IT* and references the tragic fire at the Black Spot recounted in Hanlon's father's story mentioned earlier – and *11/22/63*, including a chance meeting between protagonist, Jake Epping, and members of The Loser's Club from *IT*, Beverly Marsh and Richie Tozier.

Taking all of the above into account, King has developed his imaginary world diachronically, casting transfictional anchors in order to pull disparate texts – which *become* 'micro-narratives' from the perspective of world-building – into a hyperdiegetic 'macro-structure' (Ryan 1992, 373). This leads us to The Dark Tower saga, a series of eight novels that over time further establishes and develops transfictional relationships via the employment of 'retroactive linkages', permitted by significant alterations to the ontological rules governing 'the world.'

Retroactive Linkages and The Dark Tower

'The man in black fled across the desert and the gunslinger followed' (King, 1). So begins and ends King's self-described magnum opus, The Dark Tower, a series of eight novels[6] amounting to over 4,000 pages that recalibrates the rules of the imaginary world so that all of King's fiction could be enveloped into an overarching multiverse comprising parallel worlds. As Tony Magistrale puts it, 'The Dark Tower'

> can be appreciated as a means for unpacking the King canon, an umbrella text encompassing the whole of the writer's fictional oeuvre ... The Dark Tower is therefore a kind of Unified Field Theory for King ... The Dark Tower is a multi-layered universe in which multiple worlds co-exist.
>
> (Magistrale 2010, 150–151)

Although there is no scope in this chapter to offer a detailed synopsis of the saga – readers wanting something of that ilk can check out Vincent (2013) or Wiater, Golden and Wagner (2003) – it is worth describing the story in a nutshell. Written between 1970 and 2003, along with an 'intraquel',[7] *The Wind Through the Keyhole* (2012) – which chronologically fits in between the third and fourth volumes, *The Waste Lands* (1991) and *Wizard and Glass* (1997) respectively – The Dark Tower series concerns protagonist, Roland Deschain, the last gunslinger, as he journeys across the lands of Mid-World – and across alternate worlds – in order to find and protect the titular Tower, which stands at 'the point in time, space and reality where all dimensions meet' (Wiater et al. 2003, 22). The Tower, we come to learn, is under attack from dark forces led by the Crimson King, whom readers do not meet until the final book, *The Dark Tower* (2003). In the first book, *The Gunslinger* (1982, 2003), Roland is hot on the heels of The Man in Black, chasing him across the Mohaine desert for reasons not quite clear at this stage. Along the way, Roland meets Jake Chambers, who we learn has been murdered in another world – *our* world, what comes to be known as 'Keystone Earth' in the multiverse, one world among many. Roland sacrifices Jake in order to continue after the Man in Black, who, upon recognizing his fate, utters the oft-quoted words, '[g]o then. There are other worlds than these' (King 2003, 210), illustrating that death is but a doorway to a distinct, but interconnected, reality. As Roland finally catches up with the Man in Black, the reality of the tower, and the multiverse, is revealed:

> Imagine the sand of the Mohaine Desert, which you crossed to find me, and imagine a trillion universes – not worlds but universes – encapsulated in each grain of sand of that desert; and within each universe an infinity of others. We tower over these universes from our pitiful grass vantage point; with one swing of your boot you may knock a billion billion worlds, flying off into darkness, in a chain never to be completed ... Yet suppose further. Suppose that all worlds, all universes, met in a single nexus, a single pylon, a Tower.
>
> (2003, 229–230)

In the second volume, *The Drawing of the Three* (1987), Roland plucks Eddie Dean and Susannah Holmes from Keystone Earth and is re-joined by Jake Chambers in *The Waste Lands*, forming a Ka-tet ('one made from many'). In the final book, Roland reaches his destination alone and climbs the stairs to the Tower, only to discover that the answers he so desperately seeks evade him as he is hurtled back to the beginning of his quest (or, at least, to the beginning of *The Gunslinger*), cursed to battle for the survival of the Tower over and over again, trapped in a time loop (hence, the repetition of the first line in the saga as the final line in the series). However, rather than this 'loop', or cycle, being a form of Nietzschean 'eternal recurrence', whereby time is repeated verbatim for eternity, each 'turn of the wheel' represents a different journey for Roland and he is theoretically capable of changing his fate (although he does not remember his previous adventures). How many 'cycles' Roland has experienced thus far is not known to readers, although it is implied that 'the gunslinger has repeated and resumed his quest many times before' (McAlfeer 2009, 27). Keeping this in mind, King revised the first book, *The Gunslinger*, in 2003 so as to establish greater continuity, tone and tenor with the later novels, and so we could reasonably view the original version as an earlier iteration of Roland's cycle, rather than rendered illegitimate and non-canonical by the newer, revised tale.

This introduction of the multiverse concept, of a nexus of parallel worlds with the Dark Tower as lynchpin, afforded King the opportunity to begin constructing transfictional bridges between (what was at that point) two incommensurable worlds in order to fuse them together. For over two decades – or even further back if we accept that King wrote the first sentence in 1970 – The Dark Tower novels were 'marked by unique alterities' (Csicsery-Ronay Jr. 2012, 502), and deemed such 'a distinct departure' (McAleer 2009, 9) from King's other works, that they were occluded from the hyperdiegesis explicitly developed in what we can call 'Keystone texts' to differentiate between Tower and non-Tower novels. King has, in actual fact, provided a series of reflexive commentaries, or 'peritexts' (1997, 8), that explicitly show that it was not until the nineties that he *learned* that both worlds co-existed hyperdiegetically. Writing in the 'Afterword' to fourth volume, *Wizard and Glass*, King explains that he is 'coming to understand that Roland's world (or worlds) contains all the others of my making' (1997). Following publication of the final novel in 2003, King again reflected on this as a *discovery*, explaining that, '[m]y idea was to use The Dark Tower stories as a kind of summation, a way of unifying as many of my previous stories as possible beneath the arch of some *über*-tale' (King 2004, 685). Here, King states that it was during the writing of *Insomnia*, a Dark Tower book in all but name, that he consciously began to view the two worlds as commensurable and compossible, ultimately building transfictional bridges during the period in earnest. In so doing, the ontological rules permitted by the parallel universe novum modifies and remediates The Dark Tower, from outlier fantasy world occupying the fringes of the imaginary world, or even existing outside of it, to hyperdiegetic centerpiece. It is not that 'all of King's work [is] an outgrowth of the Dark Tower series', as Wiater et al. argue (2003, 22), but the other way around: The Dark Tower is an outgrowth of King's work (although perhaps it would be best to view the worlds as dialogic). That is to say, the panoply of transfictional crossings and incorporations that weave King's fiction into a narrative tapestry began not with The Dark Tower books, but in Keystone fiction, in *Cujo*, *IT*, *Needful Things*, *The Dead Zone*, *Pet Sematary*, and so forth. Without such anchors and bridges, it would not have been possible to activate continuity cascades, with references and quotations ricocheting from one node to another across the narrative network, providing the structure of the world with ontological heft. King's Dark Tower novels may stand at the center of the (hyperdiegetic) space-time continuum, but the ontological rules governing the multiverse required extending in order to subsume non-series elements into a unified hyperdiegesis.

Moreover, many Dark Tower concepts were not introduced in the series, but in Keystone texts, with multiple transfictional bridges pointing *toward* The Dark Tower, as well as in the other direction, thickening the associations between worlds. In *Insomnia*, for example, King developed the notion of the multiverse comprising multiple 'levels'[8] of the Tower, each level containing an infinite number of parallel worlds, which is further expanded in *Wizard and Glass* when Roland and his Ka-Tet cross into an unfamiliar apocalyptic world and, in the process, trans-fictionally crossover between diegetic realms. In Roland's world, the borders between worlds have started breaking down, leading to fissures between alternate realities, so when the Ka-Tet come across a newspaper with the headline, 'CAPTAIN TRIPS' SUPERFLU

RAGES UNCHECKED' (King 1997, 90–91), a transfictional bridge is constructed between The Dark Tower and *The Stand*, fusing the two worlds (although Roland's world and the world of *The Stand* exist on different levels of the Tower).

It was in fact during the nineties that King began building transfictional bridges from The Dark Tower to non-series Keystone books and back again, pulling as many texts as possible within the shadow of the Tower. The concept of 'Breakers,' psychic children with the power to topple the Tower, is introduced in the novella, 'Low Men with Yellow Coats,' contained in *Hearts in Atlantis* (1999), along with Chief Breaker, Ted Brautigan, who readers meet again in the final volume. The mythos is developed further in *Black House* (2001), a sequel to *The Talisman* (1984), both co-written with Peter Straub. Perhaps the most significant transfictional bridge, however, occurs in the fifth book, *Wolves of the Calla* (2003), wherein Roland meets Father Callahan, a character from his second novel, *'Salem's Lot* (1975), who perished at the hands of vampire, Barlow, and woke up in Mid-World ('there are other worlds than these'). From this perspective, *Wolves of the Calla* functions partly as a sequel to *'Salem's Lot*, and short story, 'Jerusalem's Lot' (1978). Here, King's fiction becomes less for casual airport readers and more for Constant Readers (or, more accurately, King's 'Tower junkies'), demanding extensive encyclopedic competences (Eco 1984, 7) to follow what is happening in the story. A Keystone novel, such as *Insomnia* or *Black House*, thus becomes difficult, if not impossible, to follow completely without at least some knowledge regarding The Dark Tower. It is perhaps for this reason that The Dark Tower novels have not sold as well as King's other works (which is not to say that they are poor sellers by any stretch).

The fact that these various transfictional bridges are constructed in hindsight dovetails with Wolf's concept of 'retroactive linkages', which, as he puts it,

> are most commonly found in the work of author's who have created two or more imaginary worlds and wish to bring them together into one larger creation, so they can be considered as a form of worldbuilding … the term "multiverse" is sometimes used, which describes overall structure resulting from the connection of two or more universes.
>
> (2012, 216)

Of course, it could be argued that King employed the use of retroactive linkages to unify his various fictions, always looking backward in a rearview mirror. But the concept is most often used to explain the conjoining of two (or more) distinct realities, as with Edgar Rice Burroughs' fusing together of the world of his Pellucidar, 'a land inhabited by an intelligent species of pterodactyls,' with the world of Tarzan (Scolari, Bertetti and Freeman 2014, 12).

In 2004, the final volume of The Dark Tower spelled the end of a four-decade journey for King (although he would return to Mid-World with both Kindle novella, *UR*, and novel, *The Wind Through the Keyhole*, and has said he may revisit it at some point in the future). But the ontological status of the world – of the multiverse – allowed for the existence of multiple texts existing on different planes of reality, on different levels of the tower, as it were, to coagulate and solidify narratively. This would allow for the emergence of an expanded universe spearheaded by King's author-function as creative consultant, but which would become trans-authorial and transmedial. The next section explores The Dark Tower comics, published by Marvel, as unsettling binaries between adaptation and the utopian promise of Jenkins' (2006) seminal, but arguably utopian, definition of transmedia storytelling. I also consider the role of 'orienting paratexts' of the kind that Saint-Gelais (1999) describes as 'xenoencyclopedia' as a way to further explain and expand the world's – or worlds' – ontological rules outside the parameters of the (narrative) world itself.

The Dark Tower Expanded Universe

In 1999, King was involved in a life-threatening accident, and Roland's quest was in peril, The Dark Tower verging on collapse. During recovery, King promised, not for the first time, that he would write the remaining three volumes of The Dark Tower back-to-back. However, due to the lengthy gaps between instalments, King claimed that the world had become so labyrinthine that he required a guidebook, a story bible that he could consult to ensure continuity between the various books in the series without having to break the flow of writing and risk the story 'growing cold' (King 2012, xiii). To this end, King hired Robin Furth as his research assistant, the result of which was a detailed concordance, designed 'to limit these aggravating pauses by putting Roland's world at my fingertips – not just names and places, but slang terms, dialects, relationships, even whole chronologies' (ibid).

In 2007, Marvel Comics announced a comic series based on The Dark Tower novels. Beginning not with *The Gunslinger*, but with the backstory of Roland's early years as depicted in *Wizard and Glass*, the first mini-series, *The Gunslinger Born*, works as an adaptation of King's fourth series novel. The series was overseen by King as creative consultant, thereby utilizing his 'author-function' to brand the comics as legitimate entries in The Dark Tower mythology, and plotted/outlined by Furth. Although King did not write the script – that was superhero comic alumni, Peter David – his authorship is evoked in promotional paratexts as with, for example, a press release from comic distributor, Diamond:

> King is directly involved in the creative aspects of the project, supervising all editorial and visual content ... Robin Furth ... is outlining the Dark Tower comic book series, providing scene-by-scene plotting and maintaining the continuity and consistency of each story arc'.
>
> (quoted in Vincent 2013, 145)

By indicating King's active involvement, paratexts can work to convince readers that the comics will be faithful to the novels and should be considered authentic contributions to the hyperdiegesis. King, of course, always maintains his position as grand poobah, or 'pope of the magisterial,' offering 'definitive, official rulings on matters of canon' (Parkin 2007, 252). But he also endorses Furth as a 'secondary author,' perhaps bolstered by her painstaking *Stephen King's The Dark Tower Concordance* (which has since been published in two volumes and then collected as a single compendium amounting to almost 700 pages of imaginary world facts and details), which, perhaps most importantly, is (paratextually) blessed by the pope himself. As with authorship discourse in general terms, King's stamp of approval, his imprimatur, serves a commercial function, a promotional strategy that points toward authenticity. By constructing authorship hierarchically, with King and his oeuvre occupying the highest level, it emphasizes that the hyperdiegesis is not democratic, whereby all texts are awarded equal footing, but, instead, underwritten by several layers, or strata. Within such a *stratified hyperdiegesis,*[9] the King imaginary world can be seen as comprising multiple levels of text as with, for example, the canonical rules that governed the Star Wars universe prior to Disney's takeover in 2012, whereby a hierarchical taxonomy was introduced, providing readers of the Expanded Universe of texts *outside* the cinematic saga with official rulings from the Pope – here, George Lucas, or proxy-body Lucas Licensing – describing the various levels of canonicity (Proctor and Freeman 2017). In so doing, the Star Wars film series consistently remains the lynchpin of the imaginary world, the saga's own Dark Tower.

Viewing The Dark Tower comics as *only* adaptation, however, is complicated by narrative details and scenarios that:

> expand on things that are not mentioned or only briefly alluded to in the novels. The journey back to Gilead is greatly expanded. For the first time, readers learn how Carson's forces regroup after their defeat in Hambry and rise against Gilead, eventually sacking it. The climax of the series is the battle of Jericho Hill, where the gunslingers made their last stand.
>
> (Vincent 2013, 144)

In this light, the current 'no adaptation rule' (Dena 2018) in transmedia storytelling becomes freighted with cultural distinction, continuing the 'constant denigration of the general phenomenon of adaptation' in academic terms (Hutcheon, 2006, xi; see also Stam and Raengo 2005). 'Transmedia storytelling is not *mere* adaptation', writes Ryan, the term 'mere' constructing a binary relationship, or 'moral dualism' (Hills 2002), between 'good' (integrated, coherent) transmedia and 'bad' (parasitical, redundant) adaptation. In Henry Jenkins' seminal definition (2006), both adaptation *and* licensed spin-offs are deemed unworthy of the transmedia storytelling appellation. The idea that 'an adaptation is understood as a version or retelling of the original, whereas an extension goes beyond the original' (Jenkins 2017) is complicated and confounded by The Dark Tower comics, which ultimately work, *contra* Jenkins and Ryan, by collapsing the dualism between the two models. Neither, though, should we consider adaptation as a form of transfictional process, as Saint-Gelais argues:

> precisely because of this goal of diegetic equivalence, which is incompatible with the profoundly transfictional actions of extrapolation and expansion: adaptations do not intend to continue the story, much less suggest new adventures for the protagonists.
>
> (quoted in Wells-Lassagne 2017, 8)

This notion of 'diegetic equivalence' dovetails with Jenkins' 'redundancy' and Ryan's 'mere' distinction; that is, adaptation is primarily nothing more than straightforward replication and reproduction, an equivalency that is transported across platforms monolithically. The Dark Tower comics, however, work as adaptation, transfictional and transmedia storytelling, as 'an extension of The Dark Tower series, one that provides additional tales to supplement the original tales and additional depictions of the scenes and characters' (McAlfeer 2009, 24). I am not suggesting we venture down the post-structural rabbit-hole, casting aside signifiers and concepts as we go: it is vitally important to construct theoretical models with which to examine popular artefacts. Indeed, how else would scholars be able to analyze texts and worlds without coherent framing principles? King's multiverse, however, convincingly illustrates that general ('one size fits all') rulings often fail to cope with the complexity of imaginary worlds. To this end, I would argue that each world needs to be explored and examined based on its own identity, idiosyncrasy, and narrative architecture.

To complicate matters further, Furth admittedly contradicted several events depicted in The Dark Tower novels, which led to questions and queries from fan-readers regarding the canonical status of the comics. To explain how the comic books could be conceived as compossible, then, Furth addressed the aporia directly in an essay contained within the first issue of mini-series, *The Man in Black* (2012):

> When I think about differences between the novels and the comics – and there are many of them – I always keep in mind Jake Chambers' famous phrase, "there are other worlds than these". The Dark Tower contains many levels, and within those levels are parallel worlds which mirror each other, but which are not exactly alike … I always view the Dark Tower comics as existing in one of these parallel worlds. If the Dark Tower novels exist in Tower Keystone [Roland's world], or the central world of The Dark Tower universe, then the Dark Tower comics exist in a spin-off world.
>
> (Furth 2013, 4)

At this stage, King had all but become *deus absconditus* (2015, 84), and left Furth to wander areas not fully developed or explored in the mythos (although King's author-function would remain active as creative consultant and executive producer):

> I monitored them really closely at the beginning. I wanted to make sure everything was on track and going the right way … After they went off on their own, I didn't want to junk up my head with their storylines … I've got this one book coming out, *The Wind Through the Keyhole*, and there might be more after that, but if they are, they won't be influenced at all by whatever's going on in the comics. You know what Roland always says: there are other worlds than these.
>
> (King, quoted in Vincent 2013, 105)

On the one hand, this certainly appears to be a narrative gimmick, a 'get-out-of-jail-free' card that aims to address and resolve the fannish commitment to 'textual conservationism' (Hills 2002, 28). On the other hand, however, the ontological rules of the imaginary world expressly license the inclusion of multiple worlds, with The Dark Tower at the center, so the comics can be viewed as occupying a different (perhaps lower) level of the Tower, but, perhaps most importantly, legitimately part of the (stratified) hyperdiegesis. Discursively evoking the multiverse in such a manner aims to envelop compossible and non-compossible texts into a *trans-compossible* structure, thus serving those who read for hyperdiegesis. Whether or not fans embrace these rulings as legitimate is another question entirely and beyond the scope of this chapter. In any case, the point here is not specifically about defending ontological rules, but about the way in which King and Furth discursively engage with readers to convert discontinuity into contiguous hyperdiegetic framings.

That said, such strategies are not developed in imaginary world co-ordinates, but, instead, via what Jason Mittell describes as 'orienting paratexts,' which reside:

> outside the [hyper]diegetic storyworld, providing a perspective for viewers [and readers] to help make sense of a narrative world by looking at it from a distance – although as with all such categorical distinctions, actual practices often muddy such neat dichotomies. Orientation is not necessary to discover the canonical truth of a storyworld but rather it is used to help figure out how the pieces fit together or to prose alternative ways of seeing the story that might not be suggested or by or contained within the original narrative design.
>
> (2015, 261–262)

From this perspective, worldbuilding occurs not only in the textual world, the dominion of narrative, but also in paratexts, through the delivery of exposition and explication. Viewing these elements as somehow 'outside of the world' is problematic, however: '[a]nalyzing worldbuilding narratives is nearly impossible without acknowledging that one of their major constituents is the proliferation of various appendices, additions, expansions, supplements or paratexts' (Krzysztof 2015, 87). As Jonathan Gray argues, *the text* 'is a larger unit than any film or show [or comic, novel, etc.] that may be part of it; *it is the entire storyworld as we know it*' (2010, 7, my italics). Paratextual framings are thus integral components of worldbuilding, actively forming part of 'the text' rather than reduced to 'a body of extra-diegetic supplementary commentary' (Csicsery-Ronay, Jr. 2012, 502). Just as the Tower contains an infinite number of levels, each level comprising an infinity of universes, as a narrative component of the text-world, so, too, does the Tower function on a meta-textual level, drawing attention to its own construction. Taking this into account, then, The Dark Tower comics can be viewed as a kind of *reflexive transmedia storytelling*, whereby the multiverse concept is invoked paratextually to reflect upon, account for, and resolve, the hyperdiegetic tension between compossible and non-compossible texts.

Consider, also, the film 'adaptation,' *The Dark Tower*. Released in 2017, after over a decade in 'development hell,' the film takes significant liberties with the source text(s), setting the ground for fidelity complaints from Tower junkies. Indeed, *The Dark Tower* film is in no way a reductive 'diegetic equivalent' of *The Gunslinger* but, instead, transposes and translates elements from across the mythos, selecting and re-appropriating from various books in the series. Remembering that Jake Chambers was murdered in Keystone Earth, his death opening the doorway to Mid-World, and being sacrificed by Roland as he feverishly pursues the Man in Black across the Mohaine desert, it is noteworthy that neither event occurs in the film. In the lead up to the film's theatrical release, promotional paratexts explicitly marshalled *The Dark Tower* film not as adaptation but as a sequel. By taking Roland's end-point in the novels as a starting point (his continuous looping through time), the film represents the beginning of his quest as a new turn of the cycle, a fact supported within the text as the Man in Black says, 'once more around the wheel, old friend (thus also showing that he is aware of Roland's destiny). 'It is, in fact, a continuation,' claims director Nikolaj Arcel, before name-dropping King and (re)activating authorship discourse. 'It is a canonical continuation. That's exactly what we intended and what Stephen King signed off on' (quoted in Lussier 2017).

Incidentally, Roland's loop is enforced by lack; that is, according to Furth, Roland requires the Horn of Eld, a novum that he left on the battlefield of Jericho Hill, to enable him to break the curse upon reaching the Tower. Until Roland is in possession of the Horn, his 'journey must endlessly repeat' (Furth 2012, 468). So it is that King himself tweeted an image of the horn with the words 'last time around' attached, describing the film as potentially Roland's final spin of the wheel. Indeed, our first sight of Roland in *The Dark Tower* film shows that he is clearly in possession of the Horn of Eld.

Despite the film failing to set box offices alight – although, according to Box Office Mojo, it has collected $111 million against a budget of $60 million, hardly an out-and-out failure – plans are in the works for the development of a television series based on the prequel elements in *Wizard and Glass*, illustrating that Jenkins' transmedia storytelling model may be in the series' future, although only time will tell how this will turn out. As a sequel, the film also constructs several transfictional/transmedial bridges that lead back toward King's non-series work, including *IT*, *The Shining* and *Cujo*. This neatly brings us full circle.

Conclusion: Trans-Worldbuilding?

As a case study in worldbuilding, then, the Stephen King Multiverse shows that (fetishized) transmedia storytelling is but one element in a complex chain of trans-associations. Saint-Gelais' concept of transfictionality shares common principles with transmediality, most notably those crossings and incorporations that occur intra-medially before spinning off into transmedial, and transauthorial, locations. Viewing 'true' transmedia storytelling as *the* dominant factor in imaginary world architecture needs re-adjusting to account for the variable ways that such worlds are constructed, whether diachronically or otherwise. As has been shown, worldbuilding can sometimes be quite messy and knotted, *contra* utopian transmedia storytelling. This chapter, however, has only scratched the surface of King's multiverse. I have not yet touched on the 'trans-temporal' (Freeman 2015) attributes of the world, nor have I engaged with King's oeuvre as *trans-generic* (which is not the same as generic hybridity although that is certainly a factor). King may be best known for horror fiction, but works such as *Dolores Claibourne* (1992), *Gerald's Game* (1992) and *Different Seasons* (1982),[10] to name a select few, obscure the author's bibliography and compartmentalize it into neat and tidy genre-boxes. Whether or not King eventually returns to Roland's world as promised, perhaps filling in gaps between instalments or spinning off into other co-ordinates, the world of The Dark Tower continues to be adapted and augmented in comics, film, on Kindle (The Dark Tower novella, *UR*), and an online alternate reality game, *Discordia*, which introduces new character, Arina Yokova, who upon learning about Roland's loop sets out to break him free. Yet despite these many instantiations, Roland's journey may only be at the beginning. As King constantly reminds us, destiny – or Ka, in the vernacular of Mid-World – is but a wheel. One thing, however, remains the same in all iterations hitherto:

'The man in black fled across the desert, and the gunslinger followed.'

Notes

1 Perhaps the most famous example of PWYW was Radiohead's *In Rainbows*, although King pipped them to the post by almost a decade.
2 Author/industry contracts of this kind usually include licensing rights to produce sequels.
3 Adaptations of Shakespeare plays and texts based on Frankenstein and Sherlock Holmes, for instance, far exceed adaptations based on King's work in terms if quantity.
4 The concept of the 'shared universe' is commonplace in comic books, pulp fiction and science fiction worlds (see Scolari, Bertetti and Freeman, 2014).
5 Although *Needful Things* concludes with the demise of Castle Rock and was promoted as the final novel to be set there, King has at various times returned to the small town. In 2017, it was announced that J.J. Abrams and Stephen King would be collaborating on an anthology series featuring many of King's popular characters called *Castle Rock*, which will be available on streaming platform, Hulu, sometime in 2018.
6 In chronological order, the Tower novels are as follows: *The Gunslinger* (1982, 2003); *The Drawing of the Three* (1987); *The Wastelands* (1991); *Wizard and Glass* (1997); *The Wind Through the Keyhole* (2012); *Wolves of the Calla* (2003); *Song of Susannah* (2004); and *The Dark Tower* (2004).
7 Wolf describes an intraquel as 'a narrative sequence which fills in a narrative gap within an already-existing sequel element' (2012, 378).
8 This idea of a multiverse comprising layers is featured in Michael Moorcock's *The Sundered Worlds* (1961), the first book to use the term 'multiverse', which was coined by Moorcock himself (and not the quantum physicists) (for more on multiverses in popular culture, see Proctor 2017).
9 Thanks to Matt Hills both for suggesting the term, 'stratified hyperdiegesis,' and for discussing this idea in personal communication. I am grateful for Hills' permission to use the concept in this chapter.
10 *Different Seasons* is an anthology of novellas and includes 'Rita Hayworth and the Shawshank Redemption,' 'The Body' (filmed as *Stand by Me*) and 'Apt Pupil.'

Bibliography

Breznican, Anthony. "IT All Connects." *Entertainment Weekly: The Ultimate Guide to Stephen King* (2017): 16–17.

Browning, Mark. *Stephen King on the Big Screen*. Bristol: Intellect, 2009.

Browning, Mark. *Stephen King on the Small Screen*. Bristol: Intellect, 2011.

Csicsery-Ronay, Jr. Istvan. "Of Enigmas and Xenoencyclopedia." *Science Fiction Studies*, 39, 2012: 500–511

Dena, Christa. "Transmedia Adaptation: Revising the No Adaptation Rule." In *The Routledge Companion to Transmedia Studies*, edited by Matthew Freeman and Renira Rampazzo Gambarato. London and New York: Routledge, 2018.

Doležel, Lubomir. *Heterocosmica: Fiction and Possible Worlds*. Baltimore, MD: The John Hopkins University Press, 1998.

Eco, Umberto. *The Role of the Reader*. Bloomington, IN: Indiana University Press, 1984.

Freeman, Matthew. "'Who Knows About the Future? Perhaps Only the Dead': Configuring the Transtemporal Timespan of Planet of the Apes as a Transmedia Saga." In *Time Travel in Popular Media*, edited by Matthew Jones and Joan Ormrod, 165–179. Jefferson, NC: McFarlane, 2015.

Furth, Robin. *The Dark Tower: The Complete Concordance*. London: Hodder & Stoughton, 2012.

Furth, Robin. "Dear Fellow Constant Readers." In *The Dark Tower – The Gunslinger: The Man in Black* (Collected Edition). New York: Marvel Comics, 2013.

Genette, Gérard. *Palimpsests: Literature in the Second Degree*. Lincoln: University of Nebraska Press, 1997.

Gray, Jonathan. *Show Sold Separately: Promos, Spoilers and Other Media Paratexts*. New York: New York University Press, 2010.

Hills, Matt. *Fan Cultures*. London: Routledge, 2002.

Hills, Matt. "Traversing the 'Whoniverse': Doctor Who's Hyperdiegesis and Transmedia Discontinuity/Diachrony." In *Worldbuilding: Transmedia, Fans, Industry*, edited by Marta Boni, 343–361. Amsterdam, Netherlands: Amsterdam University Press, 2017.

Hoppenstand, Gary. *Stephen King (Critical Insights)*. Ipswich, MA: Salem Press, 2010.

Hutcheon, Linda. *A Theory of Adaptation*. London: Routledge, 2006.

Jenkins, Henry, and John Tulloch. *Science Fiction Audiences: Watching Doctor Who and Star Trek*. London: Routledge, 1995.

Jenkins, Henry. *Convergence Culture: Where Old and New Media Collide*. New York: New York University Press, 2006.

Jenkins, Henry. "Adaptation, Extension, Transmedia." *Literature/Film Quarterly* 45:2 (2017).

King, Stephen. *Salem's Lot*. New York: Doubleday, 1975.

King, Stephen. *The Shining*. New York: Doubleday, 1977.

King, Stephen. "Jerusalem's Lot." In *Night Shift*, by Stephen King. New York: Doubleday, 1978.

King, Stephen. *The Dead Zone*. New York: Viking Press, 1979.

King, Stephen. *Cujo*. New York: Viking Press, 1981.

King, Stephen. *The Dark Tower Volume One: The Gunslinger.* London: Sphere Books, 1982.

King, Stephen. *Different Seasons.* New York: Viking, 1982.

King, Stephen. *Pet Sematary.* New York: Doubleday, 1983.

King, Stephen. *IT.* London: Hodder and Stoughton, 1986.

King, Stephen. *The Dark Tower Volume Two: The Drawing of the Three.* London: Hodder & Stoughton, 1987.

King, Stephen. *The Dark Half.* New York: Viking Press, 1989.

King, Stephen. *Needful Things.* New York: Viking Press, 1991.

King, Stephen. *The Dark Tower Volume Three: The Wastelands.* London: Hodder & Stoughton, 1991.

King, Stephen. *Gerald's Game.* New York: Viking, 1992.

King, Stephen. *Dolores Claibourne.* New York: Viking, 1992.

King, Stephen. *The Dark Tower Volume Four: Wizard and Glass.* London: Sphere Books, 1997.

King, Stephen. *Hearts in Atlantis.* New York: Scribner, 1999.

King, Stephen. *Riding the Bullet.* New York: Simon and Schuster, 2000.

King, Stephen. *The Plant.* StephenKing.Com, 2000. http://stephenking.com/library/other_project/plant_zenith_rising_the.html.

King, Stephen. *Dreamcatcher.* New York: Scribner, 2001.

King, Stephen. *The Dark Tower Volume One: The Gunslinger* (Revised and Expanded Edition). London: Hodder and Stoughton, 2003.

King, Stephen. *The Dark Tower Volume Five: Wolves of the Calla.* London: Hodder and Stoughton, 2003.

King, Stephen. *The Dark Tower Volume Six: Song of Susannah.* London: Hodder and Stoughton, 2004.

King, Stephen. *The Dark Tower Volume Seven: The Dark Tower* (Revised and Expanded Edition). London: Hodder and Stoughton, 2004.

King, Stephen. *UR.* Amazon Kindle, 2009.

King, Stephen. "Foreword." In *The Dark Tower: The Complete Concordance,* edited by Robin Furth. London: Hodder & Stoughton, 2012.

King, Stephen, and Joe Hill. *In the Tall Grass.* Amazon Kindle. New York: Esquire (Magazine), 2012.

King, Stephen, and Stewart O'Nan. *A Face in the Crowd.* New York: Simon and Schuster Digital, 2012.

King, Stephen, and Peter Straub. *The Talisman.* New York: Viking, 1984.

King, Stephen, and Peter Straub. *Black House.* New York: Random House, 2001.

Krzysztof, Maj. M. "Transmedial World-Building in Fictional Narratives." *Image* 22 (2015): 83–96.

Lapointe, Julien. "'He Doesn't Look Like Sherlock Holmes': The Truth Value and Existential Status of Fictional Worlds and their Characters." In *Worldbuilding: Transmedia, Fans, Industry,* edited by Marta Boni, 62–76. Amsterdam, Netherlands: Amsterdam University Press, 2017.

Lussier, German. "Yes The Dark Tower Movie is a Sequel to the Books." *IO9* 19 June 2017. Accessed 21 August 2017. https://io9.gizmodo.com/yes-the-dark-tower-movie-is-a-sequel-to-the-books-1796235912

Magistrale, Tony. *Hollywood's Stephen King.* New York: Palgrave Macmillan, 2003.

Magistrale, Tony. The Films of Stephen King: From Carrie to the Mist. Basingstoke: Palgrave Macmillan, 2008.

Magistrale, Tony. *Stephen King: America's Storyteller*. Santa Barbara, CA: Praeger, 2010.

McAlfeer, Patrick. *Inside The Dark Tower Series: Art, Evil and Intertextuality*. Jefferson, MO: McFarlane, 2009.

Mittell, Jason. *Complex TV: The Poetics of Contemporary Television Storytelling*. New York: New York University Press, 2015.

Parkin, Lance. "Canonicity Matters: Defining the Doctor Who Canon." In *Time and Relative Dimensions in Space: Critical Perspectives on Doctor Who*, edited by David Butler, 246–259. Manchester: Manchester University Press, 2007.

Powers, Kevin. "SDCC News: Marvel Bringing Stephen King's N. to Your Phone." *Comics Bulletin* July 25, 2008. Accessed 21 July 2017. www.comics-bulletin.com/news/121699557028597.htm.

Proctor, William. "Schrodinger's Cape: The Quantum Seriality of the Marvel Multiverse." In *Make Ours Marvel: Media Convergence and A Comics Universe*, edited by Matt Yockey, 319–346. Austin: University of Texas Press, 2017.

Proctor, William, and Matthew Freeman. "'The First Step into a *Smaller* World: The Transmedia Economy of *Star Wars*." In *Revisiting Imaginary Worlds*, edited by Mark J.P. Wolf, 221–243. London and New York: Routledge, 2017.

Ryan, Marie-Laure. "The Modes of Narrativity and Their Visual Metaphors." *Style* 26:3 (1992): 368–387.

Ryan, Marie-Laure. "Ontological Rules". In *The Routledge Companion to Imaginary Worlds*, edited by Mark J.P. Wolf, 74–81. London: Routledge, 2017.

Saint-Gelais, Richard. *L'Empire du pseudo: Modernité de la science-fiction*. Quebec: Nota Bene, 1999.

Saint-Gelais, Richard. "Transfictionality." In *The Routledge Encyclopedia of Narrative Theory*, edited by David Herman, 612–613. London and New York: Routledge, 2005.

Saint-Gelais, Richard. *Fictions Transfuges: Transfictionnalité et ses enjeux*. Paris: Seuil, 2011.

Scolari, Carlos, Paolo Bertetti, and Matthew Freeman. *Transmedia Archaeology: Storytelling in the Borderlines of Science Fiction, Comics and Pulp Magazines*. Basingstoke: Palgrave Pivot, 2014.

Stam, Robert, and Alessandra Raengo. *Literature and Film*. Oxford: Blackwell Publishing, 2005.

Vincent, Bev. *The Dark Tower Companion*. New York: New American Library, 2013.

Wells-Lassagne, Shannon. *Television and Serial Adaptation*. London: Routledge, 2017.

Wiater, Stanley, Christopher Golden, and Hank Wagner. *The Stephen King Universe*. Los Angeles, CA: Renaissance Books, 2003.

Wolf, Mark J.P. *Building Imaginary Worlds: The History and Theory of Subcreation*. London and New York: Routledge, 2012.

Wood, Rocky. *Stephen King: A Literary Companion*. Jefferson, NC: McFarland, 2011.

7   Canada

Transmediality as News Media and Religious Radicalization

Marie-Ève Carignan and
Sara Marcil-Morin

Between 2014 and 2017 there have been numerous attacks, claimed by terrorist groups, on key social symbols that altogether raise a number of questions about the role and responsibility of the mainstream media in covering violent radicalization and terrorism. As a phenomenon closely bound up with the expansion of the internet and social media in conjunction with the emergence of multiplatform communication, transmediality has strongly influenced both the course and the coverage of recent attacks. Indeed, the influence of the internet and social media is undeniable today, be it in terms of the creation of websites and social media accounts used by terrorist groups to recruit new followers, the reproduction in traditional media contexts of information and videos published on web-based platforms (Niemeyer 2016) or the direct influence such platforms have on the course of events. Examples include the 'safety check' Facebook application allowing users to tell their friends they are safe, the 'open door' hashtag created on Twitter to assist those seeking refuge during the Paris bombings and the posting of eyewitness photos and videos documenting the words and deeds of attack perpetrators or law enforcement (a situation that, during the October 2014 attacks on Canada's Parliament Hill, led Ottawa police to ask citizens to refrain from sharing such information for the sake of general safety) (Ottawa Police Services 2014).

Combined with the substantial number of attacks in recent history, this new context in Canada is pushing the mainstream media to award an enormous amount of coverage to such events with a focus on the perpetrators of the attacks and on the phenomenon of radicalization leading to violence – a term that appears to be gaining prominence in the lexicon of the Quebec media. In this chapter, we aim more specifically to shed new light on the Quebec media's representation of radicalization leading to violence and the violent attacks that took place in Quebec in 2014, with a view to elucidating their role in the public's understanding of these phenomena and to assessing the role of transmediality in their coverage. In the following pages, we will outline how perceptions of terrorism and radicalization are developed in a society of mediatized risk, as well as the potential impact that journalistic practices can have on public understandings of related phenomena. We will then present the findings of two complementary studies, namely an analysis of the way that radicalization leading to violence is represented in the main daily newspapers of Quebec followed by a case analysis of the province's media coverage of the 2014 attacks in Saint-Jean-sur-Richelieu and in Ottawa, in order to revisit the social responsibility of the media in covering such topics and the transmediality of the news.

Terrorism and Radicalization Leading to Violence

Since 2014, the phenomenon of radicalization has been growing and giving rise to misunderstandings across the international community, which tends to rapidly link radicalization to violence. Nevertheless, it is important to distinguish between non-violent radicalization, radicalization leading to violence, and terrorism. Bélanger et al. (2015) set forth specific criteria by which to define non-violent radicalization, which they describe as the 'process whereby a person is initiated to an ideological message and encouraged to replace his moderate beliefs with extreme opinions. In this regard, radicalization means adopting beliefs that most people do not' (Bélanger et al. 2015). Hence, '[s]ometimes people who are firmly entrenched in their own beliefs may adopt positions that while radical may not necessarily be opposed to democratic norms and values: Such radicalization would not be considered violent' (Center for the Prevention of Radicalization Leading to Violence (CPRLV) 2017).

Radicalization leading to violence, meanwhile, itself a phenomenon that we are particularly interested in given its extensive media coverage across channels, is defined by the CPRLV as a characteristic of 'people [who] adopt extremist belief systems – including the willingness to use, encourage or facilitate violence – with the aim of promoting an ideology, political project or cause as a means of social transformation' (2017). It is this type of radicalization that we have found to be predominant in the coverage of the Quebec media. But it is also important to decouple radicalization leading to violence, on the one hand, and terrorism, on the other, even if the two terms are related. Terrorism has no widely agreed-upon definition in the international community, given that it is 'a fragmented reality whose diverse manifestations make it elusive to categorize and lead to repeated revisions' (Brodeur and Leman-Langlois 2009, 37). Of course the term 'terrorism' has a strong negative connotation in that it 'constitutes a means to an end. As such, its nature varies considerably depending on the case at hand. Only the general and purely utilitarian principle, and a few modus operandi, tend toward a single, unified representation of the phenomenon' (Larousse 2015). Thus many researchers have urged caution in using the term. In spite of this lack of consensus, a legislative definition of terrorism can be found in section 83.01 of the Criminal Code of Canada, which defines terrorist activity as an act committed 'in whole or in part for a political, religious or ideological purpose, objective or cause' (Criminal Code of Canada 1985).

Beyond this legislative definition of the concept, though, several researchers (Brodeur and Leman-Langlois 2009; Campana and Hervouet 2013; Garcin-Marrou 2007) have also suggested alternative versions of terrorism. This chapter will particularly draw upon the concept of media-oriented terrorism developed by Nacos, in which 'terrorists seek to spread fear in the population and provoke governments into reacting in order to give voice to their espoused cause, which is not usually covered by the media and politicians' (Nacos 2005, 36). In the context of terrorist attacks, it would be suggested that terrorism also seeks to use the news media as a megaphone to massively broadcast their message of hate, to make claims, or to help recruit new followers (see Nacos 2005).

The Quebec Context: Recent Cases of Radicalization and Departures for Jihad

Since the rise of the Islamic State (IS)[1] in 2014, radicalization associated with violent Islamism has been an ongoing news topic around the world. In Quebec, the first events related to Islamic radicalization leading to terrorism were witnessed in attacks in the fall of 2014. Aside from lone-radical situations such as these, other cases of radicalization involving coordinated groups have also been found out in the province. In 2015, the Quebec population and political sphere were shocked to learn that six students from the Collège de Maisonneuve in Montreal had set off to wage Jihad and others were apprehended in their attempt to do so as well. To help the public and various government agencies address this growing phenomenon, a number of projects and initiatives have been set up in Quebec in recent years as the Observatory on Radicalization and Violent Extremism (OSR) and the CPRLV in Montreal. The CPRLV is the first North American non-profit organization aimed at preventing phenomena associated with, and assisting individuals affected by, radicalization leading to violence (CPRLV 2017).

The Quebec Context: The 2014 Attacks in Canada

Related events of 2014 sparked awareness and a certain degree of fear in the Quebec population regarding radicalization leading to violence. These events began on October 20, 2014 at a parking lot in Saint-Jean-sur-Richelieu, in the province of Quebec when Martin 'Amad' Couture-Rouleau, a 'follower of radical Isla' (Canadian Broadcasting Corporation December 9, 2014), rammed his car into two members of the Canadian Army, killing one and injuring the other before being shot dead by police. An active social networker who had been posting 'Jihadist propaganda for months' (La Presse October 20, 2014), Couture-Rouleau was known to both provincial and federal authorities. Two days later, on October 22, 2014, two shootings took place on Parliament Hill in Ottawa, Ontario. Michael Zehaf-Bibeau, also known to police authorities and described as a 'disillusioned individual with extremist beliefs' (Canadian Broadcasting Corporation October 23, 2014), fired shots in front of the Cenotaph and at Parliament Hill, killing Corporal Nathan Cirillo, before being fatally shot by the head of Parliament Hill security.

These two closely spaced attacks attracted considerable international media attention. The Ottawa attack was swiftly described by various media and political analysts as a terrorist act, and largely attributed to IS activities. A combination of the live coverage of the event, the parallel drawn with the prior attack in Saint-Jean-sur-Richelieu, as well as the way that the traditional media relayed social media content including postings by the perpetrator himself, and the live broadcasting of an emotional speech to the nation by then-Canadian Prime Minister Stephen Harper, which strongly emphasized standing up to terrorism, altogether raise questions about the coverage of the events. Indeed, this case is worth scrutinizing in order to observe whether the media acted responsibly in this instance, and to examine how transmediality may have shaped the coverage of the events.

The Perception of Terrorism and Radicalization in a Society of Mediatized Risk

With regard to the first question, Giddens (2000, 2005), Beck (2001) and Peretti-Watel (2001) all describe contemporary society as a risk society in which technological and industrial developments bring us face-to-face with new kinds of dangers that are man-made, uncontrollable and geographically unrestrained. Such a society typically confronts four major risks: ecological disaster, the collapse of economic growth mechanisms, the growth of totalitarian power and large-scale warfare (Giddens 2000). The fear that these risks will materialize creates a 'culture of risk' that nurtures dread of 'terrorist' conflicts, attacks and other acts, and serves as an important economic argument (such as for sales of insurance, medicine and arms, etc.), in addition to changing the forms of the social bond (Beck 2001).

According to the Centers for Disease Control and Prevention (CDC 2012), the likelihood of these risks materializing – particularly those linked to terrorist threats – is constantly on the rise as terrorists find effective ways to respond to counter-terrorism. Indeed, terrorists are able to leverage technological skills and strategically select vulnerable targets or cause multiple simultaneous attacks aimed at injuring or killing many people, thus attracting media attention owing to the magnitude of the events. The effectiveness of risk communication – that is, the ability to inform the public about the type, magnitude and probability of an outcome resulting from a behavior or exposure (CDC 2012) – is greatly limited by the media practice of reporting concrete and visible events, hence the interest for terrorists to cause large-scale events that will attract substantial media attention. The media thus strive to report situations that are perceptible to the public, and that meet the criteria for being 'newsworthy'. This is why we suggest that 'radicalization leading to violence' and related terms have become more commonly used by the Quebec media – not because of the magnitude of the phenomenon per se, but rather as a result of the spectacular events of fall 2014, as the first part of our research will confirm. Raboy notes that, in fact, the media must wait 'for a scenario to be provoked by a spectacular event' (1993, 102) before being in a position to investigate the underlying social problems, which are in turn further constrained by available space or airtime and by a media structure that limits their ability to 'contextualize societal information and explain its meaning' (Raboy 1993, 84, based on Carey 1986; Miège 1986; Tuchman 1978).

At the same time, risk perception tends to be affected by the mediatization of risks, namely because of the sheer extent of disaster coverage and the internationalization of news. This internationalization is made possible by new technologies, which bring the news closer to the public and creates the perception that even very distant risks are looming directly before them (Boutté 2006). In this context, studies of risk perception (Fischhoff et al. 1978) indicate that the public overestimates 'imaginary risks' and the frequency of spectacular and highly publicized events (attacks, murders, suicides, etc.), even if they are in fact relatively infrequent, and underestimates the least publicized natural risks (such as diseases and accidents), which are the most frequent. The media coverage of a given subject thus plays a key role in the risk perception of individuals, who are likely to size up events by comparing them to prior, highly publicized ones (Boutté 2006).

The Impact of Transmedia Storytelling on Coverage of Attacks and Radicalization

Although the concept of transmediality is often used in reference to fictional universes related to culture or entertainment, transmediality also applies to a media context where 'it is used to describe the multimedium strategies deployed' (Schmitt 2015, 23), such as those outlined previously in this chapter. These transmedia strategies, which are used across a wide range of new media platforms in addition to traditional media outlets, make it possible to reach larger audiences, but also to take advantage of tremendous flexibility in terms of the types of news selected and the time of its publication. Technological advances are creating a context conducive to the development of transmediality in the global news industry, and as such, the application of transmediality to the journalistic context has already been the subject of numerous studies (see Alzamora and Tárcia 2012; Canavilhas 2014; Gambarato and Tárcia 2016; Moloney 2011; Renó 2014).

Further to these studies, a variety of professional transmedia practices are shaping the media representation of armed attacks and of radicalization leading to violence in the Quebec media. Indeed, the multitasking of journalists, which is necessary to meet the complementary demands of multiplatform media, is changing professional practices as well as the news content processed. As electronic media continue to develop, dailies – with their smartphone and tablet apps and the online versions of their publications – are becoming instantaneous forms of media, thereby marking a departure from their traditional focus on analysis and reflection. This change in vocation is sure to impact the nature of their coverage, as has been shown already, with the media hardly dwelling on a need to define or explain the phenomenon of radicalization leading to violence.

Moreover, it is also important to highlight the impact of transmediality on media-oriented terrorism, in which terrorists provoke violent events in order to utilize the media as megaphones to make their messages heard (Nacos 2005). This synergy of different media platforms is now enabling these groups to refine their communication strategies and to use a diversity of platforms to broadcast more complex messages (Preston 2011). In particular, terrorist groups are using social media to recruit new followers, to circulate their messages, to claim attacks and to disseminate videos. As Monaci demonstrated, IS accumulates considerable online presence and produces high-quality magazines, such as *Dabiq*, which draws on synergies among various media and applies a comprehensive transmedia propaganda strategy to reach targets in Western countries, 'particularly the so-called foreign fighters' (Monaci 2017). The traditional media in Canada will sometimes relay this kind of transmedia content, as was the case for the October 2014 attacks, thus altogether raising questions in the academic community about where the public interest ends and public curiosity begins (thereby playing into the hands of the armed groups).

Methodology

In order to analyze the media representation of radicalization leading to violence, and also to take stock of its evolution over time and the transmedial link traced with other media, our methodology is based on a thematic content analysis of a corpus of articles published in the Quebec written press in 2014 and 2015. In conducting this analysis, we selected the two French-language Quebec dailies most widely read in the province, namely *La Presse* and the *Journal de Montréal* (Centre d'études sur les médias 2015).[2] Studying the *Journal de Montréal* seems particularly relevant to our research aims considering the way that the newspaper belongs to the conglomerate Quebecor, a corporation that is often accused of focusing on concentration of ownership, convergence of content, journalistic convergence within each of its channels and infotainment (Carbasse 2010), where the border between information and entertainment is difficult to trace. Given that Freeman (2016) states that infotainment is the concrete manifestation of transmediality for nonfictional content and that several critics believe that the Quebecor model affects journalistic practices at Gesca (owner of *La Presse*), this element is fundamental to our study. To deepen the idea that information flows from one media to another in these two conglomerates, we looked at the number of references to other media per article in our corpus. For the *Journal de Montréal*, only two references (to *Radio-France International* and an article by a fellow journalist) were found. As for *La Presse*, no mention of other media was noted. Although surprising, these results can be explained by the fact that the content analyzed in the newspapers will therefore affect the different platforms of the two media groups. In doing so, the newspapers can be understood as the transmedia 'tent pole' of the Quebecor and Gesca media groups, since they both produce the main information content that 'supports a number of other different media related experiences' (Davidson 2010, cited in Monaci 2017). In that sense, the representation of radicalization on both sets of newspapers will work to orient the representation of the phenomenon in and across all related media platforms.

In putting together our corpus, we obtained articles from *La Presse* by querying the Eureka.CC[3] database with the keyword 'radicalization'. For the year 2014, we identified 52 articles, and for the year 2015, 149 articles. To obtain articles from the *Journal de Montréal*, we conducted research using a monthly subscription to the electronic version of the newspaper. When also using the keyword 'radicalization', we identified 49 articles for 2014 and 165 articles for 2015. We then developed the corpus using a multi-stage sampling method. First, we rejected the articles in which the keyword 'radicalization' was used in a context other than politico-religious radicalization, which can be defined as a 'form of radicalization associated with a political interpretation of religion and the defence by violent means of a religious identity perceived to be under attack' (CPRLV 2017). Next, we rejected articles from news agencies in order to retain only those by journalists from the selected newspapers. Finally, we eliminated articles under 200 words in length in order to ensure sufficient content for analysis. We then conducted systematic random sampling based on the total number of articles. To obtain a significant number of articles for the year 2014, we used a sampling ratio of one out of every two articles. For the year 2015, we performed one-in-three sampling. In total, the analyzed corpus consisted of a sample of ninety-six articles.

Finally, an analytical grid was developed to collect several types of data. It includes variables to facilitate the identification of articles, such as month and year of publication, article type and author name. It also contains variables related to the vocabulary used, the metaphors for the phenomenon of radicalization and adjectives used to describe radicalized individuals. More specifically regarding the representation of radicalization leading to violence, we based ourselves on a list of subjects that was drawn up subsequently based on a first reading of the articles in order to code the principal, secondary and tertiary ideas addressed by the author. Regarding radicalized individuals, we coded different criteria that was set out by the CPRLV (2017), namely vulnerability factor, motive and participation level. Lastly, in terms of variables for identifying radicalized individuals, we coded sex, age group and background. The data were collected, and reports generated using the SPSS statistical analysis package.

Based on our research observations of Quebec dailies' representation of radicalization leading to violence, and given that the events of 2014 seem to have played a key role in this representation, the next phase of analysis was to take a particular interest in the attacks that had occurred in Canada in October 2014. Based on this case study, we sought to verify the Quebec media's compliance with the ethical principles recognized by the journalistic profession when covering such events, and to assess the impact of transmedia practices on journalistic choices that were made. This second phase of the research consisted of gathering printed copies of the Quebec newspapers *Le Devoir, La Presse, The Gazette, Le Soleil, Le Nouvelliste, La Tribune, La Voix de l'Est* and *Le Droit* published between the dates of 20 October 2014 and 27 October 2014. In addition to sourcing these newspapers, we also included materials from an online press review covering the websites of *Radio-Canada, TVA Nouvelles,* the *Journal de Montréal* and the *Journal de Québec.* The aim was to determine whether any potential breaches might be observed and any ethical questions raised in relation to the professional practices used to cover these events, and in turn whether a link can be observed in the use of different media to cover the subject. We used the SPSS statistical data processing package to analyze the corpus with a coding grid developed from previous research (Carignan 2018).

Findings

Since 2014, media coverage of radicalization has increased significantly in Quebec, as the preliminary results of our content analysis demonstrate. The results will be presented in three sections: first, the definition of radicalization in the context of the Quebec written press; second, the main issues addressed in relation to this phenomenon; and third, the portrait of the radicalized individuals.

With regard to the first point, our analysis uncovers an interesting element in terms of how radicalization is described, and which tends to support our hypothesis that this phenomenon has entered the media language but is scarcely explained in spite of its complexity. For example, out of the ninety-six articles analyzed, only three contain a partial or complete definition of the term. While it is true that a definition couched in scholarly language may be difficult to include in a journalistic article with a limited number of words, any definition, even a simplified one, can be helpful in order to increase public understanding of a recent complex social phenomenon. We also observed the journalistic practice of relying on metaphors to illustrate radicalization-related events. Our sample included expressions such as 'it's like cancer, you think it only happens to other people', 'a cancer with no immediate cure', 'young people haven't breathed in the bacteria of radicalization', 'our country is not immune to contagion' and 'perceived as a cure, this cobbled-together Islam becomes their oxygen'.

Although these kinds of metaphors enable the public to grasp the seriousness of cases of radicalization, they provide no real insight into the global context and complexity of the issues in play. The term 'radicalization' is nevertheless widely used across the whole of Quebec media, which might suggest that it has been thoroughly assimilated by the public. Ultimately, though, this lack of a clear definition, in conjunction with the use of generalized metaphors, may impact public understanding and hinder critical reflection on the issue at hand. It would also be worthwhile to measure the public's understanding of radicalization using additional instruments, and to observe how social media contributes to related representations. An adequate definition of the phenomenon seems fundamental to the public's understanding of it and in turn to preventing radicalization leading to violence, especially since this phenomenon is subject to widespread media coverage and the fact that terrorist groups use both social and mainstream media channels to attract sympathizers (Linera Rivera 2016) as part of a synergetic, multimedia strategy.

In the context of our research project, we drew up a list of eight main topics that are likely to be found in media coverage of violent and non-violent radicalization. In total, twenty-four of the ninety-six analyzed articles dealt primarily with 'policy and legislation'. Meanwhile, twenty articles had the 'phenomenon of radicalization' as their main topic, fifteen articles centered around 'terrorism and attacks', eleven on 'violent radicalization', ten on 'security', seven on 'religion', five on 'other' issues, two on the 'motives of radicalized individuals' and two articles focused on questions of 'prevention and research'.

It is not surprising to note the strong presence of the topic of 'politics and legislation', given that radicalization is a highly politicized issue in Canada. More specifically, in the articles published following the attacks in Saint-Jean-sur-Richelieu and in Ottawa, we found numerous references to the shortcomings of the Canadian legislative system. The legislative response of Parliament was to pass Bill C-51, the Anti-Terrorism Act which granted greater powers to security forces. The third most frequently addressed topic, 'terrorism and attacks', confirms that coverage of radicalization and terrorism is closely linked to major news events. This is consistent with Hénin's statement that, 'With each criminal outburst, our media engage in a frenzy that fulfills the wish of the IS to impose itself on our agenda' (Hénin 2015, 229). Another analyzed element reveals that twenty-two of the ninety-six analyzed articles dealt with a 'terrorist' attack of some kind. Altogether this allows us to conclude that the media coverage of radicalization is by and large linked to terrorism.

Furthermore, our results provide a portrait of the media representation of radicalized individuals based on vulnerability factors for radicalization, motives, levels of engagement and various adjectives attributed to these individuals. It is interesting to note that the vulnerability factors for radicalization identified by the CPRLV (2017) are relational, personal, social identity-related, psychological and external. In our analysis, fifty-one articles mention vulnerability factors for radicalization. Proportionally speaking, 45% (23 articles) attribute radicalization to relational factors, mainly illustrated by mosque attendance, links with Imams known for their radical discourse, and ties with radicalizing agents in college settings. This is all the more paradoxical given the frequent mention of the 'lone wolf' concept especially in connection with the events of autumn 2014 and the fact that lone wolves are frequently associated with online self-radicalization, a factor referred to in only 14% (seven) of the articles. Only one article mentions all of the above vulnerability factors, which was itself written by a researcher and thus may explain its exhaustiveness.

Regarding the motives of radicalized individuals, we analyzed the press articles according to four types of potential motives, all set forth by the CPRLV. These four motives are altruism and solidarity, heroism, thrill-seeking, and rebellion and revenge. In all, twenty-two of the analyzed articles address the motives of radicals. Of these articles, half give rebellion and revenge as motives. These articles exhibit harsh discourse, such as statements like '[radicalized individuals] are fed on religious fundamentalism and hatred of the West' (Journal de Montréal 2014). As for the other data generated by this variable, 32% (seven) of the articles point to heroism as a motive and in 18% (four) articles, altruism and solidarity is key. It is surprising to note, however, that none of the analyzed articles cite thrill-seeking as a motive for radicalization. This particular motive is raised in many writings that discuss the radicalization of young people in Quebec, who nevertheless 'know and understand little of the ideology for which they are fighting' (Bélanger 2015 quoted by

Bourdon, 2015). Hence, 'the strength of the Islamic State resides in its ability to convince lost young people that "jihad is cool"' (Hénin 2015, 218) and join them via social media in a variety of ways, including creating sensational games.

We also analyzed the level of radical engagement exhibited by the individuals mentioned in the articles. This engagement was measured by active support, participation and self-sacrifice (CPRLV 2017). Sixty-two articles made reference to radicalized individuals' levels of engagement. Of this number, 52% (32 articles) attributed their engagement to participation, while 47% (29) to self-sacrifice, and just 1 article to active support. Once again, these data indicate that radicalization garners greater coverage on the occasion of major events, which also confirms Raboy's suggestion that a major event must occur before a given social issue is addressed. This coverage of major events may encourage the media to seek out 'spectacle and... raw emotion' (Tourangeau, quoted by the Canadian Broadcasting Corporation 2015), making it poorly suited to explaining complex phenomena such as radicalization, to providing context, or to analyzing issues in depth. Another element that tends to corroborate this emphasis on event-based coverage is that only two of the ninety-six analyzed articles have prevention and research as their main topic.

The results of this content analysis – which tend to demonstrate Quebec newspapers' partiality to spectacular events, in turn raising challenges for addressing social issues and risks as well as producing only partial coverage of radicalization leading to violence – prompted us to carry out a case analysis based on the Quebec media coverage of the 2014 attacks. The purpose of this second analysis, as an outgrowth of the first, is to observe the place given by the media to the perpetrators of these attacks, and to analyze the qualifiers that perpetrators are attributed, as well as possible instances of ethical misconduct, and the role of transmediality and the expansion of social networks in the coverage of these attacks. A number of media were fast to link the events in Saint-Jean-sur-Richelieu to those in Ottawa in light of their quick succession and certain similarities between the perpetrators – for example the fact that they had previously been radicalized and both attacked representatives of Canadian military institutions. This link may have increased public fear by suggesting the presence of terrorist acts by organized terrorist groups, thus further supporting the earlier-mentioned potential impact of media coverage on public perception of risks. Indeed, certain media displayed pictures of Zehaf-Bibeau and Couture-Rouleau side-by-side when illustrating the events, despite the fact that the Royal Canadian Mounted Police (RCMP)[4] subsequently stated that it had no information connecting the two attacks.

It is these kinds of connections and links between different media representations that allow us to discuss the transmediality of the image of the perpetrators and the overall importance of transmediality in terms of the news coverage of Canada. As mentioned earlier, the principle of media-oriented terrorism posits that terrorists use the media as sound boxes to make their messages heard (Nacos 2005). Using this media resonance, terrorists seek to spread fear in the population and provoke governments into reacting in order to give voice to their espoused cause. Nacos (2005), following on from Tsfati and Weimann (2002), consequently describes a terrorist act as an act of joined-up political communication. According to Nacos, terrorists hope that the media, confronted with spectacular acts of political violence, will broadcast the information surrounding the events, including the messages they have cleverly orchestrated, whether or not they choose to claim responsibility for the acts committed. This leads us to raise the question of media responsibility in covering attacks. It is thus legitimate to question whether the perpetrators of attacks seek to use the media to secure a measure of glory and to exploit them as a sound box for their messages. The methods used by the IS on the internet and social media indeed reflect such an approach. A number of researchers are now pointing to the potential dangers of giving too much space and importance to those responsible for violent events, and of spreading their propaganda (see Berthomet 2015; Brillon 2007; Carignan 2014; Hénin 2015), which would in turn glorify these groups and spur copycats to reproduce similar acts of violence. Along these same lines, the Sûreté du Québec[5] deemed that the dissemination of images or videos prepared by radicalized individuals could 'fuel terrorism' by 'turning the message bearers into stars', urged the media to 'search their conscience' after the December 2014 broadcast of a video featuring 'a Canadian Jihadist threatening Canada in the name of the armed group IS' (Canadian Broadcasting Corporation and The Canadian Press 8 December 2014).

In the case of the October 2014 attacks, then, once again those responsible for the events were accorded significant importance in and across the media. The country main media channels even visited the secondary school attended by Zehaf-Bibeau in Laval, Quebec, nearly twenty years prior to the events. Various media, including published images of the school, a yearbook portrait, class photos of Zehaf-Bideau and broadcast footage of a video released to the public by the Commissioner of the RCMP in March 2015 and shot by Zehaf-Bibeau in his car mere moments before the Ottawa attack, worked transmedially as a way of partly citing his motives for committing the violent acts.

The personal accounts of both Couture-Rouleau and Zehaf-Bibeau on various social media channels were also scrutinized by journalists. These accounts allowed the media to reproduce various images of the two men and to revisit the extremist messages they had published on their accounts, primarily as a means of converting new followers. Among other things, the media scrutinized the Twitter and Facebook pages of Couture-Rouleau, one of which he managed under the name Ahmad LeConverti and another, under the name of Ahmad Rouleau. Newspapers including the Montreal daily *La Presse* reported that Couture-Rouleau had attempted to leave Canada for Pakistan in July 2014 in order to join his 'best Facebook friend', a resident of Karachi, before being intercepted by police (Sioui 24 October 2014), and that before he was converted, he had long been a *bon vivant,* posting Facebook pictures in which he was seen sharing beer with friends around a pool. The media also reported conspiracy theories and statements associated with radical Islam found on Couture-Rouleau's accounts (Peritz, Thanh Ha and Perreaux 21 October 2014). Among other things, a screenshot of his Facebook account was widely circulated across other forms of print and broadcast the media. The image shows the last posts on the page, dated 17 October 2014, which displays two doors, one leading to hell and the other to paradise. Along very similar lines, pictures of an armed Zehaf-Bideau were spread on IS-affiliated Twitter accounts before being relayed by the traditional media. These media should likely be particularly cautious about the information they take from websites linked to terrorist groups and radicalized individuals, considering the fact that the 'Internet is playing a major role in all the phases of the radicalisation process from pre-radicalisation to operations' (Precht 2007, 58), and that terrorist organizations often now use journalist techniques to disseminate their propaganda on their media outlets, on social media, but also to reach mainstream media (Linera Rivera 2016).

As we have seen, then, these various social and online media publications largely informed the traditional media. It thus appears particularly important to address the question raised by the QPC ethics guide (2015, 2003) of whether the media may, even unwittingly, act as accomplices to those people or groups who wish to spread a message and complete it as a form of transmediality by using the media to relay images and statements across various platforms, not to mention the question of whether too much attention and interest is given to the perpetrators of such acts. Moreover, the fact that social media facilitates access to this type of content leads us to suggest that ethical guidelines specifically pertaining to journalists' use of information found on social media may help them better assess the relevance of related coverage. This case study confirms Chaouch's (2016) observation that the temporal and economic pressure that journalists face today actually benefits terrorists who can take advantage of the speed of treatment and the lack of retreat and analysis to impose images across multiple platforms that they themselves have staged. In this way, it can be claimed that terrorists seek to use the mass media in order to publicize their messages of hatred, their demands, to recruit new followers (Mannoni and Bonardi 2003; Cohen-Almagore 2005), or even to claim related attacks they have not commanded themselves by echoing their message across media.

Conclusion

As the CDC (2012) once mentioned, the growing presence of risk in society is leading to a significant rise in the number of critical events that are occurring, including terrorist attacks. The media are by their very nature impelled to cover such events, particularly the major and spectacular ones, leading them to pay close attention to armed and other attacks; in this last context, however, they have a limited ability to address the broader social issues at stake. As the findings of our study reveal, the Quebec media appear reluctant to explain certain phenomena, such as radicalization leading to violence. Yet although they only partially discuss the causes of radicalization and provide few explanations on the topic, they extensively cover the portraits of the radicalized individuals, especially when the individuals themselves comment on attacks or spectacular events. New forms of media are changing today's information sources and seem to be encouraging the media to grant even more attention to these individuals, thus at times catering to curiosity and raising questions about whether their coverage is, in fact, in the public interest. The picture sketched by newspapers of radicalization leading to violence in Canada does not seem to allow the public to understand the nuances of the phenomenon or to develop an informed opinion on the topic. This type of media coverage may lead to prejudice within society, an issue also raised by the January 2017 attack on a mosque in Quebec City that prompted the country to question its understanding of Islam and issues of radicalization. These recent events have given rise to numerous questions about the influence of social media – and especially the social media accounts managed by extremist right-wing groups – in the radicalization of individuals. They have also raised the issue of the media's potential responsibility in sparking prejudices within civil society, as displayed by Quebec City radio shows known for their confrontational style.

This first analysis of the treatment of radicalization leading to violence ultimately emphasizes the relevance of analyzing the coverage of radicalization by other Quebec media, and of undertaking comparative analyses in order to better observe distinctions between the coverage generated in different countries. Finally, our study strongly indicates that it would be worthwhile to further examine the impact of transmediality on the local public understanding of terrorism and radicalization leading to violence.

Notes

1 In this chapter, we will be designating the Islamic State terrorist organization by its original name ('Islamic State') given that it is the name appearing on the official list of terrorist entities established by Public Safety Canada (2016) and in official documents of the UN (De Pierrebourg and Larouche 2015).

The Quebec news media instead refer to it as the 'Islamic State group' or 'armed group Islamic State'.

2 The results presented in this chapter are drawn from an analysis of this corpus that will be supplemented with articles from the Montreal daily *Le Devoir*, which ranks as the third most-read newspaper in Quebec. The analysis will be made available in the Master's thesis of Marcil-Morin (2017) at the Université de Sherbrooke.

3 Eureka.CC is an 'On-line press information service', 'specially designed for public and academic libraries' (Eureka.CC website).

4 The RCMP is the Canadian national police service and comes under Public Safety Canada. On his website, the RCMP presents an 'Awareness guide – radicalization to violence' that includes 'cases of extreme radicalization in Canada and elsewhere in the world'. Among these cases include those of Michael Zehaf-Bibeau and Martin Couture-Rouleau.

5 The Sûreté du Québec is a 'national police force' that 'act[s] under the authority of the Minister of Public Security and [has] jurisdiction to enforce law throughout Québec' (SQ 2017).

Bibliography

Alzamora, Geane and Lorena Tárcia. "Convergence and Transmedia: Semantic Galaxies and Emerging Narratives in Journalism." *Brazilian Journalism Research* 8:1 (2012): 23–34.

Beck, Ulrich. *La société du risque : Sur la voie d'une autre modernité.* Paris: Flammarion, 2001.

Bélanger, J. J., N. Nociti, P. E. Chamberland, V. Paquette, D. Gagnon, A. Mahmoud, and C. Eising. "Bâtir une communauté résiliente dans un Canada multiculturel: trousse de renseignements sur l'extrémisme violent." Université du Québec à Montréal. 4 April 2015. Accessed 1 September 2017. http://fqde.qc.ca/wpcontent/uploads/2013/09/Trousse_Renseignements_Extremisme_Violent.pdf

Bernier, Marc-Francois. *Le cinquième pouvoir. La nouvelle imputabilité des médias envers leurs publics.* Québec: Presses de l'Université Laval, 2017.

Berthomet, Stephane. *La Fabrique du djihad: radicalisation et terrorisme au Canada.* Montréal: EDITO, 2015.

Boutté, Gilbert. *Risques et catastrophes : comment éviter et prévenir les crises?.* Paris: Éditions du papyrus, 2006.

Brillon, Phillipe. "Un peu de retenue S.V.P.". *La Presse,* 19 April 2007.

Brodeur, Jean-Paul and Stephane Leman-Langlois. *Terrorisme et antiterrorisme au Canada.* Montréal, QC: Presses de l'Université de Montréal, 2009.

Campana, Aurélie and Gerard Hervouet. *Terrorisme et insurrection: évolution des dynamiques conflictuelles et réponses des États.* Québec: Presses de l'Université du Québec, 2013.

Canavilhas, Joao. "Jornalismo transmídia: Um desafio ao velho ecossistema midiático [Transmedia Journalism: A challenge to old media ecosystem." In *Periodismo Transmedia: Miradas Múltiples* [Transmedia Journalism: Multiple Perspectives], edited by Carolina Eugenia Campalans Moncada, Denis Renó, Sandra Lucia Ruiz Moreno and Vicente Gosciola, 53–67. Barcelona: Editorial UOC, 2015.

Carbasse, Renaud. "Du solide et du concret: concentration de la propriété et convergence journalistique au sein du groupe Quebecor Média." *Canadian Journal of Communication* 35 (2010): 585–594.

Carey, James W. "The Dark Continent of American Journalism." In *Reading the News*, edited by Robert K. Manoff and Michael Schudson, 146–196. New York: Pantheon, 1986.

Carignan, Marie-Eve. "Analyse de la couverture médiatique des attaques survenues en octobre 2014 à Ottawa et à Saint-Jean-sur-Richelieu: quelles limites pour la responsabilité sociale de la presse?" *Sur le journalisme*, numéro thématique Journalisme, danger et risques, 2018.

Carignan, Marie-Eve. "La modification des pratiques journalistiques et du contenu des nouvelles télévisées, du quotidien à la situation de crise: analyse France/Québec." PhD diss., Université de Montréal et Sciences-po Aix-en-Provence, 2014.

"Centers for Disease Control and Prevention". *Crisis and Emergency Risk Communication* (2012). Accessed 21 April 2016. http://emergency.cdc.gov/cerc/resources/pdf/cerc_2012edition.pdf.

"Centre de prévention de la radicalisation menant à la violence." *Type de radicalisation*. 2016. Accessed 3 May 2016. https://info-radical.org/fr/radicalisation/definition/.

"Centre d'étude sur les médias". *Portrait de la presse quotidienne*. 2015. Accessed 4 June 2016. www.cem.ulaval.ca/publications.php

Chaouch, Maxime. "La représentation médiatique du terrorisme: Analyse de la construction médiatique de l'événement terroriste et approche des implications psychosociales." MA diss., Université de Caen Basse Normandie, 2016.

Cohen-Almagore, Raphael. "Media Coverage of Acts of Terrorism: Troubling Episode and Suggested Guidelines." *Canadian Journal of Communication* 30 (2005): 383–409.

"Conseil de presse du Québec." *Guide de déontologie journalistique du Conseil de presse du Québec.* n.d. Accessed 14 May 2017. http://conseildepresse.qc.ca/wp-content/uploads/2015/08/Guide-de-d%C3%A9ontologie-journalistique_CPQ.pdf

"Conseil de presse du Québec." Droits et responsabilités de la presse (3rd edition). 2003. Accessed 14 May 2017. http://conseildepresse.qc.ca/wp-content/uploads/2011/06/droits-responsabilites-de-la-presse_fr.pdf

Criminal Code of Canada. 1985. Accessed 12 May 2017. http://laws-lois.justice.gc.ca/eng/acts/C-46/.

De Pierrebourg, Fabrice and Vincent Larouche. *Djihad.ca*. Montréal, QC: La Presse, 2015.

Fengler, Susanne. "From Media Self-Regulation to 'Crowd-Criticism': Media Accountability in the Digital Age." *Central European Journal of Communication* 5:2 (2012): 175–189.

Fengler, Susane. "Media Journalism… and the Power of Blogging Citizens." In *Media Accountability Today… and Tomorrow: Updating the Concept in Theory and Practice*, edited by Torbjörn von Krogh, 61–67. Göteborg: Nordicom, 2008.

Fischhoff, Baruch, Paul Slovic, Sarah Lichtenstein and Barbara Combs. "How Safe Is Safe Enough? A Psychometric Study of Attitudes towards Technological Risks and Benefits." *Policy Sciences* 9:2 (1978): 127–152.

Freeman, Matthew. "Small Change-Big Difference: Tracking the Transmediality of Red Nose Day." *VIEW Journal of European Television History and Culture* 5:10 (2016): 87–96.

Gambarato, Renira Rampazzo and Lorena Tárcia. "Transmedia Strategies in Journalism: An Analytical Model for the Coverage of Planned Events". *Journalism Studies* (2016): doi: 10.1080/1461670X.2015.112 7769.

Garcin-Marrou, Isabelle. *Des violences et des médias*. Paris: L'Harmattan, 2007.

Giddens, Anthony. *Les conséquences de la modernité*. Paris: L'Harmattan, 2000.

Giddens, Anothony. *La constitution de la société : Éléments de la théorie de la structuration*. Paris: Presses Universitaires de France, 2005.

Hénin, Nicholas. *Jihad academy: Nos erreurs face à l'état islamique*. Paris: Fayard, 2015.

Jenkins, Henry. *Convergence Culture: Where Old and New Media Collide*. New York: New York University Press, 2006.

"Larousse Encyclopédie." Terrorisme Consulté. 15 April 2015. Accessed 6 May 2016. www.larousse.fr/encyclopedie/divers/terrorisme/96706.

La Haye, David. "Lebel garde un œil sur le débat sur la laïcité". *Journal de Montréal* 12:26 (2015): 14–28.

Le Monde et AFP. "Attentat à Ottawa: le tireur espérait partir pour la Syrie." *Le Monde*. 23 October 2014. Accessed 14 January 2017. www.lemonde. fr/ameriques/article/2014/10/23/le-canada-traumatise-apres-l-attaque-du-parlement-par-un-tireur-isole_4510844_3222.html.

Legault, Josee. "Fusillade d'Ottawa : réflexions de la mère de Zehaf-Bibeau". *Le Journal de Montréal*. 25 October 2014. Accessed 14 January 2017. www. journaldemontreal.com/2014/10/25/fusillade-dottawa-reflexions-de-la-mere-de-zehaf-bibeau.

Linera Rivera, Rafael. "Social Representation of Threat in Extended Media Ecology: Sochi 2014 Olympics, Jihadist Deeds, and Online Propaganda." PhD diss., Fielding Graduate University, 2016.

Mannoni, Pierre and Christine Bonardi. "Terrorisme et mass médias." *Topique* 2:83 (2003): 55–72.

Marquis, Maris. 2014. "Attentat de St-Jean: un acte terroriste?." *La Presse*. 21 October 2014. Acceeded 15 July 2017. www.lapresse.ca/actualites/dossiers/attentat-a-st-jean-sur-richelieu/201410/21/01-4811177-attentat-de-st-jean-un-acte-terroriste.php

Miège, Bernard. *Le JT : Mise en scène de l'actualité à la télévision*. Paris: La Documentation française, 1986.

Moloney, Kevin T. "Porting Transmedia Storytelling to Journalism." MA diss., University of Denver, 2011.

Monaci, Sara. "Explaining the Islamic State's Online Media Strategy: A Transmedia Approach." *International Journal of Communication* 11 (2017): 2842–2860.

Nacos, Brigitte L. *Les médias et le terrorisme*. Montréal, QC: Éditions Saint-Martin, 2005.

Niemeyer, Katharina. 2016. "Les Unes internationales du 8 janvier 2015. Entre uniformité et singularité." In *Le défi Charlie : Les médias à l'épreuve des attentats*, edited by Pierre de Lefébure and Claire Sécail, 19–48. Paris: Lemieux Éditeur.

"Observatoire sur la radicalisation et l'extrémisme violent." *Qui sommes-nous? Notre mission.* 2015. Accessed 16 April 2016. https://observatoire-radicalisation. org/notre-mission/

Peretti-Watel, Patrick. *La société du risque.* Paris: La Découverte, 2001.

Peritz, Ingrid, Tu Thanh Ha and Lisa Perreaux. 2014. "Martin Couture-Rouleau's Shift into Extremism Played Out on Social Media." *The Globe and Mail.* 21 October 2014. Accessed 13 September 2016. www.theglobeandmail. com/news/national/extremism-in-canadasborders/article21217185/.

Precht, Theon. "Home Grown Terrorism and Islamist Radicalisation in Europe: From Conversion to Terrorism." *København, Denmark: Danish Ministry of Justice.* 2007. Accessed 18 May 2016. www.justitsministeriet.dk/sites/default/ files/media/Arbejdsomraader/Forskning/Forskningspuljen/2011/2007/Home_ grown_terrorism_and_Islamist_radicalisation_in_Europe_-_an_assessment_ of_influencing_factors__2_.pdf.

Preston, Jennifer. "Multiple attacks on transport infrastructure: an inter-disciplinary exploration of the impact of social networking technologies upon real time information sharing, response and recovery." 2011. Accessed 12 May 2017. www.csap.cam.ac.uk/media/uploads/files/2/preston-et-al-unpub-lished-social-networking-on-info-sharing.pdf.

Raboy, Michael. "Crise des médias, crises de société: Les femmes, les hommes et l'École polytechnique de Montréal." *Communication: Information, Médias, Théories, Pratiques* 14:1 (1993): 82–111.

"Radio-Canada avec La Presse canadienne." *Société Radio-Canada.* 8 December 2014. 15 Acceeded June 2016. http://ici.radio-canada.ca/nouvelles/ national/2014/12/08/002-conseil-national-musulmans-john-maguire-video-terrorisme-etat-islamique-canada.shtml.

Renó, Denis. "Transmedia Journalism and the New Media Ecology: Possible Languages." In *Periodismo Transmedia: Miradas Multiples*, edited by Denis Renó, Carolina Campalans, Sandra Ruiz and Vincente Gosciola, 3–19. Barcelona: Editorial UOC, 2014.

"Sécurité publique Canada." *Lutte contre le terrorisme.* 2016. Accessed 17 September 2017. www.securitepublique.gc.ca/cnt/ntnl-scrt/cntr-trrrsm/ index-fr.aspx.

"Service de police d'Ottawa." La puissance des médias sociaux. 2014. Accessed 17 September 2017. www.ottawapolice.ca/fr/annual-report-2014/Power-of-social-media.asp?hdnContent=&hdnPage=.

Sioui, Marie-Michele. "Martin Couture-Rouleau: il avait le cœur noble et le cerveau déprimé." *La Presse.* 24 October 2014. www.lapresse.ca/actualites/ dossiers/attentat-a-st-jean-sur-richelieu/201410/23/01-4812127-martin-couture-rouleau-il-avait-le-coeur-noble-et-le-cerveau-deprime.php.

"Société Radio-Canada." *Société Radio-Canada.* 6 March 2015. Accessed 12 June 2016. http://ici.radio-canada.ca/nouvelles/politique/2015/03/06/001-devoilement-video-zehaf-bibeau.shtml.

"Société Radio-Canada." *Société Radio-Canada.* 9 December 2014. Accessed 12 June 2016. http://ici.radio-canada.ca/sujet/attentat-saint-jean-sur-richelieu.

"Société Radio-Canada." *Société Radio-Canada.* October 23 2014. Accessed 12 June. http://ici.radio-canada.ca/nouvelles/societe/2014/10/22/015-famille-michael-zehaf-bibeau-passe.shtml.

Schmitt, Laurie. "Le transmédia un label promotionnel des industries culturelles toujours en cours d'expérimentation." *Les enjeux de l'information et de la communication* 16:1 (2015): 5–17.

"Sûreté du Québec." *Accueil.* 2017. Accessed 2 September 2017. www.sq.gouv. qc.ca/index.jsp.

Tuchman, Gaye. *Making News: A Study in the Construction of Reality.* New York: The Free Press, 1978.

Tsfati, Yariv and Gabriele Weimann. "www.terrorism.com: Terror on the internet." *Studies in Conflict & Terrorism* 25:5 (2002): 317–332.

8 Colombia

Transmedia Projects in Contexts of Armed Conflict and Political Change

Camilo Andrés Tamayo Gómez and Omar Mauricio Velásquez

Colombians have suffered almost six decades of armed conflict. It is a war sustained by structural sociopolitical causes that cannot be won militarily, but has not been resolved by peace or political agreements either. The shocking reality of violence in Colombia (more than 6 million victims in the last twenty years and more than 4 million internally displaced [OCHA 2013; CHM 2013]) underpins important questions regarding the nature of the conflict and the role of civil society in armed conflict contexts. Revisiting the academic work of García-Durán (2004) and Wills (2006) by international standards, the magnitude of the Colombian conflict can be described as a war. However, the multiplicity of factors and actors involved in the armed confrontation could designate a clear situation of multipolar violence (Vásquez 2010), the degradation of the conflict can show a scenario of war against society (Pecaut 2004) or the influence of the United States in Colombia (and the focus of its foreign policy after 11 September 2001) can equally suggest the Colombian conflict as an anti-terrorist war (Hernández 2004). As a consequence, some Latin-American academics use the label 'the war without name' (García-Durán 2004; Wills 2006) to stress how the Colombian armed conflict would appear to have a little of all these elements, highlighting the need to adopt a complex and multidimensional approach in order to understand the nature, and future solution, of this conflict.

Since 2010, and after three decades of failed peace efforts in Colombia, a Colombian model of conflict resolution is emerging that aims for the institutionalization of peace as a state policy rather than as a presidential policy. This approach addresses ethical values and norms of International Humanitarian Law and International Human Rights Law in order to recognize guerrilla groups as valid political interlocutors. Embracing the idea that peace will entail structural changes in social and political terms, the central element of this model of conflict resolution is the active role of civil society and, particularly, the development of communicative and collective actions to promote peace and reconciliation in the country. This model of conflict resolution understands the role of civil society to shape a better future, recognizing victims' collective action as a mechanism to restore a sense of citizenship, collective belonging and construction of processes of memory, recognition and solidarity in the midst of armed conflicts.

With this context in mind, this chapter focuses on the relationship between communicative actions, civil society's collective action and human rights in the midst of the Colombian armed conflict. It analyzes the communicative and expressive dimensions of civil society's collective action as a mechanism to restore a sense of citizenship through the development of transmedia projects. It shows how collective belonging and human rights are constructed through processes of memory, recognition and solidarity, where the development of transmedia projects is key in order to catalyze social cohesion in fragile communities. The case study of this chapter is the city of Medellin (the second biggest city of Colombia), analyzing particularly the transmedia social project #noescomolapintan. A key objective of ours is to understand what kind of citizen processes this transmedia project can open up within contexts of armed conflict and how these practices have been affecting the claiming of human rights in Medellin from a civil society perspective.

We establish in this chapter that it is evident for the Colombian case that the development of transmedia projects as part of different civil society groups can generate processes of construction of social memory, recognition and solidarity from a counter-public perspective. Furthermore, one of the principal arguments is that the development of a set of transmedia social projects for citizens is crucial to restoring a sense of citizenship inside victims' groups, and to promoting processes of national reconciliation and transition to democracy from a civil society perspective. We also argue that collective action and transmedia narratives plays a key role in mobilizing civil society in times of conflict, taking over part of the tasks normally performed by the state, inducing the formation of strong political identities and sociopolitical scenarios for conflict resolution. For this research, it is our aim to understand the role of civil society and the impact of transmedia projects and victims' collective actions in the midst of armed conflicts. We believe that if Colombia wants to start real long-term processes of peace and reconciliation in the future, then the voice of civil society and victims needs to be at the center of the process.

This chapter is divided into four sections. The first section introduces contemporary discussions regarding the role of civil society in contexts of armed conflict. The second section shows information regarding the armed conflict in Colombia, addressing particularities for the case of Medellin in the light of political change. The third section analyzes the transmedia social project #noescomolapintan within the context of the Colombian armed conflict and within frameworks of stigmatization. In the final section, we present the conclusions for this work, emphasizing the idea that victims of armed conflicts, addressing expressive dimensions of collective social action through transmedia projects, can reestablish social, political and cultural bonds with their local communities in the aim of promoting peace and reconciliation.

The Role of Civil Society in Contexts of Armed Conflict

Since the end of the Cold War, it is extensively documented in the literature that civil society played a crucial role in armed conflict societies, particularly in two macro issues: first, delivering or supporting processes of peace-making or peace-building; and second, generating waves of democratization in fragile contexts (Kaldor 2013; Marchetti and Tocci 2009). Ross (2000) and Rufer (2012) argue that non-state actors are more efficient in working for peace and national reconciliation than state actors, being able to talk to different parties without losing credibility and being more suitable to support transitions to democracy in post-armed conflict societies. Thus, in armed conflict contexts, people organize themselves to defend common interests or work for social and political transformations. Notably, they have an important role in four particular areas: preventing violent conflict and military operations against civilians; working with local communities in zones of high violence to deliver humanitarian aid; supporting peace negotiations; and endorsing reconstruction and reconciliation in post-conflict societies. In short, civil society groups and victims' social movements are decisive for the continuation of anti-war efforts and they are key actors to develop sustainable peace in the long-term.

Orjuela (2003) argues that in the context of armed conflicts, the primary responsibility of civil society groups is to create social cohesion, developing a sense of trust and a spirit of collaboration to promote peace, cooperation and reconciliation between different sections of society. For Orjuela, the main consequence of an active civil society is the prevention of future armed conflicts, underlining the importance of the civic sphere in normalizing the living conditions of former victims and improving human rights records in conflict zones. The particular role of victims' social movements in promoting peace negotiations is fundamental in terms of positive influence on public opinion and in expressing victims' perspectives in the political arena. When a peace process is under way, victims' organizations can contribute to improving the legitimacy of political negotiations, addressing their claims and grievances during the process to the leaders and the general public opinion. On the other hand, in post-conflict contexts, civil society groups and victims' groups are crucial to build trust between former combatants and civilians, especially to consolidate democracy and good governance to rebuild broken societies. Thus, the principal threats for civil society in armed conflict contexts are the possible suppression of human rights, limitations of basic civil society activities, undermining of trust and erosion of social capital, as well as partial lawlessness. In this context, the free press and independent media are drastically controlled, depriving civil society organizations of communication channels connecting to other social groups, citizens and political institutions.

Importantly, the deterioration of civil society activities in armed conflict contexts makes social recovery after war even more difficult. Fear, mistrust, insecurity, uncertainty, prompted by years and years of armed conflict, all go to obstruct citizens, social groups and common people from participating in local community developments or activities. This decline is sometimes a consequence of the exile or forced displacement of different civil society groups or key social actors, undermining the capacity of social and civic organizations to remain in times of war. At the same time, the development of collective actions of victims' social movements and civil society groups in armed conflict societies can be crucial to restore participatory democracy and all forms of associational and communicative activity. In some contexts, collective action is a mechanism that strengthens the bonds between different victims' communities across armed conflict regions, restoring the sense of citizenship and collective belonging among them. In addition, civil society's collective actions are central to formulating the demands for respect of human rights in the midst of armed conflicts, facilitating processes of democratization in post-authoritarian societies, and supporting processes of construction of political and cultural memory, recognition and solidarity during and after the conflict. In summary, collective action plays a key role to mobilizing civil society in times of conflict, taking over part of the tasks normally performed by the state (for example, assisting humanitarian work) and inducing the formation of strong political identities (such as victims' or survivors' political identities) and sociopolitical scenarios for conflict resolution.

According to Marchetti and Tocci (2009) and Kaldor (2013), the interaction between contexts, identity, frameworks of action, communicative resources and political opportunity structures determines the impact of civil society in contexts of armed conflict. For these scholars, impact is taken to mean both the direct results of a particular action as well as the influence upon the wider context underlying a particular manifestation of conflict or post-conflict. Civil society's direct and contextual impact is determined by the wider conflict or post-conflict context, by the identities of civil society, by their actions within the four main frameworks of action (conflict escalation, conflict management, resolution and transformation), and by the political structure within which they operate. In other words, contexts of conflict or post-conflict shape the identities of civil society. Those identities determine their frameworks of action. In turn, the ability of civil society to navigate the political opportunity structure of conflicts defines their overall direct and contextual impact, the latter of which feeds back into the original conflict or post-conflict contexts.

Furthermore, for Marchetti and Tocci (2009) and Della Porta (2015), during the last two decades three main macro-impacts of civil society in contexts of armed conflict can be highlighted. First, they can fuel conflict by, for example, intensifying the initial causes leading to further securitization. Second, they can hold a conflict in its current state, preventing an escalation while laying the ground for peace, as Marchetti and Tocci note:

> At a minimum and most visible level, they operate upon the most acute symptoms of conflict such as extreme violence, poverty, health or destruction, by providing immediate relief. By doing so, they may help desecuritizing the conflict environment, thus creating a more fertile ground for an ensuing tackling of its roots causes in the long term.
>
> (Marchetti and Tocci 2009, 216)

The third macro-impact of civil society in contexts of armed conflict is peace-making. It involves the range of impacts that civil society can have on reconciling incompatible subject positions by desecuritizing the conflict environment. Revisiting the work of Kalyvas (2012) and Wood (2015), we can argue that in post-armed conflict democracies with a strong military presence and militarized culture, civil society is often related to the push for full democratization and the civilization of politics, thus threatening the state. However, we must also be aware that the state is central to shaping the nature and role of civil society. When a state does not exist, or it is weak or failing, civil society comes to occupy part of the space normally filled by the functioning state. In contexts of armed conflict, when the state lacks stability, sovereign or independence, civil society can shape the actual nature of the state in question. In this context, from a political science perspective (Della Porta 2015; Marchetti and Tocci 2009), civil society needs to be both permitted and protected by the state; its existence, nature and role is determined by democracy, outlining the scope of associative freedom, as well as by the existence of other basic rights and freedoms normally protected within democratic states.

Nevertheless, we argue that when these freedoms and rights are curtailed, civil society is expected to act beyond legal boundaries, often aiming to subvert the state rather than interact with it, problematizing further the distinction between 'civil' and 'uncivil' civil society actors. In contexts of armed conflict, the shape of civil society is affected also by the specific nature of the democratic order in question. In other words, civil society functions and roles are fundamentally shaped by the specific armed conflict context in question. As a result, civil society is both an independent agent for change and a dependent product of existing structures, where 'civil' and 'uncivil' actors carrying a wide range of actions can interact within the state, both influencing and being influenced inextricably by it.

From the perspective of this research, a lack of a communicative approach limits the analysis of civil society's collective action in contexts of armed conflict. Therefore, a number of questions need addressing. What is the role of communicative agency in these contexts? How are the communicative dimensions of collective action helping civil society to address the three main macro-impacts (fuelling conflict, holding conflict, and peace-making)? And what is the impact of transmedia projects in shaping social cohesion in fragile or contested contexts? These are questions that need to be answered in order to fully understand the contemporary role of civil society and communicative strategies in fragile social contexts. If we can better understand the communicative and expressive dimensions of collective actions, it is possible to analyze how civil society creates social cohesion, developing a sense of trust and a spirit of collaboration to promote peace, cooperation and reconciliation in fragile social contexts. Our main argument here is that civil society is one of the principal social actors that has to develop a new type of socio-communicative regime in armed conflict societies, demanding in different spaces, fields or 'sociopolitical arenas' the recognition of communicative rights as citizen rights. Thus, this recognition is crucial to start a process of communicative democratization, where citizens' collective social action and the development of transmedia projects are principal resources.

Medellin and the Colombian Armed Conflict

Colombia has a population of 48 million, a landmass of $1.139.000 \, km^2$, with 5 million internally displaced people, 480,000 refugees, two left-wing guerrilla groups/armies and more than six new right-wing paramilitary groups/armies called BACRIMS. Also, Colombia has the most unequal distribution of wealth across the continent, with 30% of its population living in poverty, and it is experiencing one of the longest armed conflicts in the world, lasting almost 50 years (Fisas 2009; UNDP 2010). The United Nations Development Programme identifies five structural factors underlying the chronic armed conflict in the country: drug trafficking, limited and ineffective regional and local government, persistent inequality and exclusion, the incapacity of the state to establish democratic institutions and the apparent indifference of political and economic elites (UNDP 2003, 2010). According to Sanchez and Meertens (2001), Pecaut (2004) and Wills (2006), the principal cause of the Colombian conflict is the asymmetric war between the Colombian army and other irregular military groups (guerrillas, paramilitaries, drug dealers) for control over territory and the incapacity of the state to develop democratic mechanisms in the country. From 2002 to 2010 this was exacerbated by the Government's redefinition, which informed policy of the armed conflict as a 'terrorist threat' (Republic of Colombia – Ministry of National Defence, 2010).

In 2002 Colombia started to undergo deep sociopolitical change. After a failed peace process between the guerrilla group of the Revolutionary Armed Forces of Colombia (FARC-EP) and the government of conservative president Andrés Pastrana (1998–2002), a new president, Alvaro Uribe Vélez, was elected with the support of paramilitary groups and extreme right parties (Lopez 2010; Romero 2007). This right-wing president introduced a new policy called Programme of Democratic Security which was based on the militarization of the civilian population and military combat against the guerrillas. This program was supported by the government of the United States through the Colombia Plan (Fisas 2009). After four years of Uribe's government, the president, using his political influence, changed the constitution to get a second term in 2004. As a result of his eight years in office (2002–2010), he established a strong relationship between paramilitary groups and official political parties, where the reconfiguration of the state in favor of illegal groups was the principal consequence. During these years, 77% of Colombian MPs were paramilitary group supporters, which resulted in huge damage to democracy in the country (HRW 2010; Lopez 2010). Furthermore, a radicalization of public opinion into two groups (the supporters of Uribe's government vs. the critics of Uribe's policies) shaped the stereotypical and misleading image of both sides: groups who upheld the extreme right policies were associated with paramilitary groups, while groups who supported center and left policies were associated with guerrilla's groups (Gonzalez 2010; UNDP 2010).

Another consequence of the implementation of the program of 'democratic security' during these years was government's persecution of journalists, trade union workers, teachers, human rights activist, United Nations employers, lawyers, Colombian MPs, Supreme Court judges and NGO activists; particularly in principal cities, such as Bogotá, Medellin and Cali and regions with the highest levels of violence as Caquetá, Putumayo, Montes de María and Antioquia (HRW 2010; UNDP 2010). In 2010, Juan Manuel Santos, former Minister of Defence of Uribe's administration, was elected as new Colombian president for a period of four years (2010–2014) in order to continue the development of these right-wing policies. However, president Santos distanced himself from this ideology and opened up peace talks with the FARC-EP in 2012, although still keeping heavy military operations across the country and his government receiving technical cooperation in defense issues from the United States. In 2016, and after a long process of negotiations, the Colombian Government and this guerrilla group signed a ceasefire deal. However, the Colombian public rejected this agreement in a plebiscite. Nevertheless, The Colombian Government and the FARC-EP signed a revised peace agreement that it is pending approval by the Colombian Congress.

As a result, the principal victims of the Colombian armed conflict are civilians. The Colombian research center 'Program for Peace' states that 86% of the 6 million victims of the Colombian war in the last twenty years were noncombatants, out of which 71% were women (Program for Peace 2010). Thus, Medellin (the capital city of the County of Antioquia) is the city with the highest number of victims of interurban forced displacement in the country (more than half a million victims) and the highest number of victims of forced disappearance with more than 100,000 people reported missing or kidnapped by illegal groups. Furthermore, Medellin supplied 43% of child soldiers to the conflict, and Antioquia is the county with the highest number of victims of the Colombian armed conflict (1.2 million) (Medellin City Council Victims Unit 2017).

However, the principal aspect to consider in the case of Medellin is the permanent suffering of civilians in the midst of the armed conflict. The citizens of this city had experienced all the possible consequences of war (stigmatization, forced displacements, massacres, persecutions, marginalization, extra-judicial executions, tortures, etc.), and they are victims of all forms of violations and human rights abuses. Thus, three main aspects can characterize Medellin as a representative example of the dynamic of war in Colombia: first, the ongoing fighting between different illegal and legal armed groups for control over the local territory and its resources; second, the co-optation of civilians by illegal forces to affect social cohesion and trust; and finally, the establishment of illegal economies around drug trafficking, kidnapping and extortion that strongly affects the urban economy.

According to García de la Torre and Aramburo (2011) and Duncan and Eslava (2015), it is possible to establish three main characteristics of the humanitarian crisis in Medellin. First, it is the rise of an 'uprooting generation' with immediate effects in the social structure of the city; where the negative process of interurban forced displacement has deeply undermined social and cultural ties of families and communities with this particular territory. The second characteristic is the establishment of a culture of fear and distrust between local communities of the urban areas of Medellin as a result of the asymmetric armed conflict. Often erroneously, illegal groups have been related to some particular neighborhoods, creating an environment of dangerous stereotypes and rumors inside the population. As a consequence, the justification of some military operations was often based on those erroneous generalizations, targeting specific people as local leaders, politicians or human rights defenders. A good example of this it is the case of 'Operation Orion' in Comuna 13 (a poor neighborhood in Medellin) in 2002, where it is evidence of a military collaboration between the Colombian army and paramilitary groups and where five female social leaders were killed in a heavily populated urban area of Medellin. The third characteristic is the targeting of civilians as a method of war. This strategy is utilized by both illegal and legal armed groups, and became the main objective of their military operations. By killing innocent bystanders, they prove their power, superiority and ownership of specific urban areas to their rivals, as well as undermining the social and cultural base of support for another armed group. Regarding this third characteristic, the International NGO Amnesty International notes:

> All the parties to the conflict – guerrilla groups, the security forces and paramilitaries – have been responsible for widespread and often systematic human rights abuses and violations of IHL mostly, but not exclusively, committed against civilians. Such abuses include threats against and killings of civilians; enforced disappearances; hostage taking; forced displacement; torture and other cruel, inhuman or degrading treatment; and indiscriminate and disproportionate attacks against the civilian population. These abuses constitute crimes under national and international law. Most victims have been either campesinos or community leaders who the security forces have falsely claimed were guerrillas killed in combat. The victim is typically taken from their home or place of work in front of witnesses and taken to another location to be killed. The body is presented wearing army fatigues by the security forces, although witnesses testify that the victim had been wearing civilian clothes when detained. Many of the victims are buried as unidentified individuals despite being identified by family members. The bodies also often show signs of torture.
>
> (Amnesty International 2008, 25–26)

In summary, it is possible to argue that the current situation in Medellin is a good reference to understand in holistic terms the contemporary dynamics of the armed conflict in Colombia. This particular case reveals the main strategies that illegal groups have been developing in Colombian cities since 1993, and how some war tactics were implemented first in Medellin in order to replicate it in other Colombian urban areas. For example, Medellin was the first place where guerrillas groups used human shields to prevent territorial control for part of the Colombian army, or where paramilitary groups implemented massacres against civilians as a war strategy in order to spread fear and terror.

The Case of the Transmedia Social Project #noescomolapintan

La Loma neighborhood is a geographically strategic area for the armed conflict in Medellin city, where guerrillas and paramilitary groups have been using this territory as a main corridor to transport war supplies and illegal materials. According to the Victims Unit of Medellin City Council one guerrilla group, The Revolutionary Armed Forces of Colombia (FARC-EP), five particular paramilitary groups, Carlos Castaño's Self-Defence group, Magdalena Medio Self-Defence group, Metro bloc, Cacique Nutibara bloc and Heroes of Granada bloc, and, on the other hand, the Colombian Army and Medellin's Police forces, have been struggling to gain control over this territory and its resources for more than twenty-five years (Medellin City Council Victims Unit 2017).

In order to understand the impact of the armed conflict in La Loma neighborhood one fact is relevant: since 1980 more than 234 families were interurban displaced as a consequence of the military actions between legal and illegal forces in this territory. Furthermore, in the last three decades in La Loma more than 154 people have disappeared or kidnapped, thirty-five massacres happened (72% of victims were women) and seventeen mass graves have been discovered in neighboring rural areas (Colombian Government 2003; Medellin City Council Victims Unit 2017). However, the principal impact of the war in La Loma is that the neighborhood is territorially divided into areas controlled by gangs (known as 'combos') loyal to one side or the other, creating a phenomenon called 'invisible borders' that divide the territory into criminal territories, undermining the social cohesion of the local community.

In this context, since 2013 the inhabitants of La Loma started a socio-communicative project to generate processes of solidarity, recognition and memory in the local community. This project, called 'The Social Initiative of La Loma neighbourhood', aims to create social cohesion in this territory by developing communicative and transmedia initiatives. As a result of an alliance between the Victims Unit of Medellin City Council, EAFIT University and the Historical Memory report, 'Medellin Enough Already!' In 2014, the transmedia social project #noescomolapintan began to show the process of resistance that this urban community has been doing since 1980 in the midst of the armed conflict. A key objective of this project was to fight against stigmatization, stereotypes and discrimination by developing transmedia products where the local community presented nonofficial narratives regarding the war, and using victims' perspective to understand the dynamics of contestation in the construction of memory, recognition and solidarity during the conflict.

From 2015 to 2016, this transmedia social project created a Media-Lab in La Loma to develop five strategies. The first strategy called Communicative Citizenship was an effort to involve the community in public discussions about the war, victim reparation and reconciliation from a communicative perspective. The aim of this strategy was to build communicative and political agency to the inhabitants of this neighborhood to imagine new forms of collective action with transmedia narratives as a principal tool. The second strategy, named Cartographies of Resistance and Hope, was focused on to develop social, territorial and sound cartographies from a victims' perspective to recognize two elements: first, the repertoire of actions of resistance made by this community to overcome the war since 1980, and, second, the expressive and communicative dimension of the territory of La Loma from the inhabitants' point of view. The third strategy was the Narrative Strategy. This strategy wanted to bring storytelling skills to the participants in order to create stories that help the construction of collective memory from the point of view of the local community. Developing writing exercises and collaborative storytelling workshops, the participants created eight stories to be implemented in the final transmedia product.

The fourth strategy was the Creating Content Strategy, where members of La Loma Media-Lab developed a variety of communicative products in order to create the transmedia project #noescomolapintan. Specifically, products such as collaborative cartographies, video games, illustrations, timelines, stop-motions videos, comics, video clips, short videos, photographs and radio programs were produced to present the history of La Loma neighborhood, and provided this community with social and cultural strategies for dealing with the impacts of the armed conflict. In short, the overarching strategy of this transmedia project was to have a main narrative (that of the original history of La Loma neighborhood from the victims' point of view) and extend this original narrative into five different products in order to create a transmedia product.

The final phase, the Dissemination Strategy, aimed to present and disseminate the results of this transmedia project to other civil society and victims' groups through the alliances made between La Loma Media-Lab and nongovernmental organizations. In order to do this, we disseminated the results in three levels: first, we delivered an academic seminar and workshop at EAFIT University in Medellin in May 2016 to present the results to academics and organizations from Antioquia. Furthermore, we presented the results developing another academic seminar and workshop at Javeriana University in Bogotá (the capital of Colombia) to present the results to academics, NGOs, INGOs, mass media and organizations based on the capital of the country. The presentation of results was directed toward two key institutions of the Colombian Government: the Centre of Historic Memory (CNRR) and the Colombian Human Rights Office. Following this first level, we then focused on disseminating the results inside the community of La Loma by delivering workshops, presentations and organizing a cultural festival in December 2016. The rationale behind the organization of this event was to show to the community how it is possible to claim justice, truth, reparation and human rights in context of violence using communicative and transmedia strategies. For the final phase, we presented the results of this transmedia project internationally. We disseminated an 'informative pack' about this initiative presenting this project and key results using the networks of our project partners UNHCR (The United Nations Refugee Agency), COALICO (The international coalition against the involvement of boys, girls and youth in the armed conflict in Colombia) and EAI (Audiovisual School Project) in order to address stakeholders and key institutions.

Components of the Transmedia Social Project #noescomolapintan

As we described earlier, one of the main characteristics of the armed conflict in Medellin city is that, often erroneously, illegal groups have been related to some local communities, creating an environment of dangerous stereotypes and rumors inside the population. In the last twenty-five years, some actors such as paramilitary and guerrilla groups and the Colombian army had tried to establish symbolic orders in urban social contexts around the idea that 'killing civilians is allowed in this neighborhood because these people do not support our actions and they are against us' (Program for Peace 2010, 34–35). For this purpose, they were creating this stigmatizing narrative inside those communities and neighborhoods, introducing a dangerous symbolic dichotomy between the good people (civilians supporting legal or illegal armies) and the bad people (civilians supporting no-violent actions, claiming human rights in the midst of the conflict and protesting against any kind of ties with legal or illegal army groups). Those constructions of stigmatization are part of narrative strategies that legal and illegal actors have been developing in La Loma to create new symbolic orders and, through them, gain the support of civilians in the midst of this armed conflict. Thus, it is clear that this approach is highlighting the militarization of civil society as a war strategy, and particular constructions of official and nonofficial narratives are the result of this operationalization of ideology into public collective narratives. The result: the official narrative of stigmatization that if you are an inhabitant of La Loma in Medellin you are a dangerous person who probably support guerrilla or paramilitary groups and lives in a 'no-go area' of the city.

In this context, and after developing different workshops with the residents of La Loma, we found that this stigmatization is one of the main problems of the community in terms of building social cohesion and recognition. Furthermore, in order to establish interpretations about what has been happening in more than three decades in La Loma, this transmedia project is an example of the permanent tension between official narratives about war created by the Colombian government, the Colombian army, paramilitary and guerrilla groups ('the official warriors'), and nonofficial narratives created by civil society organizations, social movements, civilians and victims ('the unofficial war actors'). In other words, one of the main contributions of this transmedia project was to present these nonofficial narratives regarding the armed conflict in La Loma from the victims' perspective, analyzing how these narratives evidence the expressive dimensions of victims' collective action and resistance in the public sphere and their impact.

The principal narrative component of #noescomolapintan is the main story regarding the history of the neighborhood. In order to create this first narrative element, the inhabitants of La Loma made a collaborative story, called 'Our History', during the workshops, using timelines, cartographies and photography. In this story, three residents of the families that founded the neighborhood in 1940 are the focus point to introduce main historical events important for the community, showing processes of communal resistance in the midst of the armed conflict. The community also created four different stories, focusing on different groups of residents to expand the principal story and create a transmedia narrative. The components are video clips presenting the story of the 'Paniagua Folk Music Band', the video game 'Talla de Reyes' that address the tale of the collective of street art of La Loma, stop motions showing the anecdotes of two religious collectives that celebrate Easter week making processions every year, and the comic 'La Loma Salsa Club' that highlight the story of the salsa club in the neighborhood. As a result, this transmedia project created a website and a Facebook page where it is possible to access all these transmedia products.

Furthermore, and following the experience of the project of the Children's Audiovisual School (EAI) of Belén de los Andaquíes in Caquetá, Colombia, #noescomolapintan offered training and education in new technologies, storytelling, audio and video production for children of La Loma during the time of the Media-Lab project. One of the main aims of the EAI is to inspire children to create, develop and disseminate multimedia narratives, audio-visual stories, chronicles and news about their personal social context, recreating through these audio-visual narratives their own visions of themselves and their territory. Any children of the area (older than seven years) can approach the EAI with a story to tell, and the school offers him/her different alternatives to produce it. The child has to conduct the whole process: create the narrative, take pictures, do the editing and develop the digital soundtrack, receiving help from tutors (usually former members of the EAI). As a final stage, the audio-visual product is projected on a big screen placed out in the street in front of the producer's residence, transforming the street into a space where town people can watch the audio-visual piece and discuss local issues. Finally, we followed this methodology by producing three short videos with children of the neighborhood to address the role of new generations in the construction of the collective future of La Loma.

After different working sessions with the participants, it was decided that the best method for addressing the history of resistance of the inhabitants of La Loma in the midst of the armed conflict was presenting La Loma neighborhood from a counter-public point of view. The meaning of the Spanish sentence 'no es como la pintan' in English is 'it is not what you think it is'. This sentence was the catalyst for creating the main narrative of this transmedia product, and the reason behind the name of the project #noescomolapintan. For this community, some people cannot have senses of belonging with the territory as a consequence of the war, and they feel shame of belonging to a neighborhood where everybody believes that it is a place of horror and sadness. A few residents believe that one of the biggest impacts of the armed conflict in La Loma is the impossibility to be part of your community again, after you witnessed armed conflict actions, such as massacres or extrajudicial killings. Therefore, the stigmatization or defamation to particular groups of people inside those communities (including human rights defenders, victims or witnesses) are some of the main consequences of this long-term armed conflict; affecting the construction of collective narratives of belonging and representations of cultural memories for part of those social groups. As a result, one of the aims of #noescomolapintan is to overcome this problem and change these perceptions inside the community itself.

Conclusion

This transmedia project highlights how the community of La Loma had understood cultural memory, social recognition and solidarity as social and generational institutions, and therefore they had developed transmedia narratives to provide senses of memory, recognition and solidarity to generations that do not have a formalized memory as a consequence of a lack of fixed points with the past. As a consequence, #noescomolapintan became the realization of sociocultural belonging, affection and assimilation that shapes the dynamics of association and dissociation in La Loma. The narratives and representations developed at #noescomolapintan are establishing historical truths about what happened in armed conflict confrontations, providing degrees of reparation and symbolic restitution to the victims. Thus, the efforts of the inhabitants of La Loma are addressing the idea of the public sphere as a place to disclose memories, identities and narratives in the communicative activity, corresponding with the human condition of plurality and freedom through visibility, recognition and representation in public spaces.

Furthermore, this transmedia project is addressing the relationship between trauma theory and constructions of traumatic memory as a tool to contest the past in La Loma for part of victims' groups. It is clear that in this neighborhood this aspect of traumatic memory is crucial to understand how particular groups of victims can apprehend and create transmedia narratives about their past after witnessing traumatic events, such as massacres, displacements or other experiences of violence. In this context, the development of transmedia narratives is a clear example of how constructions of memory, recognition and solidarity are a healing process for victims in contexts of armed conflict. Thus, the development of transmedia products to construct memory narratives is based on expressive activism as an instrument to exercise political and social actions in the public spheres of this Colombian city.

In conclusion, then, the case of #noescomolapintan is an example of how subjectivity, transmedia narratives and expressive dimension can create social agency to generate collective actions of memory, recognition and solidarity in armed conflict contexts. As this case shows, feelings such as pain, suffering, fear, anxiety or rage can be the main motivators to encourage the development of transmedia projects. The construction of transmedia narratives is not just a rational or formal victims' collective action; it can also combine, at the same time, different formal or substantives levels of rationality and non-rationality. In summary, the case of La Loma is a striking example of the importance and relevance of emotional reasons and expressive dimensions as a key element behind transmedia social projects and how, through this method, human rights can be exercised from communicative perspectives in armed conflict scenarios.

Bibliography

Amnesty International. "Leave Us in Peace!" *Targeting Civilians in Colombia's Internal Armed Conflict*. London: Amnesty International Press, 2008.

Colombian Government, Los derechos humanos en el departamento de Antioquia. *Programa Presidencial de Derechos Humanos y Derecho Internacional Humanitario*. Bogotá: Vice-Presidencia de la República de Colombia, 2003.

CHM – The National Centre of Historical Memory of Colombia (CHM), *Enough Already: Memories of War and Dignity*. Bogotá: CHM National Press, 2013.

Della Porta, Donatella. *The Oxford Handbook of Social Movements*. Oxford: Oxford University Press, 2015.

Duncan, Gustavo and Adolfo Eslava. *Territorio, crimen, comunidad. Heterogeneidad del homicidio en Medellín*. Medellin: EAFIT University Press, 2015.

Fisas, Vicenç. *Yearbook on Peace Processes*. Barcelona: Icaria Editors, 2009.
García de la Torre, Clara and Clara Aramburo. *Geografías de la guerra, el poder y la resistencia. Oriente y Urabá antioqueños 1990–2008*. Bogotá: ODECOFI, 2011.
García-Durán, Mauricio. "Colombia: Challenges and Dilemmas in the Search for Peace." *Accord* 14 (2014): 1–23.
Gonzalez, Francis. "Gracias general Uribe por salvar la patria" *Cien días vistos por Cinep*. 70 (2010): 12–24.
Hernández, Esperanza, "Compelled to Act: Grassroots Peace Initiatives." In *Alternatives to war: Colombia's Peace Processes*, edited by García, Manuel, 24–29. London: Accord, 2004.
HRW – Human Rights Watch. *World Report 2010 – Colombia*. New York: Human Rights Watch Press, 2010.
Kaldor, Mary, "Restructuring Global Security for the 21st Century." In *The Quest for Security: Protection without Protectionism and the Challenge for Global Governance*, edited by M. Kaldor and J. Stiglitz, 117–142. New York: Columbia University Press, 2013.
Kalyvas, Stathis. "Micro-Level Studies of Violence in Civil War: Refining and Extending the Control-Collaboration Model." *Terrorism and Political Violence* 24:4 (2012): 658–668.
Lopez, Claudia. *Y refundarón la patria*. Bogotá: Debate, 2010.
Marchetti, Raffaele and Nathalie Tocci. "Conflict Society: Understanding the Role of Civil Society in Conflict." *Global Change, Peace and Security* 21:2 (2009): 202–217.
Medellin City Council Victims Unit. *Armed Conflict Statistics*. Medellin: Medellin City Council Press, 2017.
OCHA – United Nations Office for the Coordination of Humanitarian Affairs, *Colombia: Humanitarian Snapshot*. Bogota: Office for the Coordination of Humanitarian Affairs of the United Nations, 2013.
Orjuela, Camila. "Building Peace in Sri Lanka: a Role for Civil Society?" *Journal of Peace Research* 40:2 (2003): 195–212.
Pecaut, Daniel. *Territorial Dimensions of War and Peace*. Bogotá: Colombian National University Press, 2004.
Program for Peace. *The Costs of the War*. Bogotá: CINEP editions, 2010.
Republic of Colombia – Ministry of National Defence. *Impacto de la política de seguridad democrática*. Bogotá: National Press Office, 2010.
Romero, Mauricio. *Parapolítica: la ruta de la expansión paramilitar y los acuerdos políticos*. Bogotá: Corporación Nuevo Arco Iris, 2007.
Ross, Marc. "Creating the Conditions for Peacemaking: Theories of Practice in Ethnic Conflict Resolution." *Ethnic and Racial Studies* 23:6 (2000): 1002–1034.
Rufer, Michael. *Politics of Memory: Social and Political Terms of the Americas – Politics, Inequalities, and North-South Relations*. Bielefeld: Bielefeld University, 2012.
Sanchez, Gonzalo and Donny Meertens. *Bandits, Peasants, and Politics: The Case of "La Violencia" in Colombia*. Austin: University of Texas Press, 2001.
UNDP – United Nations Development Programme. *National Human Development Report for Colombia*. Bogotá: El Malpensante editors, 2003.

UNDP – United Nations Development Programme. "Truth: Facts and Reasons." *Hechos del Callejon Magazine* 34:7 (2010): 8–13.

Vásquez, Teófilo. "La seguridad democrática de Uribe (2002–2010)." *Cien días Vistos por Cinep.* 70 (2010): 1–5.

Wills, María Emma. *Nuestra Guerra sin Nombre.* Bogotá: Norma editors, 2006.

Wood, Elisabeth. "Social Mobilization and Violence in Civil War and their Social Legacies." In *The Oxford Handbook of Social Movements*, edited by Della Porta, 452–466. Oxford: Oxford University Press, 2015.

9 Brazil

Reconfigurations and Spectatorship in Brazilian Telenovelas

Felipe Muanis and Rosane Svartman

The first television station to operate in Brazil was TV Tupi, in the state of São Paulo. It was founded on 18 September 1950 by Assis Chateaubriand after he sold a year's worth of advertising space to Companhia Antártica Paulista, the Sul América Seguros group, Moinho Santista and the Francisco Pignatari Organization. Even though Brazilian television channels are public concessions, television has been a private enterprise in the country from the outset. Business groups that controlled media corporations such as newspapers and radio stations ventured into the new medium. Several stations emerged, and now TV Globo holds the hegemony of audience and advertising in the industry. While the station founded by Assis Chateaubriand covered a range of only 100 kilometers, television has become a nationwide medium over the last few decades. Every day, millions of people sit down to watch TV Globo at prime time, especially its traditional telenovelas – a trend that is somewhat against the grain of the current worldwide trend of moving toward more fragmented content and audiences.

According to the Brazilian Institute of Geography and Statistics (IBGE),[1] 97.3% of Brazilian households have a television set. Even though millions of Brazilians still watch 'traditional' network television in prime time, over 100 cable stations attract about 20 million users in the country, and half the population has access to the internet – 29.5% and 48% of its households, respectively. Netflix and other Over-The-Top (OTT) services have been available in Brazil since 2011. According to Comscore,[2] in 2017, 107 million Brazilians over 6 years of age are already considered multiplatform consumers, and mobile devices account for 63% of all digital access. While ratings for free public broadcasting television are still impressive, the Brazilian audiovisual agency (ANCINE) demonstrates that its share in the audiovisual market fell from 63.7% to 41.5% between 2007 and 2014. Still, Brazilian broadcast television draws millions of people every day to its shows, especially in its prime time – from 6 pm to 11 pm. For instance, the 9 pm telenovela often reaches 35 rating points. Each point recorded by Ibope – a company monitoring and researching media and audience – means 641,286 households in the so-called National Television Panel that estimates audience ratings for free broadcast television in the country. Therefore, a telenovela chapter with 35 rating points equates to a mass audience of over 22 million people – indeed a rare phenomenon nowadays. In 2016, forty-one telenovelas, including twenty reruns, were exhibited on free broadcast Brazilian television, totaling 3,673 hours of programming.

However, the dominance of live broadcasting in Brazil does not mean that new ways of watching such content are not emerging in the country. How do trends of connected viewing and connected audiences interact and interfere with the daily telenovela, the most traditional and most penetrating of products in Brazilian television? In order to answer this question and reflect on the displacement of Brazilian television content to other media platforms and new forms of spectatorship, this chapter will examine two initiatives taken by TV Globo: first, the sharing of its 9 pm telenovela in 2017 – titled *A Força do Querer* (*The Power of Will*) – on the Globoplay platform, and second, a fanfic project and the 2015/2016 season of *Malhação* (*Young Hearts*).[3] By reflecting on the relationship between the audience and telenovelas, this chapter will discuss how the former can – in addition to influencing the development of the latter, which is the most traditional product in Brazilian television – interfere in the production and consumption of those narratives. The chapter demonstrates how telenovelas have been changing in their forms of participation and spectatorship through two experiences: sharing telenovela and soap opera content on the Globoplay Video-On-Demand (VOD) platform and initiatives involving fanfic and telenovelas.

Telenovela: Characteristics and Changes

Daily telenovelas are the most popular product of Brazilian television, despite their tendency to depict low realism and amidst criticisms of how they typically represent and narrativize the population. On the other hand, several authors see Brazilian television and particularly its telenovelas – the object of this chapter – as a cultural symbol to be valued. Jesus Martín-Barbero (2003) argues that it is a mistake to think that television would not be a topic of culture – only of communication – since signs of Latin American identity are recognizable in the melodrama of the country's telenovelas, hereby serving as a way for the industry to recover popular memory. For Martín-Barbero, no other genre was able to please as much in the region: 'If the family is still the basic audience unit for television in Latin America it is because it is the primordial situation of recognition for most people' (2003, 293). Much of what would be allegedly rejected by the discourse of culture would find its expression in television – it would be the 'popular activated by the massive' (ibid., 312). Martín-Barbero points out that telenovelas – a newer and, in his opinion, more Latin American version of the feuilleton (originally a kind of supplement attached to newspapers) – is the only cultural product that

Latin America has been able to successfully export to Europe and the US besides the great texts of magical realism.

Currently, telenovelas communicate with their audiences on several levels: they are reflections on current issues; they provide information and knowledge to social exchange; they cause viewers' identification; and they entertain and provide relaxation, fantasy and inspiration. Heloísa Buarque (2001) studied the consumption patterns for the telenovela *O Rei do Gado* (*The Cattle King*) in a small town in the state of São Paulo. She found that by addressing affective relations, telenovelas interact with viewers through these topics, thus provoking reflections on intimate and family relationships. The author sees telenovelas as cultural texts capable of promoting a kind of sentimental education through a reflexive process that viewers carry out based on their contact with the narrative. For Buarque (2001), viewers often consider sentimental aspects more realistic in telenovelas since they are real emotions that are at play in social life. By way of example, Buarque mentions mothers who use telenovelas to talk about sensitive topics, such as sexuality and love relationships. However, it should also be noted that Brazilian telenovelas have a commercial function that pervades their productions and, on reflection, this is not different from the feuilleton from which they originate. For example, the cliffhanger at the end of each chapter – that is, the suspense created in the final scene – was intended to draw the audience to the next chapter. Feuilletons and telenovelas – in essence, melodrama – have always had a commercial bent and aimed at pleasing a mass audience. Telenovela writers are well aware of the commercial and popular nature of their work. In an interview, author Aguinaldo Silva said: 'Why do we do telenovelas? To raise ratings and please viewers. It's supposed to be a hit; there is no other reason. So there's no point in going against what viewers want' (Azevedo et al. 2008, 36). In effect, a telenovela that is not pleasing some 15 million people will likely be cancelled; ratings, like in many television industries around the world, are a key part of the characteristics of such production.

Even with such industrial continuity however, and despite the audience's knowledge of the narrative formats of melodrama and telenovela and despite the tradition of the latter – broadcast for decades – its language has undergone plenty of change over the years. Brazilian telenovelas became more agile, focusing on realism and everyday life, as well as conversing with its audience in new ways – which will be the focus of this chapter. An example of such changes was TV Tupi's 1968 telenovela *Beto Rockfeller*, written by Cassiano Gabus Mendes. It is considered a landmark for focusing the telenovela narrative on more current and everyday topics. It was also the first successful telenovela to use colloquial language. At TV Globo, a year later, the departure of Cuban author Glória Magadan, who used to supervise the development of all telenovelas, also opened the door for more contemporary topics specific to

Brazilian culture rather than relying on literature and theatre classics or stories set in foreign countries. During the 1970s, considered the 'golden age' of the genre, telenovelas definitively became the most popular format in Brazilian television.

Over the last few decades, telenovelas have undergone other changes in Brazil. Recently, author João Emanuel Carneiro gave a different title to each chapter of his telenovela *A Regra do Jogo* (*The Rule of the Game*) – a practice usually associated with the television series. When writing two seasons of teen daily television drama *Malhação* and the 7 pm telenovela *Totalmente Demais*, Rosane Svartman valued subplots that were resolved on the same day, making each chapter interesting even for those who do not follow the main plot – a feature that can also be associated with serials. In an interview, telenovela author Carlos Lombardi said: 'Chapters have changed in size for two reasons: first, because they are broadcast for longer; second, because narrative rhythm has changed. If you watch old telenovelas you will say: My God, that's slow! Was it really like that?' (Azevedo et al. 2008, 307).

But with the increase in the length of telenovelas, subplots had to be extended.[4] At the same time, the number of scenes per chapter increased. In the 1990s, for instance, a telenovela scene used to last a minute and a half on average; in 2016–2017, by comparison, the length of the average scene dropped to less than a minute. With different actors and scenarios, alternating mainly indoor studio recordings with outside scenes, it is now possible to produce on several fronts with more material being recorded each day with this material pre-edited during the filming process.

In new reception models and changes in the way that audience reconfigure screen images it is also possible to observe that Brazilian telenovelas have been undergoing interferences in terms of their spectatorship and narratives. In addition, the works themselves offer new possibilities for audience-provided collaborative content, which is quite different from rejecting, influencing or celebrating a narrative proposed by the author, as will be seen shortly. John Fiske (1987) noted that a negotiation process takes place between the content proposed and the viewers' stance. For Fiske, the balance of power lies with the audience in that negotiation. According to Henry Jenkins (2006, 2013) – a key figure in theorizing the growing power of participatory television audiences – new interactive tools and platforms lead audience not only to consume the content originally produced for television in a unique way, but also to produce new content from it.

Reconfiguring Spectatorship

Even with these changes, some key ingredients of daily television drama had not changed in Brazil until recently: namely, the control of the narrative temporal flow – and thus the continuity of the story – by the author and therefore the network's control over the flow in which chapters are broadcast and rerun. For decades, telenovela chapters have been offered to the audience on television every day from Monday to Friday (or Saturday, depending on the product). Therefore, the arcs of the main plots and the secondary plots as well as the trajectory of the characters and the changes and conflicts they all go through are presented to viewers in a linear and continuous manner, although some viewers might choose not to follow that linearity of course.

Mittell (2015) sees time as an essential ingredient for every narrative, especially in television. For Mittell, three different temporal flows can be considered for all narratives: *story time* – how time passes within the story; *discourse time* – length and structure within a narrative; and *narration time* – the time during which the plot is broadcast, that is, the deadline set for the story to be told. Much the same model for classifying narrative temporal flow applies to telenovelas and, of course, time is always a major writing tool for authors. Sarah Kozloff (1992) already considered the way that time distortions help us to discover the narrator on television. The closer real time is to discourse, the more invisible and less intrusive the narrator or storyteller is. A live narrative would be the antithesis of one including repetitions, parallel actions, flashbacks or flash-forwards, temporal elasticity, etc., when the narrator – in the case of a work of fiction, the author – is easily revealed. In a television discourse, the events of a story are changed as well as their order and duration. Citing Seymour Chatman's classification of time-related tools that a narrator can use to build a discourse,[5] the author concludes that finding out the motivations for a narrator's story-time choices can help us to discover and describe an author's characteristics. Until recently, in other words, the time flow of a telenovela – be it story time, discourse time or narration time – was not something that viewers could control.

But this lack of control has changed amidst the rise of video on demand services in Brazil. Partly in order to meet the demand of increasing online audiences, TV Globo launched the Globo Play (VOD) video platform in November 2015. In recent years, all major television networks in the world have launched digital platforms that offer OTT content directly to consumers. SBT, for instance, was the first Brazilian network to have a multi-channel network where its artists and contents are all on a single digital platform. These initiatives seek to use the power of ratings in broadcast to promote their digital spaces with an eye on the future and try to synchronize the displacement of the audience to different screens along with the displacement of content and its transmedia extensions. They also seek to meet the demand of advertisers who increasingly seek to migrate their advertisements to digital platforms and operate under new business models, such as selling content or content catalogues directly to consumers. Viewers must sign up to access content on the Globoplay video platform. They can watch live streaming or browse content on the menu. The platform includes TV Globo content from several decades in the same place.

Lev Manovich (2006), speaking of digital images, argues that the new characteristics of the information society will follow a logic that is distinct from modernism, which wanted to erase the old. However, Globoplay's biggest attraction for future subscribers would not be its list of past productions but rather its unpublished content. Subscribers can watch some series before they are shown on free broadcast television. In addition, they can watch full telenovela chapters and serial episodes. Those who consume content for free have to watch them by segments on Globoplay or GSHOW – TV Globo's entertainment portal. By providing content in this way, however, the company allows viewers to appropriate the work's *narration time* and consequently *discourse time* for the first time in the history of Brazilian television. Although the company sells to subscribers the comfort of watching full chapters, by offering its content in segments, it may be inadvertently favoring a new spectatorship practice in the context of the most traditional of Brazilian television products – a product that may have changed some stylistic traits but has nevertheless maintained largely the same spectatorship model for over half a century.

Manovich (2015) further notes that while cinema and the novel privilege narrative, the computer age introduces its correlate: the database. Manovich describes the predominance of the database in new media and points to the website of a radio or television station as an example. Watching linear programming on streaming is just one option among many. Audiences supposedly tend to watch content where, how and when they want, including the telenovela usually associated with prime time of free television. An initial look into the number of views of each segment available online for primetime telenovela *A Força do Querer*, which holds the highest ratings among telenovelas playing at the same time, demonstrates that segments have quite different ratings. On 19 June 2017, for instance, the most watched segment on the Globoplay platform had 88,140 thousand views, while the least watched one had less than half of that – 31,689 thousand views.[6] It is no surprise that the most frequently watched segments are the first one and the last, i.e. the chapter's cliffhanger and its subsequent resolution in the following chapter. Similar to the newspaper feuilleton, telenovela chapters are open-ended in order to excite viewers' curiosity so that they watch the telenovela on the next day. Telenovela chapters can end with more than one cliffhanger, since they have several narrative subplots. Before and after commercial breaks, there are also smaller cliffhangers with the same purpose: to keep viewers interested in the plot.

In addition to the high number of views of the opening scene and the cliffhangers of online telenovela chapters, a look at the week's block of chapters also shows that certain plots or subplots are more successful online than others. Manovich (2015), when researching the database culture and its relation or contrast to the narrative, observes that a traditional linear narrative is one among many other possible trajectories. As already noted, a telenovela has several subplots and they may alternate in terms of protagonist. Glória Perez's telenovela *A Força do Querer* premiered on 3 April 2017 with the story of 'mermaid' Ritinha, played by actress Isis Valverde, and her love triangle with urban playboy Ruy and truck driver/eternal boyfriend Zeca. During the week of 19–24 June the telenovela (on broadcast television and online) focused on another plot, the one involving the character Bibi, played by Juliana Paes. A total of fifty-eight segments were provided with calls to this subplot while the subplot involving mermaid Ritinha had 34 segments published. However, the scenes with the most views are those of Ritinha's love triangle, which after a few months had become a quintet involving other characters. The most watched segment of the week, on 24 June, with 134,523 thousand views,[7] is part of this plot and called 'Zeca e Ruy ficam impressionados com Jeiza e Ritinha' ('Zeca and Ruy are impressed with Jeiza and Ritinha'). Naming the scenes for viewers is a feature of new digital platforms and of the new spectatorship model as this had never been done for the traditional way of viewing telenovelas on Brazilian television. But consuming content and understanding what is offered by the database would be confusing without such scene-naming. Importantly, by observing the number of views of the segments referring to this subplot, it is possible to conclude that some people watched only this particular plot and built their own trajectory in the database. It is also possible to observe that segments with strong scenes that include sensual, dramatic or violent elements have thousands more views than others, regardless of the subplots to which they belong. For example, in that same week, a car crash scene from a subplot that did not have so many online views – that of transgender character Ivana – had 86,191 views while other scenes in that subplot had only half that amount on average. But it is possible that some viewers watch only scenes from that subplot and scenes from others that are sensual, for instance, or that some people choose certain scenes to review after watching the content of the telenovela under the traditional model. Each viewer is able not only to create his or her own narrative but also to watch segments from a single chapter over several days or segments from one week all at once.

Construction Sets

Despite networks' efforts to control their content on video sharing platforms, it is not difficult to find fan-made compilations that narrate the trajectory of their favorite couples. *A história de Pedro e Karina (Perina) – Parte 1* (*The Story of Pedro and Karina (Perina) – Part 1*) is an edition featuring only scenes with the couple played by Rafael Vitti and Isabela

Santoni from Malhação. The video had 594,764 thousand views and in order to escape private content identification tools, the author blurred the corners of the image and left the edited scenes slightly out of focus. This video is not unique, and it is possible to find edited videos including scenes with several telenovela couples – whether or not they are still being broadcast. Everyone uses resources such as blurring images, framing scenes or applying color-changing filters to escape identification tools for copyright purposes. There are many differences between compilations present on video sharing platforms and customized viewing of specific segments on Globoplay by a single viewer. Compilations are narratives offered to viewers as closed products. For instance, the video of *Pedro and Karina* includes some curator work since the compilation does not include all the scenes of the protagonist couple in the 275 chapters that have been broadcast. On the other hand, watching specific segments on Globoplay requires the viewers' effort and choice at each view.

When the network offered a telenovela in segments, or scenes, it certainly did not intend to allow viewers to build their own narratives, but instead to provide those who lost part of the plot with the possibility of following what happened in the telenovela. However, many viewers, now facing the possibility of watching only the plot in which they are interested, might prefer to watch the telenovela by segments or by selecting only certain subplots rather than watching the whole thing, thus choosing their own narrative based on their own logic. The most watched full chapter of telenovela *A Força do Querer* on the week of 19–24 June was the second chapter with 54,710 views – that is, less than half of the segment most watched for free.

This process of choice can be called the *customized* telenovela, which repeats internally what would be the transmedia logic: one can choose to view only peripheral narratives within one product rather than the main narrative. Here the main narrative subplots of a telenovela can be seen as equivalent to the transmedia flagship product as suggested by Jenkins. We can compare the available segments from one chapter with what Manovich (2015) defined as the paradigmatic dimension of a database. That is, all of the images are available for viewers to create their own narratives. 'Put differently, *the database of choices from which narrative is constructed (the paradigm) is implicit, while the actual narrative (the syntagm) is explicit*' (2015, 11 [original emphasis]). It is clear that these images – differently from what Manovich describes as 'data of choice' – include an original narrative that makes sense for those who want to consume the totality of the work. Nevertheless, individualized viewing could be seen as what Manovich defines as syntagmatic dimension, since each viewer creates his or her own relationships in a narrative with meaning. For Manovich (2015), new media tend to make the database into something material and the possibilities of narrative derived from it into something virtual. The author argues that 'modern media is the new battlefield for competition between database and narrative' (Manovich 2015, 13). However, what Manovich may not have considered is the transformation of the traditional narrative itself – and no contemporary audiovisual content is seen as more traditional in Brazil than prime-time telenovelas – into a database to be later reorganized by its consumers as a customized narrative, uniting database and narrative as part of this process. And if the database is inherent in new media, as Lev Manovich (2015) claims, then as television adapts to the digital world it also provides spaces for resistance. While this transformation and the resulting offer of content by the network for the audience's personalized consumption are not intentional or at least not intended for this purpose, providing content in this way takes away an essential part of an author's power and gives it to the public: use and control of the flow of narrative time as a writing tool. This opportunity meets the demands of those viewers who do not identify with all of a telenovela's various plots. Considering all the changes telenovelas have undergone – updating narratives, division by subplots, influence of series, etc. – perhaps the next change will be precisely this new way of watching content.

A Fanfic Invades Daily Television Drama

There are several blogs and profiles on different social networks made by fans that dedicate their time to the history of telenovelas, recording new stories, characters and events and comparing them with previous ones. Baccega et al. (2016) note that most of them continue to be amateurs, regardless of the tens of thousands of followers they might have. Telenovelas have always received attention by specialized media in Brazil, but social media tools certainly increase the value of amateur commentators. Fan clubs and amateur critics with tens of thousands of followers who write for their own blogs and other social media are now considered important by television networks and are part of the communication strategy adopted to launch a new telenovela. They might be invited to a press conference or to participate in a special online event. Even though the repercussions of amateur critics and fan clubs are noticed and appreciated, until recently little of what they actually produced was returned to the closed narrative of a telenovela.

Malhação (*Young Hearts*) is a TV Globo program watched daily by approximately 15 million people in Brazil and is a notable exception to claim, granting its audience increased participation. Despite addressing the teen universe, its audience is mainly adult and female. It has been broadcast from Monday to Friday for over two decades since 1995. For each season, the cast, the universe and the narrative change and another name is added next to '*Malhação*'. Since each season now lasts a year, the company considers the product a telenovela. New scenography in and outside the studio area is built and new management and production staff are hired. The program is also a laboratory for young actors and actresses who might star TV Globo's main telenovelas. Perhaps as a result of the universe it portrays, *Malhação* is also a pioneer of *transmediality* in Brazilian television and has an extremely participative audience. The program's official Facebook profile has more than 12 million followers while its official Twitter profile has 700,000. What's more, dozens of fan profiles of the show can be found across all social media networks. And interestingly, a feature of *Malhação Sonhos* (2014/2015 season) was that it made extensive use of fan fiction, also known as fanfic, through a collaborative promotion on the program's website with episodes broadcast to millions of people.

Fanfics are texts produced by fans based on the universe of a book, film or television show – in short, they refer to texts derived from a work and its original universe. Souza (2015) conducted a study on fan fictions made for Brazilian telenovelas between 2010 and 2013. After analyzing more than a hundred productions, she found that some of the main modulations observed are precisely rewritings of the end of the works as well as changes operated in traditional characters, situations and environments. Such changes in the narrative operated by some fans in this specific environment could already be considered forms of viewers' resistance toward the work, but that still does not mean interference in the power of the author of the telenovela and its narrative. One must also take into account fans' affection for the narrative, which, according to Clay Shirky (2009, 2010), is one of the driving forces behind this production that also includes compiling favorite characters' video clips, creating characters' fictional profiles on social networks, etc. According to Jason Mittell (2015), while participatory culture has greatly expanded, most viewers still want to be mere recipients of a good story well told. But he also points out that if these viewers are disappointed, they will simply abandon the narrative.

Social networks dedicated to this type of fan-aided production[8] also include literally hundreds of fanfics about the universe and characters from *Malhação*'s various seasons. The productions usually have a rating suggested by the authors themselves (indicating if they include sex or violent scenes), a brief legal disclaimer, which admits that the universe and/or characters were not created by the fanfic's author, and a storyline, which is a summary of the characters and the plot. Fanfics can be short or have several long chapters. Most are open for comments and sharing. Authors publicize their fanfics on specialized social networks and in several other interactive web environments.

By way of example, TV Globo's *Malhação Sonhos* was based on William Shakespeare's play *The Taming of the Shrew*. The authors used the text to reverse preconceived gender caricatures, with Pedro (Petruchio) as a weak and sensitive teenager while Karina (Catarina) was portrayed as a physically stronger, violence-prone girl. Gabriel and Grijó

(2016) analyzed fan fictions derived from the universe of *Malhação Sonhos* in the social network Nyah! – one of the largest repositories of this type of production on the internet. They found 115 completed fanfics. The shortest fanfic had a single chapter while the longest one had 65. All but one chose not to create new characters and used the show's protagonists as their main characters. As Gabriel and Grijó (2016) point out, although fanfics create their own narratives, fans still connect to the original story, creating new plots around the main romantic couples. Nevertheless, several texts set the characters or main couples in different environments – for example, in college, as hospitalized or even in imaginary prisons. And several of these fan-made narratives wish to defend and support their favorite couples when the story broadcast seems to go the other way, since love triangles are a common ingredient in telenovelas.

The fan fiction 'I'm forever yours' (original title in English), with 56 chapters, written by ColorwoodGirl, had 1,286 comments and the largest number of recommendations by 12 April 2017. The author has written new stories about the telenovela's main couple, but it is set in a future time period compared to the original narrative. In the show, the couple is still in high school, but in the fanfic story they are already in their twenties. The original telenovela has an age rating of 10-plus years, but this fanfic includes drug abuse and strong scenes and is rated by its author as 13-plus. Another fanfic featuring *Malhação Sonhos*' main couple, called 'O Melhor Amigo da Noiva' ('The Bride's Best Male Friend'), includes many sensual scenes that would never be recorded and broadcast on evening television. The author suggested an age rating of 16-plus. As noted earlier, fanfic authors often write to other fans like themselves and do not expect people involved in the production to read them. However, one of the fans in this case sent the link to his work to the authors. Using the nickname Anammack, he openly disagreed with the way that the story unfolded and wanted to argue for an alternative end to a love triangle. The staff decided that some kind of dialogue between the original narrative and the fanfic material would be interesting – a dialogue that would also take place between authors and fans. Since every TV Globo production has a transmedia author and producer, the person responsible for this area suggested a promotion for choosing a fanfic to be produced by the show's staff.

Even though *Malhação* is one of the programs in which new media experimentation is more deeply researched and tested, bringing fans' transmedial content into a television program was risky, especially given copyright issues. The original idea was called *Malhação Fanfic* and was embraced by the program's scriptwriting, production, internet and transmedia staff. It would be a collaborative experience in which fans would send their texts and ideas based on *Malhação Sonhos*' expanded universe. The staff would then record the idea chosen by the program's staff (production, scriptwriters, internet) to be offered on the official *Malhação* website. The fanfics were then be posted on a blog dedicated to this initiative and linked to the program's website.[9] The project had a big impact on print newspapers and social networks at the time. The first theme – 'Sonhos de romance' ('Dreams of Romance') – received 4,801 submissions, and the story selected – 'Bianca e seus dois maridos' ('Bianca and Her Two Husbands') – ended up not only on the website but also broadcast as part of a television episode.

The selected fanfic mixed the universe of *Malhação* – playing with a love triangle that was being broadcast – and that of a famous novel by Brazilian writer Jorge Amado, *Dona Flor and Her Two Husbands*, which features a love triangle between a woman, her current husband and the ghost of her dead husband. One of the two winners of the first fanfic initiative was a 15-year-old student living in Rio de Janeiro's Favela da Rocinha, who had the opportunity to see her scene recorded at the studio. Scriptwriters then opted to adapt her fanfic for television.

The experience with this project has been positive despite the risks, but the increasingly blurred boundary between amateur and professional content can also trigger conflicts. It raises questions, such as what is the difference between a professional author and an amateur author in this context, since both create fictional content that is broadcast and consumed on television? Metrics are one means of differentiating the two. Matt Hills (2002) notes that we cannot assume that all fans are producers or associate intense consumption of a telenovela with cultural values of production. After all, thousands of people can write fanfics about *Malhação*, but the show is watched by millions every day. Jenkins, Ford and Green (2013) write about fans' voluntary work channeled through capitalist practices. It is difficult to establish a value balance when very different 'currencies' are involved in the exchange: financial return, recognition, affection, prestige, and so on. And this kind of relationship has already become common practice through social media tools.[10] It is undeniable that the fanfic experience has added value to the show as well as promoted and publicized *Malhação*. But what have fans gained in return? For winner Ana Carolina de Souza, being recognized by those who produce the program for which she has affection was certainly a bargaining chip in this type of relationship. It is the realization by the producers of the original work that what is being produced by fans is perhaps of equally high quality and value. But was it a fair exchange? One could wonder who gained more out of the experience – TV Globo or Ana Carolina de Souza – or even if the network took advantage of a fan's voluntary work to promote its own program. This boundary between voluntary work and exploitation, between recognition and misappropriation of creation, between fan and author is still to be negotiated and understood in the light of this new and expanding transmedia scenario. It is likely, at least for now, that this relationship will never be fully consolidated or perfectly balanced. Jenkins, Ford and Green (2013) sustain that the status of what is exchanged online is hybrid and often what has sentimental value for one party has commercial value for the other. The fanfic project for *Malhação* is one such case. However, once the pact is established and a balance of expectations is achieved, even if purposes and agendas are different, there may be a point of contact between a major television network and a 15-year-old member of the audience.

This fanfic project above was in fact only one of several initiatives used by Brazil's hegemonic television network and its main drama product to learn, gain strength and reinvent itself through fanfic engagement. Contrary to the unintentional offer of change in the temporal flow of telenovelas on the digital platform, this communication and absorption of collaborative content was clearly intentional. Television is made up of people and, even though they are part of a major corporation's larger strategy, they interact with social media networks and they navigate and relate to what they admire. In short, these people are not excluded from the spirit or the ethos of today's world. This experience, like others of its kind, has shown that television is permeable to collaborative content. In fact, it has always been permeable and, as it reinvents itself again, that permeability is increased and rediscovered in the process of change. TV Globo, however, did not continue with the fanfic experience – except as part of a branded content experience and with lower engagement. Engaging with such fanfics, particularly in such integrated, transmedial fashion, comes with added demands on authors producers, directors and employees – demands that not everyone is willing to accept while it is not yet common practice. Also, initiatives that do not prove to be financially profitable in this environment are likely to be discontinued.

Conclusion

Telenovelas have been broadcast since 1951 – one year after the start of television in Brazil. Today, TV Globo's telenovelas occupy five prime-time hours each day, providing national narratives, exhibiting stories, actors and actresses, showing and influencing culture. In many ways and for many people in Brazil, the telenovela is synonymous with television. The format still fulfills this cultural and industrial function today, though it cannot avoid meeting the needs of new audiences, new transmedia environments, new interactive tools and new possibilities for the audience to actively engage with and shape the work. The Brazilian audience may still be watching television preferentially in the 'traditional' way, but its interaction with content is increasingly sophisticated and is amplified by digital platforms and social media networks. Experiences and initiatives like those described in this chapter are strong indicators of the directions that Brazilian television is likely to take, shifting what is meant by television. For in Brazil, at least, the future of telenovela and the future of television are intrinsically linked.

Notes

1 Instituto Brasileiro de Geografia e Estatística, PNAD 2015: www.ibge.gov.br/
2 ComScore is a US-based measurement company conducting internet analysis in seventy-five countries. comscore.com
3 Rosane Svartman, co-author of this chapter, is a film and television director and screenwriter. She was the final writer of TV Globo's *Malhação Intensa* (2012/2013) (*Young Hearts – Intense*) and *Malhação Sonhos* (2014/2015) (*Young Hearts – Dreams*), for which she was a finalist for the 2013 Digital Emmy Award, the 2016 Emmy Kids International and the 2017 Emmy Kids Digital. With Paulo Halm, she wrote TV Globo's 9 pm telenovela *Totalmente Demais* (*Totally Awesome*).
4 Jason Mittell (2015) notes that even American series have absorbed melodrama techniques and more extensive and dramatic narrative arcs. For him, such change is not necessarily a direct influence of soap operas – American and European daily television drama without predefined duration. For Mittell, other serial works from different media such as comic books, movie franchises and 19th-century literature also influenced serials and have their own connections to melodrama.
5 *Summary*: Discourse-time is shorter than story-time; *Ellipsis*: Discourse time is zero; Scene: Story-time and discourse-time are equal (sitcom); *Stretch*: Discourse-time is longer than story-time; *Pause*: the same as stretch except that story-time is zero.
6 Data collected on 26 June 2017.
7 Data collected on 26 June 2017.
8 The main social networks focused on fanfics in Brazil include Nyah (https://fanfiction.com.br/categoria/1290/malhacao/) and Spirit (https://socialspirit.com.br/categorias/malhacao).
9 The most accessed content on the blog was: 'Soluca? Heidequina? Ruivique? Na *fanfic* tem casais que você nunca viu!', with 75,753 hits.
10 There are several experiences and examples of collaborative audiovisual projects, but they are conducted under the supervision of an artist or producer for commercial purposes. Ridley Scott produced the feature film *Life in a Day* using audiovisual content sent from several parts of the world (see www.youtube.com/lifeinaday). In 2008, Paulo Coelho provided a short story book on his blog – *The Experimental Witch* – for people to produce short films that could be part of a feature film derived from the book (a project later announced at the Cannes Film Festival). Only the winners were paid for their work, in addition to being the authors of episodes of the feature film, of course. In both cases, contributors gained visibility and recognition, and in the second case, besides the financial payment, they gained prestige and enhanced their resumes.

Bibliography

Azevedo, Camila, Carol Lorusso, Daniela Diniz, Fabíola Glenia, Iselaa Pereira, Juliana Lang, Lilian Arruda, Mariana C. Torres, Mariana Muniz, Muniky Sena, Paula Lordello and Roberta Margarit. *Autores: História da Teledramaturgia*. Editora Globo: Rio de Janeiro, 2008.
Baccega, Maria Aparecida, Maria Amélia, Paiva Abrão. "A violência doméstica representada na telenovela A regra do jogo." *Comunicação & Educação* 21:1 (2016): 109–118.

Buarque, Heloisa de A. *Telenovela, Consumo e gênero.* Tese de Doutorado, Instituto de Filosofia e Ciências Humanas, Universidade Estadual de Campinas, 2001.

Chatman, Seymour. *Story and Discourse: Narrative Structure in Fiction and Film.* Ithaca, NY: Cornell University Press, 1978.

Fiske, John. *Television Culture.* London and New York: Methuen, 1987.

Gabriel, Araujo and Wesley Pereira Grijó. "Fanfictions: Convergência, Participação e Remixagem na Resignifição do Conteúdo Midiático." Paper presented at the *IX Symposia Nacional ABCiber Conference* (Puc Sao Paulo, 8–10 December 2016).

Hills, Matt. *Fan Cultures.* London and New York: Routledge, 2002.

Jenkins, Henry. *Convergence Culture: Where Old and New Media Collide.* New York: New York University Press, 2006.

Jenkins, Henry, Sam Ford and Joshua Green. *Spreadable Media: Creating Value and Meaning in a Networked Culture.* New York: New York University Press, 2013.

Kozloff, Sarah. "Narrative Theory and Television." In *Channels of Discourse Reassembled: Television and Contemporary Criticism*, edited by Robert C. Allen, 67–100. London and New York: Routledge, 1992.

Manovich, Lev. "Image Future." *Manovich.net.* 2006. Accessed 14 June 2017. http://manovich.net/index.php/projects/image-future.

Manovich, Lev. "Banco de dados." *Revista Eco-Pós* 18:1 (2015): 7–26.

Martín-Barbero, Jesus. "Dos meios às mediações – Comunicação, cultura ehegemonia." *Coordenadoria de Comunicação da UFRJ.* 2003. Accessed 15 June 2017. www.olharvirtual.ufrj.br/2006/imprimir.php?id_edicao=121&codigo=9.

Mittell, Jason. *Complex TV: The Poetics of Contemporary Television Storytelling.* New York: New York University Press, 2015.

Shirky, Clay. *Cognitive Surplus: How Technology Makes Consumers into Collaborators.* London: Penguin Books, 2010.

Shirky, Clay. *Here Comes Everybody: The Power of Organizing without Organizations.* New York: Penguin Books, 2009.

Souza, Maria Carmem Jacob de. "Entre novelas e novelos: um estudo das fan ctions de teleno- velas brasileiras (2010–2013)." In *Por uma teoria de fãs da cção televisiva* brasileira, edited by Maria Immacolata Vassallo de Lopes, 44–58. Porto Alegre: Sulina, 2015.

Part III
Asian Transmediality

10 Japan
Fictionality, Transmedia National Branding and the Tokyo 2020 Olympic Games

Manuel Hernández-Pérez

The term 'convergence culture' (Jenkins 2006) is still one of the most influential characterizations in Cultural Studies and Communication Studies. As has been commented throughout this book, this concept concerns a global phenomenon that includes other technological, sociological and communicative aspects. Among other impacts, Jenkins points to discursive fragmentation, a global trend toward content-recycling, and the participation of active (often digital) audiences (ibid.). While certainly implicit, others have preferred to emphasize this sociological aspect of the audiences' empowerment. The concept of digital storytelling, for example, refers to an audience that not only can but also feels the need to tell more stories (Couldry 2008). These two aspects of transmedia communication – the multiplication of formats and products and the multiplication of increasingly individual and subjective voices – have aroused interest in the theorization of fictional transmediality.

Fictionality, the key theoretical focus of this chapter, can be considered a transmedia feature but, importantly, is not necessarily fictional storytelling. While storytelling etymologically addresses the narrative features of a given form of communication, as this chapter is intended to show, transmediality is not necessarily linked to fictional narrations. Still, the transmedia phenomenon can be studied through the lens of narrative theory. In the field of journalism, for example, it is common to find a distinction between cross-media (which many understand to be multiplatform adaptation) and transmediality (a scattered narrative) (Veglis 2012). Though it is clear that we do not refer to genres or fictional contexts (journalism at least tries to tell the truth), there should still be room for the introduction of fictional elements. Thus, 'fictionality' can be understood as either a quality or a mode of fictive discourse to which we all have access. Audiences know that a text or part of a text is not real, but this is accepted as a way of establishing an argument or a pleasure. In this model of rhetoric and cognition, fictionality is seen as a universal quality, defined as 'intentional use of invented stories and scenarios' (Nielsen, Phelan, and Walsh 2015). However, if a fictional model informs a transmedia narrative, then this model needs to be understood through a communication scheme. As has been suggested elsewhere, fictionality 'resides in a way of using a language, and its distinctiveness consists in the recognisably distinct rhetorical set invoked by that use' (Walsh 2007). This definition, however, is questionable, for as any theory of communication explains, there can be a difference between what is intentional and what is finally recognized. For example, can it be considered a fictional narrative if audiences respond to it as a case of nonfiction? Imagine the extreme case of mock-documentaries, by way of further example. Perhaps, if the definition of 'genre' depends on a dialogue with the audience, a definition of fictionality can be inclusive, creating media products that are both fictional and nonfictional at the same time. Such ambiguity between fiction and nonfiction, conceived of through the lens of transmediality in the context of the Japanese media landscape, is the focus of this chapter.

This hybridization between fiction and nonfiction is even more tangible in those contexts where popular culture plays a more dominant role. It is possible, after all, that the most active media users today are young people and that popular culture is a substantial part of their consumption practices and production habits. Equally, the most consumed and shared transmedia stories in the world today belong to fictional narratives, with a high prevalence of fantasy worlds and science fiction (Scolari, Bertetti and Freeman 2014). It is thus arguably fictional stories that inspire greater participation from audiences and contribute to the creation of additional media texts in both specialized fandoms and in popular culture more generally.

It is my aim in this chapter, however, to counter such an assumption. I intend to link with narrative theory, as the main axis for a communicational and rhetorical study of Japanese media and transmedia culture. First, I will explore the main Japanese communication agents and the current state of the convergence process in this country, taking into account both technological and sociological aspects. Second, I will summarize from a historical perspective the main working elements of the Japanese media industries in relation to their use of fictionality and their convergence with media ecosystems and institutional communication systems. Finally, I will examine these various issues through an exemplar case study, assessing how the reformulations of nonfictional national branding strategies aligned to the popular 'Cool Japan' fictional narratives created for the Tokyo 2020 Olympic Games. Ultimately, I will demonstrate that it is almost impossible to build cultural (or nonfictional) messages across multiple media platforms that avoid replicating or at least referencing elements from other communication structures, notably fictional narratives.

Japanese Media Ecosystem: A Brief Overview

Following the global trend, since the beginning of the century there have been many attempts by the Japanese government to foster technological convergences and to stimulate the creative industries by embracing transmedia trends. In the case of Japan, the rapid onset of new technologies (particularly the internet and mobile technologies) is the result of an 'interventionist' policy, which has been defined in terms of 'integration' and 'digitalization' (Menon 2006). The term integration refers to how the media can share the same technological infrastructure. For example, mobile, internet and television can now all be offered by the same provider through high-speed internet connections. On the other hand, this digitalized integration is more oriented to the treatment of content, and in particular the transformation of content into digital formats. Political and historical factors have contributed to a rise in platforms and transmedia agents, although largely in a different way to other countries.

Indeed, it is important to orient this chapter by outlining some contextual information concerning the workings and cultures of the Japanese media industries. With regard to the television and video streaming, it is notable that despite the progress of social media and the internet, 51% of Japanese audiences still watch television on a daily basis, particularly to be informed about news or other nonfictional content (Reuters Institute 2016b). In terms of the consumption of fiction-based entertainment products, however, the most popular media platforms are YouTube and the Japanese distributor NicoNico Video. Over the years video streaming has been highly popular for both the consumption of news and the consumption of entertainment. Of great importance to this trend are the multiplatform tools of newspapers, such as NHK or Tokyo TV. In fact, reports indicate that watching the news on the online site (39%) is more common than through social media networks (15%) (Reuters Institute 2016b). In Japan, everything points to a shift toward the convergence of multimedia platforms, due to the dominance of Kadokawa, the largest Publisher in Japan, as a content generator.

In the Japanese context, however, the regional press is used more frequently as a news source on a weekly basis (21%), followed by nationals Yomiuri Shimbun (16%), Asashi Shimbun (14%) and lower level Mainichi Shimbun (5%) and Sankei Shimbun (4%) (Reuters Institute 2016a). The continued interest in the local press in Japan may be linked to the interest of the Japanese people in political participation. The population has been re-politicized at the local level in response to the disapproval of national policy (Foljanty-Jost and Schmidt 2006). This kind of citizen participation can be found on social media, itself a form of expression that if not completely free is at least not directly controlled by the government. In that sense, the freedom of the national press in Japan has been questioned, due to the powerful influence of media conglomerates. An example of this influence would include *kisha clubs* ('reporters' club), which are associations that have a monopoly and exclusive access to numerous institutional sources. This high level of access eventually contributes to the homogeneity of news content and its ease of manipulation around the country (Au and Kawai 2012).

Yet the survival and prevalence of news aggregators like Yahoo News or BuzzFeed Japan are justified by the confidence that is generated by the quality and ideology of these portals (Reuters Institute 2016b). This, in the long term, is arguably detrimental to the emergence of a competent digital native press. Compared to other countries, aggregation behavior in Japan is a common and successful practice, similar in its frequency to other countries such as Korea or the Czech Republic. There is a large market for the news and many native digital platforms (along with other social applications like LINE or Mixi) have already taken emerging positions at the table. Interestingly, however, many Japanese people are more interested in 'soft' news such as entertainment and celebrity stories, as well as lifestyle news, arts and culture, and sports. Recent research indicates that audiences most interested in these topics are mainly women (44%), and between 18 and 24 years old (58%) (Reuters Institute 2016b). Consistent with other commented data, the news consumer profile in contemporary Japan is mainly passive: by which I mean that only 40% acknowledge that they engage with any form of news participation at all during an average week (Reuters Institute 2016b).

This passivity is countered by the growing attitudes toward mobile and social media, though. The Japanese government's commitment to technology is particularly geared toward the democratization of the internet environment. For example, in December 2016, The Internal Affairs and Communications Ministry announced the installation of 30,000 Wi-Fi access points prior to the Olympic events. This huge investment, which involved doubling the number of free points of access available in 2016 (Kikuchi 2016), aimed to provide free and immediate access to the internet to the victims of natural disasters. Although this move can be considered to have been highly beneficial to the tourism industry at all, especially on a commercial level, the immediate impact was nevertheless mainly local and cultural.

More broadly, so-called digital media have gradually replaced mass media in many respects. In Japan, where the population pyramid has been clearly inverted for decades, the bulk of internet users are over 35 years old, the same early adopters of mobile email some years ago (Boase and Kobayashi 2008). Despite the common image of Japan as a technology heaven and a mediatized society, in many respects the Japanese are less active in social media networks than their Asian neighbours. According to data from March 2015, for instance, Japan is only the fourth highest country in the Asian zone in terms of national internet penetration, with an index of 86% and the third position (84%) in unique mobile users (RVC, 2016). Furthermore, the Japanese are noted to spend less than 20 minutes a day on social media, a very low figure compared to Malaysians, Thais and Indonesian users, for example, who spend around two hours a day on said platforms. In terms of mobile social media use, Japan stands at 17%, which is below the average (22%) of the continent.

The use of the mobile for purchases or m-commerce is also low, being inferior to many countries of another continent in a list led by Asian countries like SK, China, HK, Thailand, Malaysia and Singapore. As a counterpart, it seems that, from 2015, mobile and tablets are increasingly used for the consumption of news (Reuters Institute 2016b). In relation to social media consumption, there are also slight differences to other countries in terms of user behavior. For example, while the most habitual behaviors are watching videos, reading or liking posts and checking profiles, the actions of the Japanese users tend to be more anonymous and less focused around liking posts and checking profiles. The country's relatively low index figure for streaming video consumption through social media can be explained partly by the already mentioned abundance of alternatives offered by traditional platforms via their official sites.

Much of the literature on Japanese media suggests that in the case of digital media, it is also possible to speak of a certain idiosyncrasy. Thus, the form, function and history of the creation of virtual communities in the Japanese context are different from those of other countries, including Western but also Asian ones. According to data from Asashi University (2016), the most used tools by Japanese consumers are LINE (38.6%), Facebook (28.0%), Twitter (26.6%), Mixi (9.6%) and Instagram (8.2%).[1] That being said, due to the similarity and consistency among digital platforms and the multiple overlaps in their use, it is necessary to consider the meaning of this consumption beyond the preference for a particular brand.

Mixi is a social media network more exclusive than Facebook since it aims to connect people with similar hobbies and interests only. In that sense, it is a platform more oriented toward the creation of communities. With Facebook, there is an implicit connection with other social networks by allowing the search of old schoolmates from high school or college. But with Mixi, this connection is limited to 1000 contacts. Until 2010, access to the internet was possible only by invitation. Subsequently, it became necessary to verify by mobile phone, a mechanism that limits the use of the platform to Japanese users or people already settled down in Japan. In that sense, the average profile of users up to 2015 was 44.6% between 15 and 24, also inhabitants of the populated Kanto area (Tokyo, Yokohama and surroundings). Anonymity and concern for privacy have been part of the nature of the network since its inception. During the first years, the platform saw many users adopting false profiles, supplanting celebrities. Fictional characters drawn from worlds of *manga* and anime were common occurrences. To counter this trend, in 2011 Mixi Page was established, a strategy similar to the separation that Facebook makes between personal profiles and professional pages. Also, Mixi was one of the first applications to use the footprint (*ashiato*), which lets users know who has visited their profile, when, and how many times. As a virtual community, Mixi incorporates a review function of products such as music and movies, somewhat similarly to other databases with social functions such as IMDB. In other words, Mixi is a platform that was designed for nonfictional content but, due to the culture of Japan, has drawn on an increasing number of fictional images – a trend that I will return to shortly.

For now, though, note that Mixi's monopoly began to lessen around 2008, replaced by other applications such as Twitter. Many consider that the success of Twitter in Japan is due to the coverage offered by its user's anonymous identity. That argument would be consistent with the popularity of Mixi and the fact that almost 21% of users also adopted anonymous profiles on Facebook (RVC 2016). Other technical features may also justify the popularity of these platforms. The incorporation of the internet into mobile devices was popular in Japan before it was in other countries, as the Japanese version of Twitter was released in 2008. Asian languages like Japanese or Chinese often take greater advantage of the software's 140-character limitation. In Japanese alphabets (*hiragana* and *katakana*), for example, with a syllabic basis, one character occupies half that of a Western language such as Spanish or English (even less if ideograms such as those derived from Chinese (*kanji*) are used, which can carry complete units of meaning (verbs, objects and so on) in each symbol).

Taken as a whole, then, the increase in the participation of different social media networks has grown steadily in recent years in Japan. The majority of studies indicate as a point of inflexion the Great Earthquake of March 2011 (Ikeda and Richey 2012), and understand that this event may be only the beginning of greater mobilization and political activism in the country. However, it seems that the natural participation of social media networks is not being fully used to support activism just yet. The most important virtual forums in Japan, such as Ni-Channeru, are more focused on gathering and creating communities around fictional worlds. This orientation toward escapism and fictionality can be understood as a characteristic of Japanese virtual communities. A comparative study conducted with South Korean audiences (Ishii and Ogasahara 2007) suggests that Japanese virtual communities are not as strongly related to the real group as the Korean ones. That is to say that they are formed and based primarily online only. In more recent study (Reuters Institute 2016b), the percentage of citizens that came to the SN as a primary source of news reached 7%, which is still considerably lower than other Western countries but significantly higher than the 3% figure recorded in 2015. The Japanese usually turn to YouTube (26%), Facebook (16%), Twitter (16%) and LINE (13%). In short, it seems that in the convergence of leisure and fictional products in Japan are the main tools of the country's communication, but hardly stand as the illustrative global example of convergence culture that many would naturally associate with Japan.

Japanese Transmediality

These perhaps surprising ideas about Japan's current state as a culture of convergence do not mean that the country is in any way averse to transmediality. Far from it, in fact. Japanese popular culture can be considered one of the main exportations to the global media imagery, and through its different visual styles (manga, *kawaii, chibi,* etc.) and narrative tropes the country's media has had significant influence on a huge number of transnational media industries. The most appropriate means of characterizing the Japanese media industries is arguably in relation to the *manga* medium (Hernández-Pérez 2017). This approach would emphasize the need to move from focusing on seriality – be it of retroactive or proactive origin – to focusing on cross-platform design. Centrality and reference, terminologies derived from cognitive science, are the main forms in which this model of cross-media narrative must be defined (ibid.). In this model, media franchises can be assigned to particular texts/set of texts to which all other elements refer (Genette 1989). This central text or parental is usually the first published *manga,* although there are exceptions originated in video games, light novel or anime. Japan has been the subject of a number of studies about the particularities of its media industries, and transmedia model, in which adaptations within *manga,* anime and toys are the basic mechanism of content recycling strategies, also called media mix.

The term 'media mix' in relation to the Japanese entertainment industry was officially introduced in an interview by Yoshio Irie, editor-in-chief of *Nakayoshi* magazine (Schodt 1996). This magazine, published since 1954 by Kodansha, was aimed at a teenage female audience, offering the usual serial stories of the period. It also offered articles and educational illustrations as a complement to these other ludic contents. Shortly after, due to the *manga* boom in Japan, a new market emerged based around works exemplified by Osamu Tezuka (*Princess Knight,* 1958) and Yumiko Ligarashi (*Candy Candy,* 1975–1979), in particular. In 1990, the magazine began to adopt and even prioritize the creation of stories for television scheduled to be released shortly after the corresponding *manga.* The goal, shared by many projects since then, was to reach the realization of the merchandizing potentials based on the characters, which would generate sustained commercial benefits. In fact, this model of collaboration between the merchandise industry and anime began to implant itself in the beginnings of the Japanese animation industry, beginning with *Tetsuwan Atomu* (1963), the first anime and also the first character to create a merchandise around him (Steinberg 2012).

The phenomenon of merchandizable *manga* or animation characters has since moved into institutional communication practices, causing an oversaturation of characters in institutions, companies, educational programs across Japan. This is certainly the case with *Yuru Kyara,* with its

PR agents operating in the form of mascots, and *Gotochi Kyara*, who act as ambassadors of a city or region (Occhi 2014). The most striking thing about the Kyara and its institutions is that they are characters without history or narrative, at least in the classical sense. All of them, however, possess the potential to engage audiences emotionally and therefore are able to generate an infinity of narratives. See, for example, the Twitter account of Kumamon, one of the most celebrated characters, representative of the Kumamoto area. The character reports on his activities as an ambassador almost daily through his personal Twitter account (@ 55_kumamon). Through his posted images, comments and reports about his visits to schools, museums and other institutions, the role of the Twitter account is to promote the selling of things like local agricultural commodities (such as oranges and strawberries). However, Kumamon's work can take him very far. At the end of November 2016, the popular mascot visited the French cities of Paris and Bordeaux. Kumamon also has other friends, other *kyara* that he visits in official acts of their corresponding prefectures and localities. In February 2017, he posted a picture with Ganba-kun and Ranba-chan in Nagasaki, and in December of the previous year he had visited Musubimaru, the mascot of the Miyagi Government Office. Kumamon's tweets are similar to those of a celebrity; on Facebook and Instagram, too, he speaks to his audience ('I'll work very hard this week') and wish them a good evening ('Good night (Oyakuma') while telling stories of his trips and activities. Through Kyara, Japanese institutional communication demonstrates how fictional narratives are intermingled in complex genres and communication frames that were not expected to be fictional, but in which nevertheless seem to be consumed as entertainment.

Following the model of other media mix industries, LINE similarly operates around the creation of characters with potential for transmedia expansion – a further trend of fictionality in Japanese media. LINE is an instant messaging tool similar to WhatsApp, and as part of its narrative expansion, it includes a whole family of characters led by Brown, a bear, and Cony, a white rabbit. The two characters are used symbolically in emoticons to represent the relationships of the couple, sometimes in an exclusively romantic way, since Brown is male and Cony female. In 2013, Tokyo TV channel 5 released an animated series based on these characters called *Line Town*. Finally, there is an official shop called Line Friends that can be found in the Harajuko town (Tokyo prefecture) with branches in other countries like Korea and Taiwan. LINE is popular in the Japanese youth sector on account of its strong visual identity, reinforced through its different functionalities and characters. Paid games are also quite popular. These are usually arcade or casual mini-games and can be played individually or in teams. Advertising is a great source of income for these platforms, namely due to the penetration of the tool nationally. Finally, and as an innovative feature in this sector, LINE brands its own merchandise which in turn generates further income via products such as T-shirts, games and toys. What the cases of LINE, Mixi and other social media networks in Japan reveal, therefore, is that interpersonal communication practices are significantly different compared to in other countries. In the case of Japan, both anonymity and escapism via the consumption of fictional products and characters are certainly an overarching cultural trend. But how do these characteristics play out in a large-scale Japanese cultural event?

Case Study: Tokyo 2020 Olympic Games and Brand Nationalism

On 7 September 2013, the International Olympic Committee (IOC) awarded the 2020 Games to Tokyo. The implications of this historic decision were of great importance to all economic sectors in Japan. It was also a chance to rebuild its international image, damaged by the other great event of the decade, the unfortunate incident caused by the Great Earthquake and the security breach in Fukushima. The overwhelming presence of Japanese content, especially in the field of animation and video games, has to some extent redefined the global image of contemporary Japanese culture. In the case of the West, this perception is differentiated at a generational level. Twenty years ago, for instance, Japan was seen as a threatening power whose main weapon, being a country without natural resources, was its methodology (*kaizen*). The subsequent explosion of the Japanese economic bubble dragged the country into a long recession of which it has not yet recovered. But in the midst of that economic recession, Japan seems to have found comfort in projecting an image of cultural hegemony with which it can come back to its old aspirations of leading Asia. Iwabuchi (2010) calls this strategy 'brand nationalism', rescuing in a certain way the imperialist past of Japan.

Brand nationalism was at the heart of the country's decision to host the Tokyo 2020 Olympic Games. Prime Minister Shinzō Abe had to answer questions about safety in his pitch for the concession of the Games, promising security as the main objective. Years later and with the date of the event growing closer, the international press sees the Games with scepticism. Junichiro Koizumi, a former prime minister, has accused Abe of lying about his ability to maintain adequate levels of nuclear security (McCurry 2016). Public scandals have followed in relation to various aspects of the Games and their organization, including investigations into bribery (Gibson 2016), doubts over security against cyberattacks (McCurry 2016), the resignation of the governor of Tokyo due to expenses scandals (Yoshida 2016) and even an entire change in the Tokyo 2020 logo following accusations of plagiarism (Addley 2016).

And yet when analyzed through the lens of transmediality, it is notable that the 'story' of the Tokyo 2020 Olympic Games, at least to date, has relied extensively on fictionality and on the characterization of its key players across multiple platforms, particularly social media. During the closing ceremony of Rio 2016, for instance, Shinzō Abe, Japan's prime minister, made a cosplay appearance dressed as Super Mario. His performance linked with the projection of an online video that included the expected inspirational images of Olympic athletes accompanied by some of Japan's main contributions to the collective imagination: Pac-Man, Hello Kitty, Doraemon and Captain Tsubasa. Facing the impossibility of arriving in time, Abe, now acting like a further protagonist in this fiction, is transformed into the well-known video game character. Helped by Doraemon, he finds one of the iconic trans-dimensional pipelines that will make it possible for him to reach Tokyo from his awaited appointment in Rio on time. Abe's cosplay, and in turn his fictitious performance online, connected itself with other actions from the country's past which linked to political influence through the appeal and popularity of Japanese creative industries. But where did this practice of injecting fictionality into its cultural practices of national branding first emerge from?

For years the Japanese government has promulgated policies that would improve the sale of its products and develop the 'Cool Japan' brand strategy, a direction it has taken since 1986 when Prime Minister Nakasone promoted the 'internationalization' (*kokusaika*) of the country (Daliot-Bul 2009). Interest in promoting the country's media arts coincides with a delicate moment in Japan's economic history that has stalled in a recession since the early 1990s. With the arrival of former Prime Minister Junichiro Koizumi in 2001, Japan started to be clear that it should coordinate the appropriate measures for tits production, viewing and other aspects of these arts. From that moment, media arts, including *manga*, video games, animation, among others, started to be officially promoted, with the larger aim being to attract international attention, leading to greater interest and understanding of Japan. But above all, it is considered the 'role that popular culture can play in the promotion of industry and tourism, as well as cultural exchange' (Agency for Cultural Affairs 2003). In 2004, the first Strategic Intellectual Property Program (IPSP) was created, with the purpose of 'making Japan a world leader in content' (IPSP 2006). Following this trend, Seiichi Kōndo, the Commissioner for Cultural Affairs, has repeatedly referred to the concept of 'Cool Japan' and the role that culture must play in international politics. However, for Kōndo, entertainment-oriented policy projects are an incomplete picture, and while recognizing the utility of fiction in attracting international attention, he prefers to focus on a more traditional and holistic view of Japanese culture, relative to that of other countries in the Asian sphere (Kōndo 2011).

Even so, the Japanese Council of Cultural Affairs has taken very noticeable decisions at an international level to integrate various characters such as Astroboy, Doraemon and Hello Kitty into the country's national branding strategy – often promoting these characters as ambassadors while promoting their media products. The main promoter of these products was Foreign Minister Taro Aso, who for the first time used the term 'power' to refer to the popularity of Japanese characters in Asian markets (Aso 2006). Taro Aso was then named Prime Minister after the resignation of Yasuo Fukuda in September 2007. Being a *manga* fan and having contributed to its diffusion in the Council of Cultural Affairs, Aso's appointment highlighted the power of politics to promote the media arts, and indeed vice versa. During 2009, Aso continued with his plan to promote the media arts sector, promising that the media industry would gain 4 million jobs by 2020 and increase national capital by 1.2 trillion yen. That same year he embarked on a project that would be strongly criticized by the opposition: the construction of a *manga* museum in the Tokyo district of Akibahara. However, these were to be projects and promises that he could not ultimately carry out, since his government would abruptly come to an end a few months later, drawing a resignation motivated by pressure from the opposition on account of the country's difficult economic situation.

The concept of 'Cool Japan', however, continued to live on, defining the country's approach to national branding across media. In 2010, METI established the Cool Japan Office and in January 2012 it published the Cool Japan Strategy document. The strategy was oriented toward the promotion of cultural industries and recognized the importance of Asian, European and mainly North American markets (METI Ministry of Economy Trade and Industry 2012). Although the potential of the creative industries, as well as fashion and food industries, is underlined, it is surprising that other less valuable export sectors such as express delivery services, the Japanese-style Inn, traditional arts and crafts are also included. While it is possible that 'Cool Japan' does not mean the same for international audiences as it does for those responsible for Japan's national branding in the country itself, what is important is that the strategy was based on the blending of diverse creative and cultural industries, including both fictional and nonfictional forms. During the following years, very little has been said again from the Japanese government about 'Cool Japan'. It seems that 'Cool Japan' is a cultural narrative that has slowly diluted in the press (*The Japan Times*, though, continues to include a section devoted to the concept, and it remains a topic of interest for academics in the social area). However, Japan's identity crisis after the great East Japan earthquake may have fuelled interest in this question. Japan is now at a crossroads in terms of its global agenda, its national re-branding and its economic goals (Mandujano 2013), which strongly links the tragedy of the earthquake with the need for a 'Cool Japan' resurgence.

That resurgence has come via the branding and discourse of the Tokyo 2020 Olympic Games, which has taken a logical approach to boosting and supporting these strategies, but also serves as an example of competing narratives across media. Discourses of multiculturalism and the diversity of Japan may be the most important factor here. As has been seen, the Japanese identity and, even more so, its international image, is often defined in terms of its openness and diversity. Like all national images, it serves a perception-building purpose and thus the role of national agents in the creation and maintenance of these stereotypes cannot be ruled out. Traditionally regarded as a closed country and even hostile to foreign influences, Japan has benefited from this image to build a halo of exoticism and uniqueness that in some way links with the academic discourses of the *Nihonjinron* (Japanese Uniqueness).

Importantly, in turn, it is this message of openness and diversity that most prevalently permeates through the Tokyo 2020 transmedia campaign. Mami Sato, a Japanese Paralympian athlete, for example, has publically reaffirmed throughout Tokyo 2020 media materials that 'excellence, friendship and respect can be more than words', with even more explicit references to multiculturalism made during Sato's pitch (Olympic Channel 2013). Of course, to take a step forward as a candidate for Olympism is, in itself, a commitment to diversity. The values of modern Olympism are based on the healthy sporting competition between countries and the search for improvement. The Olympic Games have traditionally been a 'force for change' in society in terms of their ideal for seeking and rewarding tolerance toward diversity (Robson 2016). In the case of Tokyo 2020, 'Unity in Diversity' is one of three core concepts (together with 'Achieving Personal Best' and 'Connecting to Tomorrow') that have been accentuated across media to define Japan's vision of the Games:

> Accepting and respecting differences in race, colour, gender, sexual orientation, language, religion, political or other opinion, national or social origin, property, birth, level of ability or other status allows peace to be maintained and society to continue to develop and flourish.
>
> (Internation Olympic Committee ICO 2013)

The official logo of the Tokyo 2020 Organizing Committee, furthermore, adapts this same message transmedially into a visual format. With the motto 'Unity in Diversity', the logo is inspired by Japanese traditional patterns and colors (namely, indigo blue) and it is 'composed of three varieties of rectangular shapes, [with] the design represent[ing] different countries, cultures and ways of thinking' (Internation Olympic Committee ICO, 2016).

Though we do not know how Japan will take advantage of such a multiculturalism discourse in terms of continuing to build its national image as a culturally diverse and open country, what is clear is that in terms of the country's approach to building Tokyo 2020 as a transmedia production, fictional characters are critical. Even in the organizing committee's pitch, the Japanese anime industry is identified as one of the key means of promotion for the proposal. More specifically, the charisma of Captain Tsubasa, a character from a popular *manga* about soccer, is used, explaining here how he inspired other world-class players such as Messi, Kaka and Uchimura (Olympic Channel 2013). Instead of adapting other discourses more specific to 'real' Japanese culture and society, or creating a corporatized image, the multiplicity of merchandising in the form of adapted fictional characters – linked to real-world figures and scenarios – has come to define the Tokyo 2020 transmedia strategy. Indeed, acting under the aforementioned label 'ambassadors', a number of characters have been part of the official Tokyo 2020 merchandise since February 2017. These characters have all been selected specifically because of their national popularity, such as Atom (Astro Boy), Bunny (Sailor Moon), Luffy (One Piece), Naruto, Goku (Dragon Ball Z), Shin-chan and Jibanyan (Yokai Watch). These more regionally specific characters are then combined with other characters across a number of interconnected media platforms, linked for example with characters that will also appeal to broader Asian markets as a way of building and sustaining its 'Cool Japan' brand message transmedially, such as the magical girls from *Pretty Cure*.

Fans, in addition, also contribute to these crossover character images. The short film *Doraemon at the 2020 Neo-Tokyo Olympic Games*, animated by Aleix Pitarch, is a fan-fiction work in the form of a mash-up. Released shortly after the Olympic nomination was known, it recreates the apocalyptic scenario of the film *Otomo Akira* (1988), drawing on the same shots from the film and trailer. It features, as protagonists, Doreamon's characters created by Fujiko F. Fujio from the late 1960s, thus marking one of the oldest instance of Japanese media mix given that over the years it has since been recycled in numerous television programs, anime films and other cultural products. *Otomo Akira* is very much part of the Japanese collective imagination on account of its transgressive and counter-cultural image. It is postmodern, visceral and sometimes horrific in its portrait of a young biker gang in a future megacity (Neo-Tokyo). And in Pitarch's fan-fiction work, there is an emphasis on intertextual references that work to subvert the original film's more dystopic images, instead favoring more messages that are in line with aforementioned ideas of multiculturalism and diversity. In particular, these intertextual messages drew heavily from characters of Fujio, who are usually considered to be a paradigm for traditional Japanese values of family in a transgressive context that is still easily recognizable by fan audiences.

This particular example of fan-fiction illustrates the contradiction inherent in all transmedia 'Cool Japan' strategies. On the one hand, national branding uses popular fictional narratives in the domestic and international spheres, with many characters derived from *shōnen* in the case of Tokyo 2020. This emphasis on fiction seems logical given the sheer popularity of the genres from which these character derive, including martial arts, sports, adventure, etc., which can all be applied semantically and emotionally to the Olympic competition. However, on the other hand, the participatory nature of contemporary international audiences – where developing one's own stories becomes increasingly central to how and why audiences choose to move across media – means that only a fragment of the audience truly becomes engaged, namely those that are drawn to such fan-based (digital) media works. And appealing to a select audience only is entirely counter to the intended message of multiculturalism, diversity and openness that the transmedia 'Cool Japan' strategy is aiming to reinforce. Perhaps this contradiction is why Ian Coundry has referred to the 'Cool Japan' movement as 'Geek Japan' (Condry 2013), even though it intends to speak to and engage the most global of markets.

Still, whatever the messages and narratives that make up Tokyo 2020 turn out to be, it seems clear that the way in which audiences consume them will be very different compared to previous Olympic events. The key difference lies in the technological and social changes promoted by media convergence. Due to the rise of the millennial audience, a large degree of participation is expected via social media and mobile apps (Bunch 2016). All signs point to Japan making a great effort to be at the forefront of new media technologies by showing their technological innovation and rank on a global scale. The increasing maturity of AR and VR media alongside the increasing quality of video and 360-video capture technology will allow for the multiplication of different experiences available to audiences around the world. It is surely a matter of time before such emerging technologies afford a proliferation of canonical cultural products and fan-created media forms, both working in dialogue. In that sense, it seems likely that fictionality will continue to cross new media frontiers in Tokyo and beyond.

Conclusion

As such, it is difficult to discard fictional production when talking about transmedia phenomena in Japanese media culture or in the production of national branding in Japan. Some forms of fictionality also have space in these scenarios. Japan takes advantage of the emotional value and the natural attraction of its fictional characters when promoting events and the country itself. The Tokyo 2020 Olympic Games, for example, involves the adaptation of a set of political narratives into journalistic media discourses and broader institutional communication. The current forms of Japanese national branding is determined by the tragic events of the 2011 earthquake and a decade of unstable strategies based on the soft power of their media industries. Tokyo 2020 aims to connect both images of Japan, rescuing positive values such as a tolerance for diversity, respect for traditions and technological innovation.

Through the study of Japanese media and its cultural exportations, I maintain the idea that Japanese transmediality is inherently narrative and fiction based. In some cases, the use of the fictional does not imply a change in the purpose of the communication in Japan (for example, Shizo Abe's cosplay as Super Mario is still a public act), but it does raise a question over its status as fiction or nonfiction given its transmedial sprawl into and across diverse cultural settings. Is such a case really a fiction? Or it is a nonfiction? Perhaps 'transfiction' is the more accurate classification, insofar as this chapter's examples altogether combine nested fictions into nonfictional structures. Regardless, it is a fact that Japan is a country with enormous potential for story creation through its rich cultural production based on the mixing of media forms, which brings new opportunities for transmediality based on practices of intertextuality and the recognizability of its cultural products in the global media landscape.

Note

1 These data of institutional origin may differ from other external sources depending on the criteria followed in the correspondent survey. For example, compared to Reuters Institute (2016a) the MIC does not seem to consider YouTube as one of the major social networks.

Bibliography

Addley, Esther. "Tokyo 2020 Unveils New Olympic Logo after Plagiarism Allegations." *The Guardian*. 25 April 2016. Accessed 3 June 2016. www.theguardian.com/sport/2016/apr/25/tokyo-2020-organisers-unveil-new-logo-olympic-plagiarism-allegations.

"Agency for Cultural Affairs 2003: Promoting the Media Arts and Films." Policy of Cultural Affairs in Japan. *Fiscal* (2011).

Aso, Taro. "A New Look at Cultural Diplomacy: A Call to Japan's Cultural Practitioners." *Ministry of Foreign Affairs of Japan*. 28 April 2006. Accessed 3 June 2016. www.mofa.go.jp/announce/fm/aso/speech0604-2.html

Au, Pak Hung and Keiichi Kawai. "Media Capture and Information Monopolization in Japan." *Japanese Economic Review* 63:1 (2012), 131–147.

Boase, Jeffrey and Tetsuro Kobayashi. "Kei-Tying Teens: Using Mobile Phone E-mail to Bond, Bridge and Break with Social Ties – A Study of Japanese Adolescents." *International Journal of Human Computer Studies* 66:12 (2008): 930–943.

Bunch, Kyle. "10 Ways Tokyo 202 Will Be Radically Different From Rio." *Campaign*. 25 August 2016. Accessed 4 August 2017. www.campaignlive.com/article/10-waystokyo-2020-will-radically-different-rio/1406791.

Couldry, Ian. *The Soul of Anime: Collaborative Creativity and Japan's Media Success Story*. Durham, North Carolina: Duke University Press, 2013.

Couldry, Nick. "Mediatization or Mediation? Alternative Understansings of the Emergent Space of Digital Storytelling." *New Media & Society* 10 (2008): 373–391.

Daliot-Bul, Michal. "Japan Brand Strategy: The Taming of 'Cool Japan' and the Challenges of Cultural Planning in a Postmodern Age." *Social Science Japan Journal* 12:2 (2009): 247–266.

Foljanty-Jost, Gesine and Carmen Schmidt. "Local Level Political and Institution Changes in Japan: An End to Politcal Alienation?" *Asia Europe Journal* 4:3 (2006): 381–397.

Genette, Gerard. *Palimpsestos: La Literatura en Segundo Grado.* Madrid: Taurus, 1989.

Gibson, Owen. "French Financial Prosecutors Confirm Investigation into Tokyo 2020 Bid." *The Guardian.* 12 May 2016. Accessed 15 June 2016. www.theguardian.com/sport/2016/may/12/french-financial-prosecutors-confirminvestigation-into-tokyo-2020-bid-olympics-black-tidings.

Hernández-Pérez, Manuel. *Manga, Anime y Videojuegos: Narrativa Cross-media Japanea.* Zaragoza: Prensas de la Universidad de Zaragoza, 2017.

Ikeda, Ken and Sean Richey. *Social Networks and Japanese Democracy: The Beneficial Impact of Interpersonal Communication in East Asia.* London: Routledge, 2012.

"International Olympic Committee ICO." *Tokyo 2020 Official Website.* Accessed 4 June 2016. https://tokyo2020.jp/en/

IPSP: Intellectual Property Strategic Program. Accessed 6 October 2014. www. kantei.go.jp/jp/singi/titeki2/keikaku2006_e.pdf

Ishii, Kenichi and Morihiro Ogasahara. "Links between Real and Virtual Networks: A Comparative Study of Online Communities in Japan and Korea." *CyberPsychology and Behaviour* 10:2 (2007): 252–257.

Iwabuchi, Koichi. "Undoing International Fandom in the Age of Brand Nationalism." *Mechademia* 5:1 (2010): 87–96.

Jenkins, Henry. *Convergence Culture: Where Old and New Media Collide.* New York: New York University Press, 2006.

Kikuchi, Daisuke. "Japan's Communications Ministry Finalizes Plan for 30,000 Wi-Fi Spots by 2020." *The Japan Times.* 26 December 2016. Accessed 15 April 2017. www.japantimes.co.jp/news/2016/12/26/national/japans-communications-ministryfinalizes-plan-30000-wi-fi-spots-2020/#.WZHHDDKPDwc

Kōndo, Seiichi. "How Can Culture Become Soft Power." *IHJ Bulletin* 31 (2011): 12–20.

Mandujano, Yunuen. "The Politics of Selling Culture and Branding the National in Contemporary Japan: Economic Goals, Soft-Power and Reinforcement of the National Pride." *The Scientific Journal of Humanistic Studies* 5:9 (2013): 31–41.

McCurry, Justin. "Abe's Fukushima 'Under Control' Pledge to Secure Olympic Was a Lie: Former PM." *The Guardian.* 7 September 2016. Accessed 4 June 2017. www.theguardian.com/environment/2016/sep/07/former-japan-pm-junichiro-koizumi-accuses-abe-lying-over-fukushima-pledge

Menon, Siddhartha. "Policy Initiative Dilemmas Surrounding Media Convergence: A Cross National Perspective." *Prometheus: Critical Studies in Innovation* 24:1 (2006): 29–80.

"METI Ministry of Economy Trade and Industry." 2012. *Cool Japan Strategy.* Tokyo: METI.

Nielsen, Henrik Skov, James Phelan and Richard Walsh. "Ten Theses about Fictionality." *Narrative* 23:1 (2015): 61–73.

Occhi, Debra. "Yuru Kyara Humanity and the Uncanny Instability of Borders in the Construction of Japanese Identities and Aesthetics." *Japan Studies: The Frontier* 1 (2014): 7–17.

"Olympic Channel: Presentation by Tokyo, Japan". 2013. *Olympic Channel (YouTube)*. 10 September 2013. Accessed 16 April 2015. www.olympicchannel. com/en/?utm_source=Google:AdWords&utm_medium=Paid_Search&utm_campaign=VML:Brand_Olympic_Channel_Tier1_Desktop&utm_content=Desktop:1000003&gclid=EAIaIQobChMI_aexnZzX1QIVzpPt Ch22hgeiEAAYASAAEgLgl_D_BwE

"Reuters Institute Digital News Report." 2016a.

"Reuters Institute Digital News Report." 2016b.

Robson, Graham. "Multiculturalism and the 2020 Tokyo Olympic." *Journal of Tourism Studies* 15 (2016): 51–58.

"RVC 2016: The State of Social Media and Messaging in Asia Pacific – Trends and Statistics." RVC Government Fund of Funds Development Institute of the Russian Federation.

Schodt, Frederik L. *Dreamland Japan: Writings on Modern Manga*. Berkeley, CA: Stone Bridge Press, 1996.

Scolari, Carlos A., Paolo Bertetti, and Matthew Freeman. *Transmedia Archaeology: Storytelling in the Borderlines of Science Fiction, Comics and Pulp Magazines*. Basingstoke: Palgrave Pivot, 2014.

Steinberg, Marc. *Anime's Media Mix: Franchising Toys and Characters in Japan*. Minneapolis, MN: University of Minneapolis Press, 2012.

Veglis, Andreas. "From Cross Media to Transmedia Reporting in Newspaper Articles." *Publishing Research Quarterly* 28:4 (2012): 313–324.

Walsh, Richard. "The Pragmatics of Narrative Fictionality." *A Companion to Narrative Theory*, edited by James Phelan and Peter J. Rabinowitz, 15–164. London: Wiley-Blackwell, 2007.

Yoshida, Reiji. "Masuzoe Resigns Over Expenses Scandal; Sakurai Vows Not to Enter Forthcoming Gubernatorial Race." *The Japan Times*. 15 June 2016. Accessed 2 July 2017. www.japantimes.co.jp/news/2016/06/16/national/politics-diplomacy/masuzoe-get-¥22-million-retirement-allowance-quitting-tokyo-governorship/

11 India

Augmented Reality, Transmedia Reality and *Priya's Shakti*

Matthew Freeman

With digital technologies continuing to develop and expand their functionality and reach, mobile devices have cemented their essentiality in the average individual's daily life. Central to this essentiality is the important role played by interactivity and participation, which also have come to epitomize transmediality. Scolari, Bertetti and Freeman suggest that there are different levels of participation in transmedia stories ranging from the consumer of a single media form to the 'prosumer' who expands the storyworld by producing new content, which thus 'represents the highest level of transmedia engagement' (2014, 3). Jenkins emphasizes that the rise of convergence culture has altogether worked to make this possible, empowering audiences by giving them the 'right to participate' (2006, 23). In the world of advertising, meanwhile, there has been a general borrowing of virtual and augmented reality elements in order to enhance interactive potentials, as demonstrated by the likes of 360-degree videos, augmented reality in Snapchat lenses and in-app deep-linking in Facebook Buy Buttons.

However, while digital forms of interactivity have been said to influence notions of fan participation (Jenkins 1992, 2006) and advertising effectiveness (Cho and Leckenby 1997, cited in McStay 2010), most of the extant literature around mobile devices specifically has tended to focus on common interactive media forms such as videos and interactive websites.

There has been little attempt to theorize the use of augmented reality technologies on mobile technologies in relation to existing understandings of transmediality. As digital technologies and mobile devices continue to bring media interfaces into the workings of our daily lives, a salient question is not so much '*what* is transmediality?' but rather '*where* is transmediality?'. While Jenkins' more recent writings on transmediality have delved into ideas of transmedia location, meaning 'the context from which transmedia products emerge' (Jenkins 2016), in this chapter, I wish to explore the idea of transmediality *as* location – by which I mean the breaking out of transmedia content into real-world environments via digital technologies.

Specifically, this chapter examines the kinds of transmedia interventions represented by *Priya's Shakti*, a creative collaboration that uses comic books, exhibitions and augmented reality, not to mention street art, to call attention to the struggles faced by women in India. I use *Priya's Shakti* as a lens through which to consider the significance of interactive mobile devices and augmented reality technology on the role of transmediality, thinking about what it now means to conceptualize the transmediation of reality and arguing that *Priya's Shakti* exemplifies the way in which transmediality can be used to reshape how we see the world. Essentially, I will demonstrate how mobile devices, comic books, augmented reality and street art murals are all used strategically and creatively in this trans-media project to draw attention to the line standing between worlds of reality and fantasy simultaneously, using the separation and technologically aided overlap between these worlds to provoke emotions.

Conceptualizing Transmedia Reality

It is now understood that 'transmedia' is not a noun, but rather an adjective in search of a noun. 'Transmedia, by itself, simply describes some kind of structured relationship between different media platforms and practices' (Jenkins 2016). Thus scholars have turned their attentions to 'transmedia storytelling' (Jenkins 2006), 'transmedia engagement' (Evans 2015), 'transmedia branding' (Tenderich and Williams 2015) and so on and so forth. But what of transmedia *reality*? How can we understand the general practice of 'using multiple media technologies to present information … through a range of textual forms' (Evans 2011, 1) as that which extends and augments the real world? By 'transmedia reality', then, I really mean the use of transmediated digital content to transform how users make sense of the real world, with the affordances of digital media technologies bringing digital and real worlds together. Before analyzing the specifics of *Priya's Shakti* and its attempts to change attitudes toward sexual violence in India via transmedial dynamics of augmented reality, I will begin this chapter by first outlining some of the key theoretical pillars needed to conceptualize transmediality as a location-based phenomenon. This means delving into existing scholarly understandings of mobile media, interactivity, locative media and indeed augmented reality.

There is no doubt that digital technologies have caused a shift in user behavior, to such an extent that they are no longer merely media but 'a part of life' (Belk 2013, 477; Fiandaca 2011, 141). Mobile devices soon came into play as they extended past telecommunications and integrated text messaging technologies into their media systems, which then permeated youth culture and led to more technical innovations as well as interactive and commercial possibilities for the platform (Goggin and Hjorth 2009). Mobiles have become an important center of media and technological convergence (Jenkins 2006, 5) or of 'multimediality' by combining various 'media forms, channels and delivery systems' in a single platform (Oksman 2009, 118), turning mobiles themselves into media (Goggin and Hjorth 2009, 3). The technological affordances of mobile devices that have democratized media by integrating tools and functions that allowed the average user to capture and edit their own photos and record their own videos, in turn facilitating user-generated content, have bridged mobile media with Web 2.0. The rise of social platforms such as Facebook amidst users' need to 'communicate and share' is one of the main factors behind the surge in mobile phones now supporting internet access (Gauntlett 2011, 12–13). The continuous changes in the uses of mobile and internet media have played a major part in the 'contemporary adoption, absorption, and retention of new technologies' (Cunningham and Potts 2009, 137), but they have also been key to the increasingly intertwined link between technology and daily life. Mobile media is fundamental to the presentation of more 'personal' and thus more interactive media messages that is itself key to understanding transmediality in more real-world terms.

Technologists would describe the concept of interactivity in connection with computer and mobile applications or its features (Johnson, Bruner and Kumar, 2006, 35), while advertisers are mainly concerned with the way in which interactivity as technology can 'add value to the communication process' (2006, 35–36), rather than how it is conceptualized. Interactivity can be seen as an official characteristic of a media technology, where it is measured by the extent to which a media can potentially allow users to exercise control on the 'content and/or form of the mediated communication' (Jensen and Toscan 1999, 59, cited in Mechant and Looy 2014, 303). In other words, interactivity itself exists on a continuum. Jensen broke this down into several dimensions based on different 'communication patterns', whether interactivity constitutes a list of options of pre-produced/accessible information or content to choose from, whether it allows the user to generate content by inputting their own data into a system, and whether it can sense and 'register information' from users and then 'adapt and/or respond' to what the user wants or does, sometimes automatically (1998, 200). Jensen's taxonomy of interactive media will be explored in relation to the transmediation of the *Priya's Shakti* project shortly, but at this stage it is also important to highlight that interactivity has a social dimension, with Mechant and Looy describing it as 'a form of information exchange between different actors', whether it be human to human or human to machines (2014, 303). This social dimension to interactivity will be important to my own analysis of transmedia reality.

As interactivity plays such a huge role in making new media attractive and beneficial to active audiences, it also impacts the range of new digital technologies that have crossed over onto mobile media platforms, including virtual and augmented realities. Virtual reality (VR), termed by and originated from Jaron Lanier while working on 'simulation projects' and 'virtual environments' in the 1980s, is most commonly known as an ideational computer-generated environment that allows users to have realistic interactions with it through the use of supporting equipment, namely VR headsets and sensory gloves (Hillis 2014, 512).

Meanwhile, augmented reality (AR), the main focus of this chapter, refers to the technologies that allow 'digital information' or virtual objects, i.e. 2D and 3D images, to interact with and merge or overlap with real-life environments (Bolter 2014, 30). Paul Milgram and Fumio Kishino (1994) posited that virtuality itself exists on a continuum, with one end of the spectrum consisting entirely of 'real objects' and surroundings (real environment) and the other end being completely virtual and synthetic (virtual environment), while other VR-related technologies that lie in the middle, consisting of a blend of real and virtual spaces, are called 'Mixed Reality'. AR falls under that category but leans closer toward the real environment as the user's perception comprises more of the physical world than the virtual (Bolter 2014, 30). Once used solely in lab research, AR has now been repurposed for commercial and cultural purposes on account of the rise of mobile devices, particularly the smart phone (ibid.). Today, there are many mobile apps that utilize this technology for mapping, gaming and social networking all around the world.

Generally, AR is divided into two types, one being 'location-aware' and the other being 'vision-based' (Petrucco and Agostini 2016, 116). Location-aware AR connects with a device's GPS and adjusts its information presentation according to a user's location. Examples include apps such as Waze and Google Maps. Vision-based AR, meanwhile, displays virtual artefacts and information (or graphics) once a user aims their mobile device's camera at an object, such as the Snow App, Snapchat and indeed the AR component of *Priya's Shakti* (ibid.). Snapchat's explosive popularity, of course, what with users enjoying interacting with quirky animated camera lenses, has prompted the company to roll out new forms of mobile media advertising. Still, beyond advertising, how can the use of AR on mobile devices be understood as a socially minded transmedia strategy for reshaping people's attitudes toward the world?

Engaging with such a question first means considering the role of locative media in today's media landscape. The term 'locative media' was coined by Karlis Kalnins in 2003 (see Hemment 2006), and is closely related to AR. But whereas the latter may have a large number of functions depending on the creator, the former concentrates mostly on social interaction with a place and with technology. Insofar as locative media projects have a social or personal background, they can encourage new ways of engaging with the layered histories, meanings and sensory experiences of landscape. By way of example, Soundlines was a locative media project carried out with school children by Strata Collective, a group of artists working with story, music and new media to create innovative learning experiences. The project involved field trips and pervasive media technology, specialist training for the children – in film, animation, music and mediascape, where media becomes layered into the landscape, itself triggered by GPS when walking with headphones and portable computers).

At a time when global media audiences are said to be losing touch with their sense of place on account of the 'traditionally interlocking components of 'place" now being absorbed by the digital interfaces of mobile media (Meyrowitz 1999, 100), the aforementioned examples and conceptions of interactivity, AR and locative mobile media all raise important questions about the potentials of communicating messages across platforms. Jenkins famously argued that transmedia storytelling is 'the art of world-building' (2006, 166) – immersing audiences in a fictional story's universe – but in straddling the boundaries between both real-world environments and digital media interfaces, the use of AR technologies on mobile devices opens up world-building to wholly new dimensions. So, let's now examine some of these new dimensions via the case of *Priya's Shakti* in India.

Priya's Shakti: An Experiential Convergence

In short, *Priya's Shakti* is an innovative transmedia project that attempts to change attitudes toward rape victims in India. Co-created by Ram Devineni and Dan Goldman and initially funded by the Tribeca Film Institute's New Media Fund and the Ford Foundation with a budget of US$250, the project began as a comic book before crossing into AR, street art and art exhibitions. The comic book launched at the 2014 Mumbai Comic and Film Convention. The idea to create *Priya's Shakti* came after the horrible gang rape and murder of a young woman on a bus in New Delhi in 2012. The incident caused an enormous outcry across India, particularly among young people. Many people called for a cultural shift in terms of empowering women in modern society and challenging deep-rooted patriarchal views that affect both women and men. As a result, Priya was created, billed as a new Indian superhero, who is a rape survivor with the capacity to inspire others and promote change.

'Shakti' – a word meaning 'female power' – is a highly transformative concept in India, where the highest profile criminal cases are related to sexual abuse (Bhomwick 2013). Contextually, gender-based sexual violence in India is deeply rooted in patriarchal views. The World Health Organization estimates that over 1 billion women worldwide have or will experience either intimate partner violence or non-partner sexual violence in their lifetime. A lot of gender-based violence is not reported due to fear and shame. Through the message of *Priya's Shakti*, the project intended to reach wide audiences in India and around the world.

But whereas the usual notion of transmediality storytelling would see audiences migrating from one media platform to another, *Priya's Shakti* exemplifies what I have previously termed 'experiential convergences' (Freeman 2016). This model of transmedia storytelling reflects the enormity of the changes dictated by digital technologies, and may be seen as a logical extension of technological convergence. Whereas important technological shifts toward 'connected viewing' may have led in some cases to 'the migration of our media and our attention from one screen to many' (Holt and Sanson 2014, 1), a project such as *Priya's Shakti* indicates that it is now time to theorize transmedia storytelling *not* as a phenomenon that relates directly to migratory audiences or even to crossing media, but as an experience of drillable multi-media consumption, as will be discussed shortly. For as Tosca and Klastrup observe, 'while stress is laid on the importance of different platforms when they investigate transmedia practices, little attention is usually paid to the aesthetic properties of the worlds or products themselves' (2016, 108). Incidentally, Tosca and Klastrup have also proposed a shift in thinking from focus on platform alone to studies of *media experience* and 'the kinds of personal or shared experiences users are constructing and re-enacting through them' (ibid.).

It is precisely this emphasis on experience that is so important to understanding *Priya's Shakti* as a transmediation of reality. Back in 2011, and addressing the use of mobile devices to extend the story of television dramas transmedially, Elizabeth Evans argued that audiences were largely disinclined to engage with mobile-based transmedia content, concluding that

> Although there is the potential … to have more positive opinions of the mobile phone as an alternative for televisual content, as far as television drama is concerned, the audience is still firmly focused on the box in your living room and not the box in your pocket.
>
> (2011, 140)

However, a lot has changed since 2011, and each of the platforms utilized by *Priya's Shakti*, including the comic book, are centered around the natural portability and daily experience of the mobile phone. In other words, *Priya's Shakti* was immediately positioned culturally as a project and indeed a story that is irrevocably entrenched into the experience of daily life.

Comic Book

Consider the above-mentioned comic book, which began the transmedia narrative. Published digitally and available for free online and via all mobile devices, the story of the comic book focuses on Priya, a human woman and ardent devotee of the Goddess Parvati, who has experienced a brutal rape as well as the social stigma and isolation resulting from it. The Goddess Parvati is horrified to learn about the sexual violence that women on Earth face on a daily basis and is determined to change this disturbing reality. Inspired by the Goddess, Priya breaks her silence by calling to the Goddess for help amidst such dire social circumstances (a common trope in Hindu mythology). She sings a message of women's empowerment that encourages thousands of women to take action against gender-based sexual violence around the world. Importantly, the form of the comic book, particularly the digital comic book, was key to communicating the project's message of sexual violence that Indian women face on a daily basis unless patriarchal norms are challenged. As co-creator Ram Devineni explains,

> We are tackling really horrific subject matters – rape, gang rape, and acid attacks in these comic books. I think the appeal of the comic book format, especially the way Dan [Goldman] has drawn the artwork to give dignity to the survivors and the characters, has made the comic books very accessible to general audiences, especially teenagers. If you tell someone this is a comic book about gang rape, most people would be very put off by that. But the mere fact that we told the story through the creation of a superhero, especially an Indian female superhero, which is unheard of, and using the context and the structure of Hindu mythology as a way of telling it – it made it appealing to audiences all over.
>
> (Dodson 2016)

Indeed, there is the sense that the target audience of teenagers and the youth culture of India would not willingly engage with a documentary, say, or a less visually attractive media form. Devineni and Goldman understood the digital needs of their audience and decided that a comic book was the ideal way to reach them. Moreover, adding the AR and interactive technology on top of the comic book acted almost like an engagement ploy to attract more audiences, as will be discussed shortly. Or as Devineni puts it, 'it really is just a perfect synergy of art, activism, and technology designed for young people' (Dodson 2016).

Even without the added use of AR, however, the *Priya's Shakti* comic book was very much designed to be rooted in reality and to extend aspects of the real world, even if utilizing a seemingly fantastical comic-book layout. The pages are borderline cartoony in design, vibrant and highly colorful. There is a deliberate mismatch, in other words, between the visual attractiveness of the comic pages and dark themes and subject matter told within. But beyond the real-world themes and social issues of the narrative lending the comic book a sense of gravitas that is not immediately palpable from the superhero-fronted nature of the story, the design of the comic book also subtly communicates reality by borrowing images from the real world. As Devineni explains: '[Dan] is one of those few comic book artists who actually merges comic book art with actual real sceneries and real things surrounding him. The backgrounds are real – they are photographs, things that exist in the real world' (ibid.).

In a sense, one might claim that the imagery of the comic book is thus interacting with the real world, with interactivity in this context constituting 'pre-produced/accessible information or content to choose from', to apply one of Jensen's earlier cited dimensions (1998, 200). In effect, the comic book's panels are digital collages, utilizing photography and hand-drawn artwork alongside each other in such a way that what is being built is, according to Devineni, 'fake worlds using photography from the real world – the surreal on top of the real' (ibid.).

Augmented Reality

Characterizing the look and feel of the *Priya's Shakti* world as the surreal on top of the real is further enhanced – or one might even say augmented – via AR technology. What is important about the project's use of AR is that, despite it working as an additional means of attracting the youth culture of contemporary India, it was not actually a marketing strategy. Instead, the use of mobile-based AR technology stemmed from Devineni wanting to use this technology as a form of storytelling specifically, thus garnering the project a transmedial dimension. In terms of the practicalities of how it works, users are required to download the free app from Blippar.com on their smart phone. Then when users point their phone at select images in the comic book, they experience another dimension to the comic, viewing animations, hearing real-life stories, watching short films and experiencing other interactive elements that pop-out of the comic book pages. QR codes are incorporated into many of the comic book pages, acting like bar codes that can be scanned by a smart phone. One image can be seen with the naked eye, but scan the same image with a mobile phone, using the app, and a transmedial dimension to the image appears.

These interactive elements, themselves reflecting Jensen's description of interactivity as that which 'register information' from users and then 'adapt and/or respond' to what the user wants or does (1998, 200), exemplify a rather cutting-edge manifestation of transmedia storytelling. The project's co-creator and comic book artist Dan Goldman explains that there is a two-tier relationship between the comic book and its AR dimension:

> For me it is really that the story has to be complete in the lowest tech version because of who our target audience is. Not everybody is going to have a phone or access to broadband, so the entirety of the story has to work on the page. The way we build out the story using the AR is really the bells and whistles for a secondary audience. So what's in the script needs to be on the page first and foremost, and we have to get all those details and emotions there first, and then we use the AR to animate and bring an extra wow factor to pull in people that have access to that stuff.
>
> (Dodson 2016)

Nevertheless, there is greater meaning to the AR component than Goldman initially indicates, particularly in terms of how we understand its transmedial functionality. To be clear, this is not 'the flow of content across multiple media... [or] the migratory behavior of audiences' that Jenkins characterized of media convergence (2006, 2). Though audiences are still assuming 'the role of hunters and gatherers, chasing down bits of the story' (Jenkins 2006, 21), they are hardly moving across media channels, nor is the story of *Priya's Shakti* existing independently on additional media platforms. The experiential nature of this particular convergence of multiple media forms afforded by the interactive AR technology enables for additional story content to be buried within the comic book. Indeed, this case demonstrates a form of transmedia storytelling where audiences are invited to follow the storytelling experience not *across* media platforms, but rather *within* a series of overlapping media platforms. It is the idea of depth, of digging deeper inside the comic – itself a visual blend of the fictional and the real – that characterizes the *Priya's Shakti* story.

And this vertical digging down rather than horizontal moving across is absolutely crucial. In an altogether physical sense that itself reflects the physicality of the social issues at the heart of the *Priya's Shakti* project, the act of placing a mobile phone in front of the comic book and looking through the mobile screen to see new content incorporated into the comic pages is fundamental to communicating the project's message: users are essentially seeing the comic book in a whole new light via their mobile phone, learning more about the real-world horrors that exist behind and within the seemingly colorful gloss on the surface of society. In other words, the transmedial use of AR in this way forces people to *look again*, to not assume that the world around them is always the place that it first appears. In effect, *Priya's Shakti* establishes transmediality as that which reshapes one's perception of the world; it is the creation of an unreal view of the world whose messages are profoundly real.

Street Art

Utilizing transmedia storytelling to draw profound attention to reality requires that the world of the story goes beyond the digital affordances of software. In the case of *Priya's Shakti*, its users are required to interact with the locales of the real world. Of course, one of Jenkins' original seven core principles of transmedia storytelling was 'performance', which concerns 'the ability of transmedia extensions to lead to fan produced performances that can become part of the transmedia narrative itself' (2009). But the type of performance being enacted by *Priya's Shakti* audiences is less to do with notions of fandom and more about capturing a sense of place. Joshua Meyrowitz (1999, 100) commented that a lot of Westerners have lost touch with their sense of place because the 'traditionally interlocking components of "place"' had been broken up by electronic media since their location did not hinder them from always being 'in touch and tuned-in' or, as most would now say, connected to or 'always-on' their portable media (McStay 2010, 3), and this also applies to any digital media and mobile user. However, at a time when the innate connectivity and shareability of digital and mobile media is also making certain strands of transmedia stories ironically fleeting, it is arguably the role of locative media and physical real-world projects to now keep audiences engaged for longer.

One such example of a locative, real-world extension of a transmedia project is the street art and its painted murals for *Priya's Shakti*. The type of highly colorful, hand-drawn images that populated the earlier discussed comic book are similar to the murals that Devineni and his team propagated on the streets of India. Four different murals were painted as transmedial extensions of the *Priya's Shakti* narrative, three in Mumbai and one in Delhi. In India, Hinduism and its iconography are ever-present, and the murals crafted were deeply intertextual images that worked to draw parallels between the fiction of *Priya's Shakti* and the reality of the social issues underpinning it. In this case, the imagery recalls the Hindu iconography of the goddess Durga – or Shakti, as she is also known. As the story goes, Durga was created by the most powerful gods in the universe to defeat Mahishasura, a demon who managed to secure a boon that rendered him killable only by a woman. Mahishasura, a half-buffalo, half-human hybrid, assumed this made him as good as immortal. But Durga, who rides a tiger and carries a colorful range of weapons, was the one to kill him. The image of the Goddess Durga astride a tiger can be found in homes, businesses and places of worship across the nation. The *Priya's Shakti* murals reference and transform this image through the image of Priya sitting on a tiger – an image that represents Priya conquering her own fears.

It was Devineni's goal to make this image of Priya on the tiger a powerful symbol for fighting gender-based violence in India. As with the comic book, all of the murals have AR features that can be viewed with a mobile phone via the Blippar app, with users able to see special animations and films pop out of the wall in front of their eyes. But the locative, real-world physicality of the murals is what is most significant in terms of their contribution to the meaning of the transmedia narrative. By placing parts of the transmedia story outside of screen-based media forms and on the wall of real locations across India, those locations essentially become characters in the unfolding story – a story that literally crosses real and virtual environments even as those environments fold in on themselves.

While I have claimed throughout much of this chapter that the transmediality represented by *Priya's Shakti* has little to do with the commercial whims of marketing and advertising, it is possible to draw a direct comparison between the street art utilized by this project and the phenomena of location-based promotion that has taken hold in the advertising industry in recent years. Scholars have long discussed the ephemeral nature of new media promotion, from YouTube content and websites to interstitials and memes (Grainge 2011; Pesce and Noto 2016). As hinted above, promotional media forms are traditionally characterized by brevity, both in terms of content duration and the audience's exposure to them. As a way of keeping audiences engaged in content, then, attaching a location-based promotional journey has become commonplace. With the rise of mobile technology, a promotional campaign now has the ability to both reach out to audiences and to guide them to specific locations as part of a broader, spatially linked experience. Broadly describing an 'internet-based... scheme employing a scavenger hunt metaphor' (US Patent number 6, 102, 406), these promotional journeys may span multiple territories, and involve multiple users. The development of these and other locative forms of promotion have seen promotion as a whole move from the circus barker to that of an explicit journey, with audiences invited to participate in one identifiable event in advance of engagement with another event. Within this nexus of various promotional stages is the complex interplay between kinds of texts and user experiences. Straddling the boundaries between the traditional real-world positioning of advertising and art installations or exhibitions, they move further and further away from being media texts in the traditional communicative sense and instead emerge as interactive and more location-based texts that communicate multiple sets of social and cultural meanings based on the experience of users.

Occupying much more of a social-activist arena than this overtly commercial promotion area, the *Priya's Shakti* street art was nonetheless devised with a number of the same motives in mind. Just as with location-based promotion, these murals sought to create a multimedia experience that transcended the screen; there is also a similar degree of interactivity that is based on users generating content for projects by inputting their own cultural meanings into how the images are experienced. There is also a comparable emphasis on equating experience to liveness, attaching location-based images to exhibit spaces that are public and shared, with the communal nature of these images and spaces directly linked to the intended messages.

In a more general sense there may well be question marks over how we should approach and define such locative forms as objects of study and how we should go about categorizing them as parts of an unfolding transmedia narrative within what are customarily screen-based forms. But as far as *Priya's Shakti* is concerned, these street art murals – though arguably drawing on rationales and principles derived from the advertising industry and big corporates – were conceived alternatively and subversively to open the discussion on the social issue at hand. By literally carving said social issue into the walls of Indian communities, garnering interest and attention via the color and visual charm of the painting and popularity of the Hindu mythology underpinning it, the street art worked to physically augment the fantasy of the comic book pages into reality, with technology, in turn, AR into fantasy.

Conclusion

Put simply, the use of each and every one of the project's platforms – namely, comic books, AR and street art – is essentially about blurring the line between digital and real-world environments, between fantasy and reality, by creating a world of 'Mixed Reality'. At any one moment, those engaging with *Priya's Shakti* are experiencing the real world and the virtual world side by side, with mobile devices and AR drawing attention to the overlap between those worlds. In doing so, users are simultaneously drawn into the project by images, narratives and interfaces of fantasy before being asked to perceive the realities of sexual violence in India, and indeed are reminded of the realities of sexual violence in the country when engaging with images, narratives and interfaces of fantasy.

Indeed, *Priya's Shakti* is a transmedia project that encourages you not to escape from reality by entering a fictional world, as one assumes to be the objective with any number of the big transmedia properties now populating Hollywood, but rather to think differently about reality by traversing the line between real and virtual. It asks us to see the world differently, and it is transmedia storytelling – with its power to immerse users in interactive practices and shared, connected experiences – that is fundamental to achieving those important social ambitions.

The social aftermath of *Priya's Shakti*, for instance, is altogether characterized by change and hope. The comic book shatters taboos around gender-based violence through art, education and a strong identifiable female character who is both rape survivor and superhero – itself communicating the project's duality as equal sites of brutal reality and whimsical fantasy. 'More importantly,' as Devineni explains, 'it changed the level of debate in India from focusing on punishing the perpetrator to focusing on how society should treat rape survivors' (TEDx 2015). In that sense, too, the combined locative/digital technologies underpinning *Priya's Shakti* point to why transmediality is now making its foray into mobile media, where the barriers of attention economy and the overly fleeting nature of many digital media forms can be overcome. Apps, I-Docs and websites may be the holy grails of interactive projects, but reality, it seems, remains a truly interactive space through which to engage digitally.

Bibliography

Belk, Russell W. "Extended Self in a Digital World." *Journal of Consumer Research* 40 (2013): 477–500.

Bhomwick, Nilanjana. "Why Rape Seems Worse in India Than Everywhere Else (But Actually Isn't)." *Time.* 8 November 2013. Accessed 5 August 2017. http://world.time.com/2013/11/08/why-rape-seems-worse-in-india-than-everywhere-else-but-actually-isnt/.

Bolter, Jay David. "Augmented Reality." In *The Johns Hopkins Guide to Digital Media*, edited by Marie-Laure Ryan, Lori Emerson and Benjamin J. Robertson, 30–32. Baltimore, MD: Johns Hopkins University Press, 2014.

Cunningham, Stuart, and Jason Potts. "New Economics for the New Media." In *Mobile Technologies: From Telecommunications to Media*, edited by Gerard Goggin and Larissa Hjorth, 131–142. New York and London: Routledge, 2009.

Dodson, Claire. "Acid Attacks and Augmented Reality: How Priya's Mirror Is Using Tech to Change India." *Fast Company*. 28 October 2016. Accessed 16 August 2017. www.fastcompany.com/3064317/acid-attacks-and-augmented-reality-how-priyas-mirror-is-using-tech-to.

Evans, Elizabeth. *Transmedia Television: Audiences, New Media and Daily Life*. London and New York: Routledge, 2011.

Evans, Elizabeth. "Building Digital Estates: Transmedia Television in Industry and Daily Life." Paper presented at the *ECREA TV in the Age of Transnationalisation and Transmediation Conference*, Roehampton University, 22 June 2015.

Fiandaca, Daniele. "Agency of the Future." In *Digital Advertising: Past, Present, and Future*, edited by Fiandaca, Daniele and Burgoyne, Patrick, 139–147. London: Creative Social, 2011.

Freeman, Matthew. *Historicising Transmedia Storytelling: Early Twentieth-Century Transmedia Story Worlds*. London and New York: Routledge, 2016.

Gauntlett, David. "Web Studies: A User's Guide." In *Web Studies: Rewiring Media Studies for the Digital Age*, edited by David Gauntlett, 2–18. London: Arnold Publishers, 2000.

Gauntlett, David. *Making Is Connecting: The Social Meaning of Creativity, from DIY and Knitting to YouTube and Web 2.0*. Cambridge: Polity Press, 2011.

Goggin, Gerrard, and Larissa Hjorth. "The Question of Mobile Media." In *Mobile Technologies: From Telecommunications to Media*, edited by Gerard Goggin and Larissa Hjorth, 3–8. New York and London: Routledge, 2009.

Grainge, Paul, ed. *Ephemeral Media: Transitory Screen Culture from Television to YouTube*. Basingstoke: Palgrave Macmillan, 2011.

Hillis, Ken. "Virtual Reality." In *The Johns Hopkins Guide to Digital Media*, edited by Marie-Laure Ryan, Lori Emerson and Benjamin J. Robertson, 510–514. Baltimore, MD: Johns Hopkins University Press, 2014.

Hemment, Drew. "Locative Arts." *Leonardo* 39:4 (2006): 348–355.

Holt, Jennifer, and Kevin Sanson, eds. *Connected Viewing: Selling, Streaming and Sharing Media in the Digital Age*. London and New York: Routledge, 2014.

"I Stand with Priya: Ram Devineni." *TEDx*. 30 May 2015. Accessed 18 August 2017. www.priyashakti.com/tedx/

Jenkins, Henry. *Textual Poachers: Television Fans and Participatory Culture*. London and New York: Routledge, 1992.

Jenkins, Henry. "Transmedia Storytelling." *MIT Technology Review*. 15 January 2003. Accessed 4 February 2013. www.technologyreview.com/news/401760/transmedia-storytelling/.

Jenkins, Henry. *Convergence Culture: Where Old and New Media Collide*. New York: New York University Press, 2006.

Jenkins, Henry. "The Revenge of the Origami Unicorn: Seven Principles of Transmedia Storytelling." *Confessions of an Aca-Fan: The Official Weblog of Henry Jenkins*. 12 December 2009. Accessed 20 February 2012. http://henryjenkins.org/2009/12/the_revenge_of_the_origami_uni.html.

Jenkins, Henry. "Transmedia What?" *Immerse*. 15 November 2016. Accessed 4 August 2017. https://immerse.news/transmedia-what-15edf6b61daa.

Jensen, Jens F. "Interactivity: Tracking a New Concept in Media and Communication Studies." *NORDICOM Review* 19:1 (1998): 185–204.

Johnson, James, Gordon C. Bruner II, and Anand Kumar. "Interactivity and its Facets Revisited: Theory and Empirical Test." *Journal of Advertising* 35:4 (2006): 35–52.

"Locative Media." *Young Digital.* n.d. Accessed 12 August 2017. www.young-digital.net/methods/different-methods-some-examples/locative-media.

Mahajan, Jaya. "The Making of Priya's Shakti: Innovative Transmedia Project That Attempts to Change Attitude towards Rape Victims in India." *I-Docs.* n.d. Accessed 14 August 2017. http://i-docs.org/2014/12/19/the-making-of-priyas-shakti-innovative-transmedia-project-that-attempts-to-change-attitude-towards-rape-victims-in-india/.

McStay, Andrew. *Digital Advertising.* Basingstoke: Palgrave Macmillan, 2010.

Mechant, Peter and Jan Van Looy. "Interactivity." In *The Johns Hopkins Guide to Digital Media,* edited by Marie-Laure Ryan, Lori Emerson and Benjamin J. Robertson, 302–305. Baltimore, MD: Johns Hopkins University Press, 2014.

Meyrowitz, Joshua. "No Sense of Place: The Impact of Electronic Media on Social Behavior." In *The Media Reader: Continuity and Transformation,* edited by Hugh Mackay and Tim O'Sullivan, 99–120. London: SAGE Publications, 1999.

Milgram, Paul, and Fumio Kishino. "A Taxonomy of Mixed Reality Visual Displays." *IEICE Transactions on Information and Systems* 12(1994): 1321–1329.

Oksman, Virpi. "Media Contents in Mobiles: Comparing Video, Audio, and Text." In *Mobile Technologies: From Telecommunications to Media,* edited by Gerard Goggin and Larissa Hjorth, 118–130. New York and London: Routledge, 2009.

Pesce, Sara, and Palo Noto, eds. *The Politics of Ephemeral Digital Media: Permanence and Obsolescence in Paratexts.* London and New York: Routledge, 2016.

Petrucco, Corrado, and Daniele Agostini. "Teaching Our Cultural Heritage Using Mobile Augmented Reality." *Journal of E-Learning & Knowledge Society* 12:3 (2016): 115–128.

Rao, Mallika. "Here's Why the Biggest Slum in India Is Honoring a Fictional Rape Victim." *Huffington Post.* 26 May 2015. Accessed 14 August 2017. www.huffingtonpost.com/2015/05/26/priyas-shakti-street-art_n_7294470.html.

Scolari, Carlos A., Paolo Bertetti, and Matthew Freeman. *Transmedia Archaeology: Storytelling in the Borderlines of Science Fiction, Comics and Pulp Magazines.* Basingstoke: Palgrave Pivot, 2014.

Tenderich, Burghardt, and Jerried Williams. *Transmedia Branding: Engage Your Audience.* Los Angeles, CA: USC Annenberg Press, 2015.

Tosca, Susana, and Lisbeth Klastrup. "The Networked Reception of Transmedial Universes: An Experience-Centered Approach." *MedieKultur* 32:60 (2016): 107–122.

12 Russia

Interactive Documentary, Slow Journalism and the Transmediality of *Grozny: Nine Cities*

Renira Rampazzo Gambarato

In the context of the contemporary Russian mediascape, use of the term 'multimedia' is pervasive to the detriment of other terminology. Although multimedia refers to the combined use of text, audio and visual content, in Russia, this popular term seems to incorporate other assumptions, including the consideration of multimedia and other concepts such as cross-media and transmedia storytelling as synonyms. This terminological confusion could be explained by late modernization, as proposed by Russian sociologists (Dubin 2011; Gudkov 2011), and the low level of civic activity and narrow choices for community participation (Gambarato and Lapina-Kratasiuk 2016). Nevertheless, multiplatform media production and its technological advancements are part of the mediascape in Russia, which is gradually absorbing the term 'transmedia storytelling' and the conceptualization that the term depicts. In addition, related terms and practices, such as interactive documentary and slow journalism, are also now beginning to permeate the media realm in Russia.

Russian society is deeply split between the mainstream public sphere, organized around traditional media (television, radio and print), whereas a parallel public sphere is structured around new media (internet, mobile media and social media) (Kiriya 2014). Even though Russia is one of the fastest-growing regions of internet users in the world, 94%–95% of Russian citizens receive information primarily from government-controlled television (Gambarato and Lapina-Kratasiuk 2016). Since 2014, numerous attempts to control the Runet (Russian internet) through several laws, which limit internet use in Russian territories, were ratified. 'Most laws and restrictions are aimed specifically at limiting the Runet, but vertical control over media content and media consumption has spread in contemporary Russia' (Gambarato and Lapina-Kratasiuk 2016, 5).

Amidst this rapidly growing digital media environment and government-controlled media outlets, this chapter examines *Grozny: Nine Cities*, a transmedia experience created by Russian documentary photographer/journalist Olga Kravets, documentary photographer/filmmaker Maria Morina and photojournalist Oksana Yushko. The collaborative project depicts the hidden layers of Grozny, the capital of Chechnya, a city that has been coping with the aftermath of two wars. The award-winning project is the combination of an online interactive documentary, an audiovisual installation, a photo exhibition, a soundtrack album, a book, a website and a social media profile. The project, developed between 2009 and 2014, provides an in-depth approach to the complex stories behind oppressed Grozny from the differing eyes and styles of the three authors. *Grozny: Nine Cities* commenced as a documentary photography project and, incorporating the experiences during the process, has transformed into a relevant example of slow journalism across multiple media platforms.

This chapter briefly discusses the premises of interactive documentary (Gaudenzi 2013; Kerrigan and Velikovsky 2016; Uricchio et al. 2015), slow journalism (Gambarato 2016; Greenberg 2012; Le Masurier 2015) and transmediality (Freeman 2016b; Gambarato 2013; Jansson 2013; Jenkins 2006) as the theoretical background referred to in the transmedia analysis of *Grozny: Nine Cities*. The methodological approach for exploring this case study is the original transmedia project-design analytical model by Gambarato (2013) aimed at outlining the features of the design process behind transmedia experiences. The research methods include a semi-structured interview with Olga Kravets, one of the *Grozny: Nine Cities* authors, which is a valuable contribution to the discussion.

Interactive Documentary, Slow Journalism and Transmedia Storytelling

Grozny: Nine Cities has as its tent-pole an interactive documentary (iDoc). Since Robert Flaherty's *Nanook of the North* (1922), generally cited as the first documentary film, the documentary genre has developed toward a convergence of cultures with the Web playing a primary role in this scenario (Gaudenzi 2013). A series of prefixes have begun to accompany the noun 'documentary', such as digital, Web, interactive, multimedia and transmedia, among others. On the one hand, 'everything is now wide open' (Kopp quoted in Cheshire 2014), states Ingrid Kopp, the director of digital initiatives at New York's Tribeca Film Institute. Kopp stresses in relation to documentary storytelling methods that 'a new form isn't going to emerge and that be the standard anymore' (Cheshire 2014). Multiple structures are in play. For instance, in the realm of journalism, what Kopp describes as 'scrollytelling projects' (Kopp quoted in Cheshire 2014) are being acclaimed, including *The New York Times* Snow Fall (Branch 2012). By contrast, authors, such as Hardie (2016, 14), remain reluctant to consider an iDoc as a documentary, and argue that 'because the format and content of an "interactive documentary" can be altered, then it is not a documentary as we have come to understand the term'.

The premise of iDocs is the active flow of information. The notion of iDoc considered here is the one presented by Gaudenzi (2013): with the support of digital technologies, iDocs presuppose that the user must be able to (physically) *do something*, which implies that audiences can form their own storyline by choosing the path to experience the story, watching a video, seeing a photo, etc. 'An interactive project allows audiences to relate to it somehow, for instance, by pressing a button or control, deciding the path to experiencing it, but not being able to co-create and change the story', thus limiting participation (Gambarato 2012, 74). Crawford (2012) highlights three core aspects that are involved in the aesthetics of interactivity: (1) speed, (2) depth and (3) choice. The first refers to the degree of responsiveness of audience actions, the second is related to how significant the subject is to the audience and the third is relevant because the choices should work together to satisfy the audience's needs (Gambarato 2016). The transmedial environment seems ideal for developing interactive stories in the sense that it integrates various levels of the storyworld and takes advantage of digital tools to do so. However, Ding (2016) warns:

> In short, documentary and legacy media institutions' current focus on transmedia approaches often prioritises their ability to build markets and audiences, rather than their ability to expand narratives or enrich conversations. At the same time, there are exciting storytelling, community building, and experiential possibilities that are being neglected.

Transmedia storytelling involves the unfolding of a storyworld (Jenkins 2006) in which instalments of the narrative are spread across diversified media platforms to engage the audience, creating an integrated experience. Although Jenkins (2003) coined the term transmedia storytelling in 2003 and refers to Marsha Kinder (1991) as the one who coined the word 'transmedia' (Freeman 2016a, 168), the phenomenon of telling stories across different media is not new, and the word 'transmedia' itself has been used for decades. In the 1970s, British journalist Bernard Levin used the title 'Transmedia and the Message' for a chapter in his book *The Pendulum Years: Britain in the Sixties* (1970). Freeman (2014, 2377), historicizing transmedia storytelling, states that 'transmedia storytelling was born out of advertising strategies', and several of the pioneering examples are storyworlds, such as *The Wonderful Wizard of Oz*, *Tarzan* and *Superman*, from the beginning of the 20th century (Freeman 2016b). Jansson (2013, 287) considers transmedia narratives as 'increasingly inter-connected and open-ended circulation of media content between various platforms, where the subjects previously known as "the audience" are increasingly involved in the production of flows'.

Even though transmedia storytelling has emerged within the entertainment realm (Kinder 1991; Jenkins 2006) and is closely related to advertisement strategies (Freeman 2014, 2016b), the concept is applicable to fictional and nonfictional stories alike, including the journalistic sphere (Gambarato,

Alzamora and Tárcia 2016; Gambarato and Tárcia 2016). Kerrigan and Velikovsky, for instance, argue that '[n]on-fiction transmedia draws on the same definitions as fiction transmedia' (2016, 233) and '[n]on-fiction transmedia is an extant and ever increasing phenomenon' (2016, 237).

Slow journalism, as a nonfictional form inspired by the slow food movement[1] (Petrini 2007) from the 1980s, informs the audience 'about the provenance of the information and how it was gathered' (Greenberg 2012, 381–382). Le Masurier (2015, 142) highlights the matter of transparency among the core features of slow journalism: 'being clear about what is original journalism and what is reproduced PR copy, being clear about how information is obtained, and in digital journalism by linking readers to source documents, background research and other relevant stories'. Greenberg (2012, 382) emphasizes that 'often, a defining aspect of the genre is that the story works on more than one level so that the specific subject matter leaves openings to other, more universal themes'. This characteristic unites slow journalism and transmedia storytelling, and is also the case for *Grozny: Nine Cities*, which takes advantage of telling the story through different levels (the nine cities) and multiple media platforms. As I have explained elsewhere of this relationship between transmedia storytelling and slow journalism:

> The connections [...] start from the focus on the story and the power of narrative. The story is number one and works on multiple levels, or dimensions, creating a dynamic storytelling experience and leaving space for the content to expand across different media platforms. A storyworld is developed to support the expansion of content and multiplicity of media channels. Both TS [transmedia storytelling] and slow journalism embrace new technologies (mobile, locative media, for instance) and devices (smartphones, tablets, etc.) to tell compelling stories able to reach a diversified public. The audience engagement is a central point for both to involve the audience as collaborators and create a more valuable experience. In order to do so, more time is invested from the side of authors/producers as well as from the public. (Gambarato 2016, 448–449)

Building on this, Kerrigan and Velikovsky (2016, 238) discuss documentary transmedia narratives and argue that 'the documentary transmedia content does more than present linear journalistic reports; it allows for deeper discussion and public debate of complex issues and allows the audience to engage and participate in story universes to create their own narrative experiences'. The non-linearity, the highest standards of storytelling craft, the interest in untold stories and the transparency of slow journalism support the argument that slow journalism, using the tools provided by iDocs, combined with transmedia strategies can tell factual and compelling stories, such as the soon to be discussed *Grozny: Nine Cities*.

Transmedia Project Design Analytical Model

The transmedia project-design analytical model (Gambarato 2013) was the method chosen to develop the case study of *Grozny: Nine Cities* due to its qualitative nature, which contributes to the understanding of the design process of projects that unfold across multiple media platforms. The model is applicable to fictional and nonfictional experiences. Ten specific topics, such as narrative, extensions and engagement, are guided by a series of practicable questions. Strickler's (2012), Jenkins' (2006) and Long's (2007) transmedial approaches are directly implicated in the analytical model.

Analysis can lead to synthesis, and therefore, the analysis of an intricate transmedia project such as *Grozny: Nine Cities* can contribute to the advancement of transmedia practices. As proposed by Freeman (2016a, 205), 'our role as media industry studies scholars is perhaps to be brainstormers and analysts to help theoretically advance cutting-edge media industry workings'. The model is briefly described in the following table (see Table 12.1). In a similar context, this model was applied to analyze the transmediality combined with slow journalism of *The Sochi Project* (see Gambarato 2016).

Transmedia Analysis of *Grozny: Nine Cities*

Premise and Purpose

The Chechen Republic (commonly referred as Chechnya) is a federal subject of Russia in the North Caucasus region. After the Soviet Union was dissolved in 1991, Chechnya declared its independence. Since then, Chechnya has been immersed in conflicts internally and with its neighbors, especially Russia. Russia's interest in the region is economic (control of the Caucasus oilfields and pipeline routes) and political. In December 1994, the First Chechen War commenced when Russian troops targeted Grozny in an effort to prevent Chechnya from seceding from the Russian Federation. The war lasted almost two years and ended in the defeat of Russian forces in August 1996. The Russian troops withdrew, and Chechnya's *de facto* independence continued (German 2013). However, Russian control of the republic was restored during the decade-long Second Chechen War (1999–2009). After Chechen terrorists attacked sites in Moscow in 1999, President Vladimir Putin sent troops back to Chechnya. This time, the Russian forces succeeded. 'By 2002 the UN named Grozny "the most destroyed city on the planet"' (Wingfield-Hayes 2009).

Although the war officially ended in 2009 and 'Moscow has been pumping hundreds of millions of dollars into Chechnya's reconstruction' (Wingfield-Hayes 2009), violence, abuse of power, intimidation, kidnappings and murders continue in the region. Chechnya's current pro-Moscow president, Ramzan Kadyrov, a young former rebel fighter with

Table 12.1 Concise description of the transmedia project design analytical model

Nr.	Topic	Practicable questions
1	Premise and purpose State clearly what it is about and the reason why the project exists.	What is the project about? Is it a fictional, a nonfictional or a mixed project? What is its fundamental purpose? Is it to entertain, to teach or to inform? Is it to market a product?
2	Narrative The structure storyworlds evoke in the transmedia milieu.	What would be the summary of the storyline? What is the time frame of the story? What are the strategies for the expansion of the narrative? Are negative capability and migratory cues included? Is it possible to identify intermedial texts in the story?
3	World-building A storyworld should be robust enough to support expansions, going above and beyond a single story.	Which is the central world in which the project is set? Is it a fictional world, the real world or a mixture of both? How it is presented geographically? Is the storyworld big enough to support expansions?
4	Characters The features of the characters and the way they appear across all of the platforms should be in unison.	Who are the primary and secondary characters of the story? Does the project have any spin-offs? Could the storyworld be considered a primary character of its own? Could the audience be considered a character as well?
5	Extensions Transmedia storytelling involves multiple media in which the storyworld will be unfolded and experienced.	How many extensions does the project have? Are the extensions adaptations or expansions of the narrative through various media? Is each extension canonical? Does it enrich the story? Do the extensions have the ability to spread the content and also to provide the possibility to explore the narrative in-depth?
6	Media platforms and genres A transmedia project necessarily involves more than one medium and can also embrace more than one genre (science fiction, action, comedy etc.).	What kind of media platforms (film, television, internet, etc.) are involved in the project? Which devices (computer, game console, tablet, mobile phone etc.) are required by the project? What is the roll-out strategy for releasing the platforms? Which genres (action, adventure, detective, science fiction, fantasy and so forth) are present in the project?

(Continued)

Nr.	Topic	Practicable questions
7	Audience and market Scoping the audience is fundamental to more appropriately deliver the transmedia experience. TS involves some level of audience engagement.	Who is the target audience of the project? What kind of 'viewers' (real-time, reflective and navigational) does the project attract? Do other projects like this exist? Do they succeed in achieving their purpose? What is the project's business model? Revenue-wise, was the project successful? Why?
8	Engagement All of the dimensions of a transmedia project, at a lower or higher level, are implicated in the experience people will have when engaging with the story.	Through what point of view (PoV) does the audience experience this world: first-person, second-person, third-person or a mixture? What role does the audience play in this project? What are the mechanisms of interaction in this project? Is there also participation involved in the project? Does the project work as cultural attractor/activator? Are there UGC (user-generated content) related to the story (parodies, recaps, mash-ups, fan communities etc.)? Does the project offer the audience the possibility of immersion into the storyworld? Does the project offer the audience the possibility to take away elements of the story and incorporate them into everyday life? Is there a system of rewards and penalties?
9	Structure The organization of a transmedia project, the arrangement of its constituent elements and how they inter-relate to each other can offer concrete elements to be analyzed.	When did the transmediation begin? Is it a pro-active or retroactive project? Is this project closer to a transmedia franchise, a portmanteau transmedia story or a complex transmedia experience? Can each extension work as an independent entry point to the story? What are/were possible endpoints of the project? How is the project structured?
10	Aesthetics Visual and audio elements should also contribute to the overall atmosphere and enhance the experience spread throughout multiple media platforms.	What kinds of visuals are being used (animation, video, graphics, a mix) in the project? Is the overall look realistic or a fantasy environment? Is it possible to identify specific design styles in the project? How does audio work in this project? Is there ambient sound, sound effects, music and so forth?

little education, is at the forefront of accusations of human-rights violations (Wingfield-Hayes 2009). Notwithstanding, he was re-elected on 18 September 2016 with about 98% of the vote, and he celebrated in a full suit of medieval armor, which included 'a conical helmet, a longsword strapped to his waist and a spear in his hand' (Tharoor 2016). Nonetheless, the stereotypes and prejudices on both sides are still very much alive, with Chechens depicted as Islamist terrorists, rebels and suicide bombers, and Russians as the villains who kill Chechens. *Grozny: Nine Cities* examines this issue and attempts to establish a necessary dialogue between Chechens and Russians, between perceived and factual realities.

Grozny: Nine Cities, indeed, is a long-term collaborative project that has evolved and unfolded across offline and online media platforms to tell the nonfictional story of the aftermath of the two Chechen wars. Kravets points out that the relevance to work on this project for five years was to show Chechnya in transformation (Holubowicz 2014). In the midst of the complex reality of North Caucasus, *Grozny: Nine Cities* was born aiming at presenting a factual portrait of postwar Chechnya. The project's authors add that:

we see the creation of this participatory project as a type of a peace-keeping mission. As Russian citizens, we feel the guilt for what happened during the two wars – ethnic cleansing, rapes, kidnappings and Islamisation. We look at Chechnya and see a reflection of the social and economic problems of a greater Russia.

(Kravets, Morina, and Yushko n.d.)

The project has been nominated for, and has won, several awards. Among other honors, the project was the Grand Prize Winner in the Multimedia Category of the 2011 Lens Culture International Exposure Awards. *Grozny: Nine Cities* has been presented at festivals worldwide in Germany, Greece, France, Peru and the United States, but not in Russia. Although the coverage of the First Chechen War is considered 'Russian journalism's finest hour' (Ellis 1999, 121) and an indication that 'Russia had broken, however imperfectly and incompletely, with the Soviet legacy of information control' (Mickiewicz 1999, 10), in the Second Chechen War 'virtually completely censorship' (Oates 2008, 126) dominated the media coverage. This topic continues to be subject to much censorship in Russia today.

Narrative

Grozny: Nine Cities is inspired by the American author Thornton Wilder's (1973) novel *Theophilus North*. In the book, the protagonist divides Newport, Rhode Island, into nine distinct but intersecting 'cities'. Every city has nine layers of existence, nine cities hidden in one. Therefore, the project deconstructs Grozny (Kravets 2013) in a clear

intermedial reference to *Theophilus North*. The nine cities of Grozny are
(1) the city of ordinary people, (2) the city of servants, (3) the city of religion, (4) the city of men, (5) the city of oil, (6) the city of women, (7) the
city of strangers, (8) the city that ceased to exist and (9) the city of war.

The nine cities function as instalments of the story that help organize
and expand the content. This logic is spread throughout the different
media extensions. For instance, Kravets explains that the exhibition is
based on the nine cities as nine chapters with nine leading images. The
photographs were selected and displayed according to their relevance for
each chapter (Olga Kravets, interview conducted by the author, Skype
recording, 10 July 2014). Each 'city' acts as a negative capability, attracting audience attention and compelling them to keep following the other
levels of the story. Migratory cues are dispersed throughout the project.
For instance, the computers displaying the iDoc in the exhibition and
all of the links available on the website and Facebook page offer ready
access to other elements of the project.

World-building

The storyworld of the project gravitates around the epicenter of the two
Chechen wars in the past twenty years: Grozny, Chechnya. Situated in
the North Caucasus, one of the poorest regions in Russia, the Chechen
Republic has been overwhelmed by conflicts and bloody battles for
centuries (Hahn 2007). The disputes involve territorial controversies,
religious altercations, natural resources, and independence insurgencies, among other ethnic, economic and political issues. Today, after a
Homeric odyssey, Grozny is under Moscow's radar: destroyed and rebuilt at a high monetary and human cost.

Yushko, describing the project's process, assumes that 'we discovered a new world of Muslim part of Russia with totally different mentality. During work we learned from each other. We tried to combine
three different points of view trying to create more objective picture'
(Holubowicz 2014). Reflecting upon the potential of nonfictional
world-building, Ding (2016) states that '[w]hile world-building usually
refers to the practice of creating expansive, detailed fictional universes
for science fiction or fantasy works, it is also a constructive lens through
which to view and explore the narrative structure of transmedia projects'. The *Grozny: Nine Cities* storyworld is robust enough to support
extensions, going beyond a single postwar story in terms of content and
extrapolating the domains of photography in terms of media platforms.
The nine primary themes explored in the project (ordinary people, servants, religion, men, oil, women, strangers, normality and war) tackle
objective and subjective narrative dimensions, enriching the possibilities of story expansion.

Characters

Grozny: Nine Cities portrays men, women and children in their ordinary lives. The characters are anonymous for security reasons because of the authoritarian government:

> Things happen to people all the time and we don't know how secure they will be, so our project allows them to stay anonymous and to tell their stories still. It was really the decision that it is easier for us: We can come, and even though I have been there 13 times (I spend a lot of time there), we can come and we can leave, but these people stay there, so it is just important to still tell their stories because they want to get it out, but to leave them safe.
>
> (Kravets 2013)

The continuing complex relationship between Chechens and Russians has been captured by the project. For instance, the authors overheard (and recorded) a conversation between two Russian soldiers guarding the only Russian Orthodox church in Grozny, which illustrates the situation:

SOLDIER 1: Well, you know, it's… it's not our country, in any case. How can it be our country? Everything is done their way, everything. You can't go up to a woman and talk to her.
SOLDIER 2: They'll look at you strangely.
SOLDIER 1: Not just look at you. They'll come and find you at your army base. And then deliver you in a bag to your bosses, in pieces. (*Grozny: Nine Cities*' Facebook Page)

Although the authors consider that 'in *Grozny: Nine Cities* the main protagonist is the user himself' (Kravets, Morina and Yushko n.d.), this impression is not necessarily the one that audiences experience. The authors state that, referring to the iDoc, the user 'is a wanderer going through nine layers of existence of the reinvented Chechen capital' (Kravets, Morina and Yushko n.d.). However, it could be argued that, in fact, Grozny itself is a prominent character, which is omnipresent throughout the entirety of the project and embraces the audience, inviting people to immerse themselves in the storyworld. As will be discussed, the lack of audience participation does not characterize the user as the protagonist of the story.

Extensions

Grozny: Nine Cities consists of an iDoc, photo exhibition and audiovisual installation, short video, soundtrack album, book, website and Facebook page. In the project's mothership (the iDoc), photos, video, audio and text are integrated in order to tell such an intricate story. Morina explains that the 'web-documentary with its additional online tools gives you a new way to tell a complicated story' (Holubowicz 2014). The iDoc is structured around a twenty-minute video and aggregates the time-line of the wars, describing succinctly the primary events since the First Chechen War. The iDoc also displays numerous texts, voice-over audio tracks and additional videos and photos that provide in-depth content. There are French-, Russian- and English-language versions of the iDoc.

The photo exhibition and the audiovisual installation are the result of a collaboration with visual musician Jose Bautista and curator Anna Shpakova. The installation comprises three projectors simultaneously presenting audiovisual content. The primary element of the installation is the twenty-minute video included in the iDoc, but extra material is incor-porated. The exhibition is structured around the nine cities as chapters with printed photos in different sizes. In total, there are forty prints: nine 55 × 80 cm, eleven 40 × 60 cm, ten 35 × 50 cm and ten 30 × 30 cm prints. According to Kravets (interview conducted by the author, 10 July 2014), the creators had planned to make available in the exhibition players/headsets linked to each of the nine cities with audio tracks (the original sound of people talking in Russian and a voice-over in English) related to the content of each chapter.

A short five-minute video (Morina 2011), produced early in the process to promote the project, was then screened at festivals, and the soundtrack album produced by Jose Bautista features the original soundscape com-posed by the visual artist as an important part of the project's atmo-sphere. The soundtrack is available on Spotify. *Grozny: Nine Cities* does not have its own comprehensive book, but the project is included in the collective photo book *War is Only Half of the Story – Vol. IV*[2] by The Aftermath Project, which is dedicated to exploring post-conflict issues through photography. The website groznyninecities.com contributes to the project in terms of content, and functions as a hub. The Facebook page serves as a space for disseminating updates about the exhibitions and the authors, and for easily sharing the project's links. However, the Facebook page does not represent a storytelling contribution. Kravets (interview conducted by the author, 10 July 2014) says that because the group responsible for the project is very small and self-funded, it has not been possible to properly tend to the Facebook page and maintain other social media channels.

Although all extensions are canonical, then, not all of the extensions expand the narrative in the sense of providing new and enriching content to *Grozny: Nine Cities*. The iDoc, installation and exhibition are signifi-cant extensions that immerse the audience in the storyworld through the installation and exhibition, and aid them in exploring the narrative in-depth via the iDoc. The other extensions function rather as accessories that contribute to publicizing and spreading the word about the project rather than expanding it.

Media Platforms and Genres

The media employed in the project are the internet (iDoc and website), video, printed media, soundtrack album and social media. Regarding devices, a computer is required to gain access to the project. Certainly, other devices could be used, including smartphones and tablets. Kravets stresses the need to choose a medium based on its relevance to the story:

> I think what's really important is to choose a medium that is suited for your very own story and material. Don't do a web-doc, just because it's trendy, think why you need it. With Grozny, I spent a lot of time explaining traditional broadcasters why I am not making a film, why it will be just what it is, an interactive doc.
>
> (Holubowicz 2014)

Documentary is the primary genre of *Grozny: Nine Cities,* and it includes documentary photography and interactive documentary. Also slow journalism permeates the entire concept behind the project. The rollout strategy was affected by the fact that this was a retroactive project that evolved from a photographic essay into a multiplatform production. Per Kravets (interview conducted by the author, 10 July 2014), the production commenced in 2009, with the first materials released in 2011. The website and the Facebook page have been active since 2011. The short five-minute video was launched in August 2011, followed by the Aftermath Project book in January 2012, the audiovisual installation/exhibition in June 2012 and the soundtrack album in October 2012. The French version of the iDoc was released in January 2014 in anticipation of the Winter Olympic Games in Sochi, Russia. The Russian and English versions were made slightly later.

Audience and Market

Initially, the project was exclusively photographic, but during the production phase in Grozny, the authors realized that if they used only photos, part of the story could not be told, especially because they could not document it visually for safety reasons, accessibility, etc. Kravets emphasizes that

> the story comes first. The story was calling to be expanded. [...] It is like an inverted pyramid, you know, starting from the small thing and then growing, growing, growing. It is basically really about expanding the content, telling as much as we can tell within every product and most important thing is they all exist for different audiences.
>
> (interview conducted by the author, 10 July 2014)

The project is designed to reach domestic and international audiences. Russian and Chechen youth are the primary target group. That is the audience for the Russian-speaking market. Kravets explains the problematic relationship between Russians and Chechens: 'the segregation is so big; they don't have the chance to talk; they don't have the chance to meet just because of the prejudices' (ibid.). The project also intends to raise awareness of the Russia-Chechnya conflict internationally. 'If I am talking about the international audience, it is really about the decision makers, the researchers, people like you, who will spread the word in a different way' (ibid.). Kravets anticipates that the international audience are likely to focus on other aspects of the project, not precisely the situation in Chechnya. However, indirectly the stories of the war will still spread. She concludes that there are two target audiences: 'international educated people, who can influence and make decisions and the young Russians and Chechens, who really need a platform of communication to start the dialogue. Our attempt is to help this interaction' (ibid.).

Grozny: Nine Cities aims to attract different kinds of users/viewers, however. In Murray's (1997) terms, the project comprises principally real-time and reflective long-term viewers. The first group of viewers eventually accesses the content, and the latter follows the entire development of the project. The three authors are independent professionals who do not have links to media corporations and who mostly self-funded the project and benefitted from small grants, such as the Magnum Emergency Fund 2013 and via Empha.is, an online crowdfunding platform for the photography community. Although Empha.is no longer exists, at the time it was successful. *Grozny: Nine Cities* asked for US$7, 500 and received around US$8, 500 (Olga Kravets, interview conducted by the author, 10 July, 2014). Kravets admits that the project was begun without a business model, and the authors did not commence planning until two years later. Although the authors applied for funding, Kravets confesses that being Russian does not help: 'by being Russians we really decreased our chances for funding' (ibid.). She attributes the difficulty to the sensitive subject, censorship and self-censorship in Russia. The World Internet Freedom Index 2016 (Freedom House 2016) classifies internet users in Russia as 'not free'. Among the 65 countries contemplated in the annual survey, Russia now ranks 52nd right behind Sudan, Kazakhstan and Egypt. Gambarato and Medvedev (2015, 169) enumerate other characteristics of censorship ratified by Russian governmental policies:

> Since 2013, the Kremlin-controlled Parliament has: 1) labelled Russian, internationally financed non-profit organisations as foreign agents; 2) authorised the government to block websites dedicated to extremism; 3) approved the anti-blasphemy law allowing jail sentences; 4) introduced fines for those who speak publicly about social equivalency for homosexual and heterosexual relations; and 5) banned the adoption of Russian orphans by US citizens.

The entire project is presented for free: the iDoc, installation/exhibition and even the soundtrack can be accessed without payment. The Aftermath Project book requires payment. However, the revenue does not go to the authors but to the foundation to support future grants (Olga Kravets, interview conducted by the author, 10 July 2014).

Grozny: Nine Cities is not the only initiative to portray the challenges of the region. For instance, the novel *A Constellation of Vital Phenomena* by Anthony Marra (2013), which made *The New York Times'* best-seller list, is situated in Chechnya and describes characters in 'an often bloody and brutal book' (Starin 2014). The *Greco-Roman Grozny*[3] documentary by Chrystal Callahan chronicles the struggles of three Chechen teenagers who aim to become Olympic Greco-Roman wrestlers. Moreover, the transmedia experience *The Sochi Project* (see Gambarato 2016) by Dutch documentary photographer Rob Hornstra and journalist/filmmaker Arnold van Bruggen depicts the hidden story behind the 2014 Winter Olympic Games in Sochi and the conflicts in the North Caucasus. *The Sochi Project* is also a well-known example of slow journalism.

Engagement

Grozny: Nine Cities embraces interactivity but does not include full participation, which means that the authors are in control of the information-flow and oversee the narrative, while audiences explore the project in varying ways without influencing the story. It is primarily an exploratory project in which the user navigates the database, deciding the path but without real impact on the storyworld (Ryan 2005). Although 'many iDocs are just linear-documentary shaped by the internet affordances' (Bonino 2011, 3), that is not the case here. Of the four modes of interaction (conservational, hitchhiking, participatory and experiential) proposed by Gaudenzi (2013, 37–71), *Grozny: Nine Cities* utilizes hitchhiking and hints of the experiential mode.

The hitchhiking (or hypertext) mode is characterized by a non-linear narrative that rearranges the fixed storyline within a closed system. In this type of iDoc, 'what is arguably more essential is an interesting narrative or a well-defined topic for the user to explore' (Gaudenzi 2013, 51). *Grozny: Nine Cities* offers the audience the opportunity to explore the nine cities in the sequence or to freely navigate through them. Each city is presented through hyper-textually linked video, photo, audio and text. In addition to the primary experience of a twenty-minute video encompassing the nine instalments of the story, other videos, voice-overs, text and photos of each city are available. An interactive time-line of the war includes precise data about the events of the two Chechen wars. Racontr, a publishing platform which showcases and shares interactive storytelling, was the authors' option to produce the iDoc without funding. Therefore, added to the monetary restrictions were technical limitations.

Hints of the experiential mode of interaction are offered by the project's installation/exhibition. The experiential mode permits audiences to experience the reality and be immersed in it (Gaudenzi 2013). Although the iDoc is not an example of locative media, the installation/exhibition with audiovisual content and soundtracks of real conversations captured in Grozny function as an immersive experience, an experiential one. The documentary nature of the story can be experienced in the first-person point of view with the direct narrative of the characters (such as in the first scene of the iDoc, when the taxi driver talks to the viewer about the destruction in Grozny) and in third-person through the narrator's perspective. The entire project works as a cultural attractor, stimulating a community of people interested in the subject formed around *Grozny: Nine Cities*.

Structure

Grozny: Nine Cities is a retroactive project. It was built as a transmedia production after the authors realized that documentary photographs alone would not be enough to tell the complex story of Grozny. Kravets (2013) comments that the involvement of multiple platforms in a transmedia production facilitates to pass through Russian censorship. The government laws and regulations imposed on the Runet, in addition to the government-controlled traditional media, characterize a media environment potentially censured.

The iDoc was produced by Chewbahat Storytelling Lab in Paris, using Djehouti, the technology integrated in the Racontr publishing platform. The project is structured as a transmedia franchise, with each extension standing alone and working as an independent entry point to the storyworld of *Grozny: Nine Cities*. Regarding the endpoint, the project has now been completed in terms of production. Nevertheless, Chechnya seems not yet beyond the authors' scope, as Yushko states:

> We are planning to come back to Chechnya with some educational programs in art and photography. This year we made a trip with a humanitarian mission of clowns from The Gesundheit Institute to the Chechen hospitals, nursing homes, schools, orphanages.
>
> (Holubowicz 2014)

Aesthetics

The visuals and the sound played a primary role in *Grozny: Nine Cities*. The soundtrack composed by Jose Bautista is a core element that elevates the quality of the project:

> Mr. Bautista has invented his own unique concept of working on audio-visual production, which he called kanseisounds. It derives

from kansei, 'sensitivity', 'sensibility', 'emotion' and 'feeling'. While Japanese engineers and designers apply kansei to build a development plan based in the emotional response of a human being while contemplating and using an object, Mr. Bautista [...] applies it to the combination of visuals and sounds.

(Kravets, Morina and Yushko n.d.)

Bautista's soundscape incorporates erudite elements (for instance, an opera singer sings without words) far from stereotypical Chechen folk music. The result is a sophisticated melody well integrated in the subject of the story and the *Zeitgeist*. The design of the project overall reflects the genuine character of Grozny, but the authors and their collaborators wanted to avoid overuse of the folk motifs commonly associated to Chechnya. Kravets stresses that 'it has to have strong connection with the place but we also shouldn't be too folk. We really wanted to show the atmosphere of the place, but at the same time be very contemporary' (interview conducted by the author, 10 July 2014).

Kravets (ibid.) emphasizes the visual inspiration from the work of Yuri Kozyrev[4] and Stanley Greene,[5] photographers who have worked in Chechnya and provided compelling coverage of the wars. She also mentions the work of Tim Hetherington, a photojournalist who used photo stories across different media, as a reference to multiplatform production, especially regarding his *Sleeping* Soldiers[6] project. In addition, Kravets' personal aesthetic references are the coverage of the Bosnia war by Tom Stoddart [7] and the video-style of the filmmaker Sergey Loznitsa.[8] His photographic approach to video is characterized by a non-moving camera, that can be seen in his documentary *Maidan* (2014) about protests in Ukraine: 'the camera doesn't so much as tilt or pan, remaining irrevocably fixed and observing straight ahead' (Grozdanovic 2014). The observational style is a distinctive feature of *Grozny: Nine Cities*.

Conclusion

Grozny: Nine Cities revives the distress caused by two recent wars and a past full of conflicts in the heart of Chechnya. Grozny, metaphorically divided into nine cities, is the epicenter of the journey this transmedia project offers to audiences. The journey is intended to raise awareness of the postwar suffering the population faces and commence the necessary dialogue between Chechens and Russians, fighting against their mutual prejudices. To thoroughly address the complexity of Grozny's story and reach a young audience inside and outside of the Russian-speaking market, the project makes use of online and offline media outlets. The relevance of the convergence of interactive documentary and slow journalism within a transmedia terrain relies on the fact that iDocs, as:

> immersive, visual and, above all, experimental narratives have developed rapidly over the past few years, offering wide-ranging examples for journalists who seek to reach new audiences, to enhance the relevance of their reporting for an informed, engaged citizenry, and to make better use of the interactive and collaborative potential of today's mobile technologies.
>
> (Uricchio et al. 2015, 5)

Ryan (2013) offers several insights into why transmedia stories are becoming more popular worldwide: (1) it is about money and consumption of as many products as possible, (2) it is a consequence of the proliferation of media and electronic gadgets, (3) it is related to the potential for transmedia stories to form communities, (4) audiences choose how much they want to explore of a certain storyworld, (5) downloadable media give audiences a more flexible timetable to experience the story and (6) cognitive investment, meaning that it takes effort to be engaged, but once the audience is immersed in the story, it is natural to continue within the storyworld.

Although part of the content of *Grozny: Nine Cities* is partially repurposed across varying platforms, transmedia features are evident, especially within the iDoc, installation and exhibition, as the transmedia analysis has illustrated. Kravets (2013) justifies that 'in this project, the content has decided for itself; it is transmedia'. At the intersection between documentary and journalism, the documental nature of the project is preserved along the extensions and is enhanced by the long-term approach of slow journalism and the expansion of the story across various media provided by transmediality. *Grozny: Nine Cities* is visually and content-wise a relevant initiative to tell a compelling story in contemporary Russia.

Nevertheless, the project's lack of appropriate planning is reflected in the outcome. Asked about what could have been done differently, Kravets answers: 'I would not have started without first funding, the budget, and the [...] project plan' (interview conducted by the author, 10 July 2014). Despite all of the difficulties with funding, with Russian censorship, she emphasizes that the complete independence of the project was, by contrast, an advantage. Above all, *Grozny: Nine Cities* is a worthy 'learning-by-doing' experience.

Gambarato and Lapina-Kratasiuk (2016) discuss particularities of transmedia storytelling in the Russian context that apply to the case of *Grozny: Nine Cities*: (1) transmedia productions often have a high level of novelty within Russia and a relatively low level of audience participation and user-generated content; (2) transmedia storytellers offer more opportunities for interaction and less participation (which would give the audience the chance to co-create and influence the story outcome); (3) the presence of mobile technologies and location-based services in the country facilitates the penetration of transmedia projects in urban areas; (4) transmedia strategies work as an alternative for projects that often have restricted access to mass media, particularly television; and (5) although technology and transmedia productions are flourishing in Russia, the social and cultural change mind-sets are still to be developed in the country. Above all, interactive documentaries, slow journalism and transmedia storytelling are tools that can contribute to changing the audience's low level of participation paradigm in Russia, introducing contemporary forms of convergence cultures.

Notes

1 The slow food movement, as an alternative to fast food, was born in Italy in 1986 and strives to maintain and protect the traditional and regional cuisines. It encourages the consumption of local and fresh products produced in a sustainable ecosystem.
2 Access *Grozny: Nine Cities* in the photo book *War is Only Half of the Story – Vol. IV*: www.youok.ru/index.php/book/.
3 Access the *Greco-Roman Grozny* documentary: www.youtube.com/watch?v=PgYd-qUWWig.
4 Access Yuri Kozyrev's work in Chechnya: noorimages.com/photographer/kozyrev/.
5 Access Stanley Greene's work in Chechnya: noorimages.com/photographer/greene/.
6 Access *Sleeping Soldiers* by Tim Hetherington: http://vimeo.com/18395855.
7 Access Tom Stoddart's *Siege of Sarajevo*: www.tomstoddart.com/gallery/siege-of-sarajevo.
8 Access Sergey Loznitsa's work: http://loznitsa.com/.

Bibliography

Bonino, Filippo. "Is Interactivity in Interactive Documentaries Exploited at Its Full Potential?" MA diss., London College of Communication, 2011.
Branch, John. "Snow Fall: The Avalanche at Tunnel Creek." *The New York Times*, 20 December 2012. Accessed 26 October 2016. www.nytimes.com/projects/2012/snowfall/?forceredirect=yes#/?part=tunnel-creek.
Cheshire, Tom. "Documentary Storytelling with You Directing the Action." *Wired*, 5 July 2014. Accessed 1 November 2016. www.wired.co.uk/magazine/archive/2014/07/features/docu-storytelling.
Crawford, Chris. *Chris Crawford on Interactive Storytelling*. Indianapolis, IN: New Riders, 2012.
Ding, Sue. "The Trouble with Nonfiction Transmedia." *Immerse*, 16 November 2016. Accessed 18 November 2016. https://immerse.news/the-trouble-with-nonfiction-transmedia-6a4813bdad16#.9cy2q16nz.
Dubin, Boris. Россия нулевых: политическая культура, историческая память, повседневная жизнь [Russia of the 2000s: Political Culture, Historical Memory, and Everyday Life]. Moscow: ROSSPEN, 2011.

Ellis, Frank. *From Glasnost to the Internet: Russia's New Infosphere*. Basingstoke: Palgrave Macmillan, 1999.

Freedom House. "Freedom on the Net 2016." 2016. Accessed 15 November 2016. https://freedomhouse.org/report/freedom-net/freedom-net-2016.

Freeman, Matthew. "Advertising the Yellow Brick Road: Historicizing the Industrial Emergence of Transmedia Storytelling." *International Journal of Communication* 8:23 (2014): 62–81.

Freeman, Matthew. *Industrial Approaches to Media: A Methodological Gateway to Industry Studies*. Basingstoke: Palgrave Macmillan, 2016a.

Freeman, Matthew. *Historicising Transmedia Storytelling: Early Twentieth-Century Transmedia Story Worlds*. New York and London: Routledge, 2016b.

Gambarato, Renira R. "Signs, Systems and Complexity of Transmedia Storytelling." *Communication Studies* 12 (2012): 69–83.

Gambarato, Renira R. "Transmedia Project Design: Theoretical and Analytical Considerations." *Baltic Screen Media Review* 1 (2013): 80–100.

Gambarato, Renira R. "The Sochi Project: Slow Journalism within the Transmedia Space." *Digital Journalism* 4:4 (2016): 445–461.

Gambarato, Renira R., and Ekaterina Lapina-Kratasiuk. "Transmedia Storytelling Panorama in the Russian Media Landscape." *Russian Journal of Communication* 8:1 (2016): 1–16.

Gambarato, Renira R., Geane Alzamora and Lorena Tárcia. "Russian News Coverage of 2014 Sochi Winter Olympic Games: A Transmedia Analysis." *International Journal of Communication* 10 (2016): 1446–1469.

Gambarato, Renira R., and Lorena Tárcia. "Transmedia Strategies in Journalism: An Analytical Model for the Coverage of Planned Events." *Journalism Studies*, 2016. Accessed 2 December 2016. doi:10.1080/1461670X.2015.1127769.

Gambarato, Renira R., and Sergei Medvedev. "Grassroots Political Campaign in Russia: Alexei Navalny and Transmedia Strategies for Democratic Development." In *Promoting Social Change and Democracy through Information Technology*, edited by Jakob Svensson and Vikas Kumar, 165–192. Hershey, PA: IGI Global, 2015.

Gaudenzi, Sandra. "The Living Documentary: From Representing Reality to Co creating Reality in Digital Interactive Documentary." PhD diss., University of London, 2013.

German, Tracey C. *Russia's Chechen War*. London: Routledge, 2013.

Greenberg, Susan. "Slow Journalism in the Digital Fast Lane." In *Global Literary Journalism*, edited by Richard Keeble and John Tulloch, 381–393. New York: Peter Lang, 2012.

Grozdanovic, Nikola. "Cannes Review: Sergei Loznitsa's Ukrainian Crisis Documentary 'Maidan.'" *Indiewire*, 26 May 2014. Accessed 1 November 2016. www.indiewire.com/2014/05/cannes-review-sergei-loznitsas-ukranian-crisisdocumentary-maidan-85482/.

Grozny: Nine Cities' Facebook Page. Accessed 1 November 2016. www.facebook.com/notes/grozny-nine-cities/overheard-in-grozny/240955985929436.

Gudkov, Lev. Абортивная модернизация [Abortive Modernization]. Moscow: ROSSPEN, 2011.

Hahn, Gordon M. *Russia's Islamic Threat*. New Haven, CT: Yale University Press, 2007.

Hardie, Harold R. "The Documentary Mind: In the Subject of a Practitioner's Perspective on Changes in Documentary Concept and Production." PhD diss., Edith Cowan University, 2016.

Holubowicz, Gerald. "Nine Questions to the Authors of Grozny Nine Cities." 2014. Accessed 15 July 2015. http://chewbahat.tumblr.com/post/75423445211/nine-questions-to-the-authorsof-grozny-nine-cities.

Jansson, André. "Mediatization and Social Space: Reconstructing Mediatization for the Transmedia Age." *Communication Theory* 23:3 (2013): 279–296.

Jenkins, Henry. 2003. "Transmedia Storytelling." *Technology Review*, 15 January 2003. Accessed 1 November 2016. www.technologyreview.com/news/401760/transmediastorytelling.

Jenkins, Henry. *Convergence Culture: Where Old and New Media Collide.* New York: New York University Press, 2006.

Kerrigan, Susan, and J. T. Velikovsky. "Examining Documentary Transmedia Narratives through the Living History of Fort Scratchley Project." *Convergence: The International Journal of Research into New Media Technologies* 22:3 (2016): 233–249.

Kinder, Marsha. *Playing with Power in Movies, Television, and Video Games: From Muppet Babies to Teenage Mutant Ninja Turtles.* Berkeley: University of California Press, 1991.

Kiriya, Ilya. "Social Media as a Tool of Political Isolation in the Russian Public Sphere." *Journal of Print and Media Technology Research* 3:2 (2014): 131–138.

Kravets, Olga. "Cross Video Days 2013." Cineuropa video, 3:19. Posted June 2013. http://cineuropa.org/vd.aspx?t=video&l=en&did=241883.

Kravets, Olga, Maria Morina, and Oksana Yushko. "Grozny: Nine Cities." Unpublished manuscript.

Le Masurier, Megan. "What Is Slow Journalism? *Journalism Practice* 9:2 (2015): 138–152.

Levin, Bernard. *The Pendulum Years: Britain in the Sixties.* London: Jonathan Cape, 1970.

Long, Geoffrey. "Transmedia Storytelling: Business, Aesthetics and Production at the Jim Henson Company." MA diss., Massachusetts Institute of Technology, 2007.

Marra, Anthony. *A Constellation of Vital Phenomena.* New York: Hogart, 2013.

Mickiewicz, Ellen P. *Changing Channels: Television and the Struggle for Power in Russia.* Durham, NC: Duke University Press, 1999.

Morina, Maria. "Grozny: Nine Cities." Vimeo vídeo, 04:59. Posted November 2011. https://vimeo.com/32580050.

Murray, Janet. *Hamlet on the Holodeck: The Future of Narrative in Cyberspace.* Cambridge: MIT Press, 1997.

Oates, Sarah. *Introduction to Media and Politics.* London: SAGE, 2008.

Petrini, Carlo. *Slow Food Nation.* New York: Rizzoli, 2007.

Ryan, Marie-Laure. "Peeling the Onion: Layers of Interactivity in Digital Narrative Texts." 2005. Accessed 1 November 2016. http://black2.fri.uni-lj.si/humbug/files/doktoratvaupotic/zotero/storage/CDQXGTTM/onion.html.

Ryan, Marie-Laure. "Transmedial Storytelling and Transfictionality." *Poetics Today* 34:3 (2013): 361–388.

Starin, Carolina. "Tolstoy Influence Felt in U.S. Chechen Book." *The Moscow Times*, 9 July 2014. Accessed 1 November 2016. www.themoscowtimes.com/ arts_n_ideas/article/tolstoy-influence-felt-in-us-chechenbook/503217.html.

Strickler, Elizabeth. "10 Questions." *Transmedia Design*, 2012. Accessed 1 November 2016. http://transmediadesign.wordpress.com/assigments/10-questions/.

Tharoor, Ishaan. "Putin Ally Celebrates Winning 98 Percent of Vote in a Full Suit of Medieval Armor." *The Washington Post*, 19 September 2016. Accessed 1 November 2016. www.washingtonpost.com/news/worldviews/wp/2016/09/19/ putin-ally-celebrateswinning-98-percent-of-vote-in-a-full-suit-of-medieval-armor/.

Uricchio, William, Sarah Wolozin, Lily Bui, Sean Flynn, and Deniz Tortum. *Mapping the Intersection of Two Cultures: Interactive Documentary and Digital Journalism*. Cambridge: MIT Open Documentary Lab and MacArthur Foundation, 2015.

Wilder, Thornton. *Theophilus North*. New York: Avon Books, 1973.

Wingfield-Hayes, Rupert. "Chechen Problem Far from Over." *BBC News*, 16 April 2009. Accessed 1 November 2016. http://news.bbc.co.uk/2/hi/europe/7974652. stm.

List of Contributors

Mélanie Bourdaa is Associate Professor at the University of Bordeaux Montaigne in Communication and Information Sciences and a researcher in transmedia storytelling and fan studies. She ran a MOOC (Massive Open Online Course) entitled 'Understanding Transmedia Storytelling' in France. She created a research group gathering scholars working in the field of Fan Studies, and also co-created a consortium on transmedia storytelling, gathering researchers and professionals in this field of expertise. She now runs the research program 'MediaNum', dealing with the valorization of cultural heritage via transmedia storytelling, funded by the Region d'Aquitaine.

Marie-Ève Carignan is Professor of Information and Public Communication at the Université de Sherbrooke. She is also co-director of the Communications and Strategic Communications graduate programs. She holds a doctorate in Information Sciences and Communication from the Institut d'études politiques d'Aix-en-Provence and a doctorate in Communication from the joint PhD program of the Université de Montréal, the Université du Québec à Montreal and Concordia University. Her research focuses on cultural industries and audiences of culture, media content analysis, journalistic practices and ethics as well as on strategic communication, including public relations, crisis communication, risk, terrorism and counter-terrorism.

María-José Establés has a degree in Audiovisual Communication (Universidad Complutense de Madrid (UCM)) and two Masters in Journalism (UCM) and in Communication and Learning in the Digital Society (Universidad de Alcalá). She is currently working on her doctoral thesis at Pompeu Fabra University and is analyzing the different processes and strategies that are present in the professionalization of fans. This work is funded by the Doctoral Training Grants 2015 program of the Spanish Ministry of Economy, Industry and Competitiveness. Her research on media literacy, journalism and fandom has been published in various indexed journals (*Palabra Clave*, *Opción*, *Prisma Social*) and edited books. She has also been a visiting researcher at the Universities of Bournemouth, UK and Jyväskylä, Finland.

Matthew Freeman is Reader in Multiplatform Media at Bath Spa University and Co-Director of its Media Convergence Research Centre. He also acts as REF Champion for the University's Communication, Culture and Media submission to REF. His research examines cultures of production across the borders of media, industries, cultures and histories, and he is the author of *Historicising Transmedia Storytelling: Early Twentieth-Century Transmedia Story Worlds* (Routledge, 2016), *Industrial Approaches to Media: A Methodological Gateway to Industry Studies* (Palgrave Macmillan, 2016), the co-author of *Transmedia Archaeology: Storytelling in the Borderlines of Science Fiction, Comics and Pulp Magazines* (with Carlos A. Scolari and Paolo Bertetti, Palgrave Pivot, 2014), and the co-editor of *The Routledge Companion to Transmedia Studies* (with Renira Rampazzo Gambarato, Routledge, 2018). His forthcoming books include *Genre/Transmedia: Rethinking Genre in a Multiplatform Culture* (Palgrave Macmillan) and *The World of The Walking Dead* (Routledge).

Renira Rampazzo Gambarato is Senior Lecturer in Media and Communication Studies at Jönköping University, School of Education and Communication, Sweden. Her Post-doctorate in Film Studies is from Concordia University, Canada and she holds a PhD in Communication and Semiotics from Pontifical Catholic University of São Paulo, Brazil, an MA in Communication and Semiotics also from Pontifical Catholic University of São Paulo, and a BA in Industrial Design from São Paulo State University, Brazil. She is co-editor of the books *Exploring Transmedia Journalism in the Digital Age* (with Geane Alzamora, IGI Global, 2018) and *Kulturdialoge Brasilien-Deutschland–Design, Film, Literatur, Medien* [Cultural Dialogue Brazil-Germany–Design, Film, Literature, Media] (with Geane Alzamora and Simone Malaguti, Verlag Walter Frey, 2008). Her current research revolves around transmedia storytelling analysis, Peircean semiotics, digital culture, international and intercultural media studies and education, film analysis, and the design of multiplatform experiences.

Camilo Andrés Tamayo Gómez is a Researcher at EAFIT University and a member of the British Sociological Association (BSA) and the International Sociological Association (ISA). He has a PhD in Politics and International Studies at the University of Huddersfield, UK. He is affiliated with the British Sociological Association's Sociology of Rights Study Group and is a Board Member of the Research Committee on Social Movements, Collective Action and Social Change of the ISA. The work that Camilo has been developing in recent years focuses on the relationship between citizenship, social movements, human rights and communicative citizenship from a sociopolitical perspective. His recent research explores how social movements of victims of armed conflicts have been using different communicative citizenship actions to claim human rights in local and regional public spheres and how these actions have been affecting constructions of political and cultural memory, dimensions of social recognition and degrees of solidarity and power.

Mar Guerrero-Pico works as a Research Assistant at Universitat Pompeu Fabra, Barcelona. She holds a PhD in Social Communication (Universitat Pompeu Fabra, 2016), an MA in Communication and Creative Industries (Universidade de Santiago de Compostela, 2010) and a BA in Journalism (Universidad de Navarra, 2007). Her thesis titled 'Historias más allá de lo filmado: fan fiction y narrativa transmedia en series de television' explores fans' textual production in television-based transmedia storytelling. Her articles have been published in peer-reviewed journals such as *International Journal of Communication, Communication & Society, Signo y Pensamiento, Comunicación y Sociedad, Palabra Clave* and *Cuadernos.info*. Her research interests include fan culture, transmedia storytelling, television shows, social media and media education.

Manuel Hernández-Pérez is Lecturer in Digital Design and Programme Leader for the Game and Entertainment Design course at the School of Arts, University of Hull. He is the author of the monograph *Manga, Anime and Video Games: Japanese Cross-Media Narratives* (2017) published in Spanish by University of Zaragoza Press. In the last few years, he has also conducted research into video games and social network-based narratives and, more recently, on Japanese media industries with a special focus on transmedia and cross-cultural readings of manga and anime products.

Matt Hills is Professor of Media and Film at the University of Huddersfield, where he is also Co-Director of the Centre for Participatory Culture. Matt is additionally co-editor on the 'Transmedia' book series for Amsterdam University Press, and has written six sole-authored monographs, starting with *Fan Cultures* in 2002 (Routledge) and coming up to date with *Doctor Who: The Unfolding Event – Marketing, Merchandising and Mediatizing a Brand Anniversary* in 2015 (Palgrave Pivot). He also edited *New Dimensions of Doctor Who* (I.B. Tauris 2013) and has published more than a hundred book chapters or journal articles on topics such as media fandom and cult film/television. This includes work on transmedia for the open access journal *Participations* and the 2017 Routledge-edited collection, *The Rise of Transtexts: Challenges and Opportunities*. Among other projects, Matt is currently working on a follow-up to his first book for Routledge, *Fan Studies*.

Indrek Ibrus is Professor of Media Innovation at the Baltic Film, Media, Arts and Communication School at Tallinn University. He is also the head of Tallinn University Centre of Excellence in Media Innovation and Digital Culture. He has authored several publications on media innovation and evolution, media standardization, mobile media, cross- and transmedia and data management. He advises on a regular basis the Estonian government, EU Commission and the Council of Europe on media and cultural policy making. He holds a PhD from the London School of Economics and Political Science and an MPhil from the University of Oslo.

Sara Marcil-Morin is an MA student in Communication at Sherbrooke University, and her thesis focuses on the representation of the phenomenon of radicalization in the Quebec press. Her research interests are related to journalism and media, particularly to crisis coverage, terrorism and radicalization.

Ana Margarida Meira works in the field of Marketing and Communication, specializing in the journalism, communication and marketing of fashion and fashion-based marketing. She graduated from Universidade do Minho with a degree in Product Design and an MA in Fashion Communication. Her academic writing spans a number of disciplines but principally concerns aspects of social theory, social stratification, communication and media studies.

Toby Miller is Distinguished Professor of the Graduate Division, University of California, Riverside; Sir Walter Murdoch Professor of Cultural Policy Studies, Murdoch University; Profesor Invitado, Escuela de Comunicación Social, Universidad del Norte; Professor of Journalism, Media and Cultural Studies, Cardiff University/Prifysgol Caerdydd; and Professor in the Institute for Media and Creative Industries, Loughborough University London. As the author and editor of over forty books, his work has been translated into Spanish, Chinese, Portuguese, Japanese, Turkish, German, Italian, Farsi and Swedish. His most recent volumes are *Greenwashing Culture* (2018), *Greenwashing Sport* (2018), *The Routledge Companion to Global Cultural Policy* (edited with Victoria Durrer and Dave O'Brien, 2018), *Global Media Studies* (with Marwan Kraidy, 2016), *The Sage Companion to Television Studies* (edited with Manuel Alvarado, Milly Buonanno and Herman Gray, 2015), *The Routledge Companion to Global Popular Culture* (edited, 2015), *Greening the Media* (with Richard Maxwell, 2012) and *Blow Up the Humanities* (2012).

Felipe Muanis is a Television and Cinema Professor at the Art and Design Institute and Post-Graduate Programme in Art, Culture and Language of the Federal University of de Juiz de Fora, Juiz de Fora, Minas Gerais, Brazil. He received his PhD in 2010 from the

Social Communication Department of the Federal University of Minas Gerais, with a Daad-Capes scholarship at Bauhaus Universität-Weimar, Germany. His thesis examines meta-images in television commercial breaks, analyzing IDs and art breaks from Brazilian television channels, such as TV Globo and MTV, and associating them with 1920s avant-garde film images. He was a Visiting Professor at Germany's Ruhr Universität Bochum (2015–2016) and Universität Padeborn (2010). His research interests span a variety of fields: television theory; contemporary movements between television, cinema and video games; digital and other media focusing on reception; different perspectives on television, their realizations in different countries and their televisiographies; and comic books, media, image and storytelling. He leads the research group 'Entelas: grupo de pesquisa em televisão, teoria, imagem e recepção' at UFF and published the book *Audiovisual e Mundialização: Televisão e Cinema/Audiovisual and Globalization: Television and Cinema* (2014).

Maarja Ojamaa is a Researcher at the Baltic Film, Media, Arts and Communication School at Tallinn University. She is also affiliated with the Department of Semiotics at the University of Tartu, where she defended her PhD thesis on the transmedial aspect of cultural auto-communication. Maarja's primary research interests lie in the transmedial mechanisms of cultural memory and in ways of diversifying the re-usage of cultural heritage. In addition to the research work, she has been teaching semiotics-related courses at all stages of the Estonian higher education system as well as in high schools.

William Proctor is Senior Lecturer in Media, Culture and Communication at Bournemouth University. He has published on various topics including Batman, James Bond, Ghostbusters, Star Wars and One Direction. At present, William is completing work on his debut single-authored monograph, *Reboot Culture: Comics, Film, Transmedia*, to be published by Palgrave Macmillan in 2018. He is co-editor on *Disney's Star Wars: Forces of Production, Promotion and Reception* (University of Iowa Press, forthcoming) and *The Scandinavian Invasion: Critical Studies in Nordic Noir and Beyond* (Peter Lang, forthcoming), both with Richard McCulloch. William is also Director of the World Star Wars Project.

Carlos A. Scolari is Associate Professor (tenure) in the Department of Communication at the University Pompeu Fabra, Barcelona. He has a PhD in Applied Linguistics and Communication Languages (Università Cattolica del Sacro Cuore, Milan, Italy) and a degree in Social Communication (University of Rosario, Argentina). He has lectured about digital interfaces, media ecology and interactive communication in more than twenty European, Latin American and Asian countries. His most important publications include *Hacer Clic* (2004), *Hipermediaciones* (2008), *El fin de los medios masivos* (with M. Carlón, 2009/2014), *Crossmedia Innovations* (with I. Ibrus, 2012), *Narrativas Transmedia* (2013), *Transmedia Archaeology* (with P. Bertetti and M. Freeman, 2014) and *Ecología de los medios* (2014). His articles have been published in *Communication Theory, New Media & Society, International Journal of Communication, Semiotica, Information* and *Communication & Society*. He is Principal Investigator of the Horizon 2020 'Transmedia Literacy' research project (2015–2018).

Rosane Svartman graduated in Film at UFF (1991) and earned her MA in Communication from the Federal University of Rio de Janeiro (2006). She is a Doctoral Student in Cinema Studies at UFF. She is an active partner of the production company Raccord Produções (raccord.com.br). She directed four feature films: *Como Ser Solteiro/How to be Single in Rio* (1998), *Mais uma Vez Amor/Once Again Love* (2005), *Desenrola/Untangle* (2011) and *Tainá – uma Aventura na Amazônia/Tainá – an Adventure in the Amazon* (2012). She wrote the books *Quando Éramos Virgens/When We Were Virgins* (2006, Casa da Palavra Ed.), *Desenrola/Untangle* (2011, Ediouro Ed.); *Onde os Porquês têm Resposta/Where the Whys Have Answers* (2003, Jorge Zahar Ed.) and *Melhores Amigas/Best Friends* (2006, Jorge Zahar Ed.). She also wrote the following plays: *Mais uma Vez Amor/Once Again Love* (2004, directed by Ernesto Piccolo), *O Pacto das Três Senhoras/The Pact of the Three Ladies* (2011, directed by Ernesto Piccolo) and *Anjos Urbanos/Urban Angels* (2012, directed by Isabel Diegues). She was Head Writer of the soap opera *Malhação/Young Hearts* (2012/2013 and 2014/2015, TV Globo) for two seasons. During that time, she was nominated for the Emmy Digital Award (2013) and the Emmy Kids Award (2015), and she wrote telenovela *Totalmente Demais/Totally Awesome/Totally Diva* (2015–16, TV Globo).

Omar Mauricio Velásquez is a Full-Time Professor and Researcher at EAFIT University. He has an MA in Literary Hermeneutics at EAFIT University, Colombia and a BA in Arts at Universidad Nacional, Colombia. The areas of work he is interested in focus on narrative and television audience studies. He has recently become interested in the relevance of configuration on the public in the creative industries, an issue that has led him to join the Research in Social Justice of Colombia group and to attend conferences about the subject of citizen participation in the media as a model of organic transmedia appropriation.

Index